Global Compassion

Global Compassion

Private Voluntary Organizations
and U.S. Foreign Policy since 1939

Rachel M. McCleary

OXFORD
UNIVERSITY PRESS

2009

OXFORD
UNIVERSITY PRESS

Oxford University Press, Inc., publishes works that further
Oxford University's objective of excellence
in research, scholarship, and education.

Oxford   New York
Auckland   Cape Town   Dar es Salaam   Hong Kong   Karachi
Kuala Lumpur   Madrid   Melbourne   Mexico City   Nairobi
New Delhi   Shanghai   Taipei   Toronto

With offices in
Argentina   Austria   Brazil   Chile   Czech Republic   France   Greece
Guatemala   Hungary   Italy   Japan   Poland   Portugal   Singapore
South Korea   Switzerland   Thailand   Turkey   Ukraine   Vietnam

Published by Oxford University Press, Inc.
198 Madison Avenue, New York, New York 10016

www.oup.com

Oxford is a registered trademark of Oxford University Press.

Library of Congress Cataloging-in-Publication Data
McCleary, Rachel M., 1953–
Global compassion : private voluntary organizations and U.S. foreign policy
since 1939 / Rachel M. McCleary.
p.   cm.
Includes bibliographical references and index.
ISBN 978-0-19-537117-8
1. Voluntarism—Government policy—United States—History.   2. Non-governmental
organizations—Government policy—United States—History.   3. World War,
1939–1945—War work—United States.   4. United States—Foreign relations—1945–1989.
5. United States—Foreign relations—1989–   I. Title.
HN90.V64M393   2009
361.7'7097309045—dc22   2008041064

1 3 5 7 9 8 6 4 2

Printed in the United States of America
on acid-free paper

Preface

Before the terrorist attacks of September 11, 2001, on the United States, societies were experiencing geopolitical fragmentation. The ideologically rigid fault lines of the cold war became fluid. National and ethnic identities reemerged, and new political alliances were created. After the 2001 terrorist attacks, transnational threats followed religious fault lines, creating a different fragmented world. Both scenarios—the cold war and post–September 11—have been the root of great human suffering and dehumanization.

The field of international relief and development is going through a radical change, not out of willfulness but because of transnational security threats that run along both ideological and religious fault lines. Current world circumstances require private voluntary organizations (PVOs) to remain operationally flexible, adapting to quickly changing circumstances while addressing security issues that historically have not been present.

Unfortunately, PVOs for all their expertise and experience lag behind rather than lead a reassessment of how relief and development should be carried out. To be viable, they must reclaim the programmatic territory they have given up to for-profit contractors and the U.S. military. They need to refocus on their institutional strengths and the constituencies they are serving.

This book is a constructive attempt, using long-term data, to show the strengths and weaknesses of the relationship between PVOs and the U.S. government. As that relationship grew closer, the U.S. federal bureaucracy expanded and PVOs gained experience and maturity, resulting in complexities.

PVOs accepting significant federal funds became interest groups losing sight of their constituencies overseas. These agencies need to wean themselves from that source of funding to become relevant and meet the challenges of aiding others in the new global context. Furthermore, in times of emergencies, when governments seek to further strengthen that dependency, humanitarian agencies should resist, retaining their independence to make sound institutional decisions.

The work of PVOs overseas is invaluable as they bring skills, education, medicine, and technology to areas of the world where governments barely provide basic services, if at all; national civil society structures are weak; and concepts of civic participation are nascent. Like many Americans, I was raised with the belief that if you gave someone the opportunity to become self-sufficient, they would accept the challenge.

Having grown up in the midst of people who dedicated their lives to working in relief and development, this book is both a personal and a professional endeavor. I dedicate this book to my parents, Paul Frederick and Rachel Pauline McCleary, who served as missionaries in Bolivia. My father, on returning from the mission field, became head of Church World Service, Save the Children, and Christian Children's Fund. After retiring, my father continued working by founding another PVO, ForChildren, Inc.

Several individuals who work in the field of international relief and development generously engaged in discussions with me, sharing their insights and experiences. As practitioners in the field of international relief and development, their experiences contributed to my gaining a broad yet nuanced perspective of issues. I would like to recognize their contribution to my understanding and this work. I wish to thank the former presidents of InterAction: Peter Davies, Julia Taft (deceased), Mary McClymont, and Ken Giunta. I am especially indebted to Judith Gilmore, former director of the U.S. Agency for International Development's (USAID's) Private Voluntary Cooperation–American Schools and Hospitals Abroad (PVC-ASHA), whose comments on the manuscript greatly helped me to think through and improve the presentation of my ideas. My gratitude is extended to the following individuals for their collegiality: Thomas Getman, James McCracken, Serge Duss, John DeHaan, Ray Martin, Jerry Ballard, Kathryn Wolford, Tom H. Fox, Elise Smith, John Garrison, Tom Keene, Frank Kiehne, Ken Hackett, Robert Seiple, Ted Engstrom, Robert Ainsworth, Richard Stearns, Michael Wiest, Cheryl Morden, Terry Hasdorff, Bud Hancock, Andrew Natsios, Vanessa Goiza, Garrett Grigsby, Ben Homan, Wesley Wilson, and John Gardner.

I wish to thank John Raisian, director of the Hoover Institution at Stanford University, for generously providing me with summer support and an office. Ronald Becker, head of the Special Collections and University Archives Department at Archibald S. Alexander Library at Rutgers University, patiently and graciously assisted me with the collection of the American Council of Voluntary Agencies in Foreign Service data. During data gathering over several years from various sources, student research assistants were invaluable. I want to express my appreciation to Brian Boyle, Matt Siegler, and Sarah Gogel. My special thanks to Emily Neill, Dana Brudowsky, Kimberly Priore, and José Ursúa. I wish to express my gratitude to Harriett Pallas and Mary Newton, who professionally manage and organize the data on PVOs at USAID. To my husband, Robert Barro, who has been a constant source of support, I wish to say thank you.

Contents

List of Figures

List of Tables

Global Compassion

1

Dispelling Common Perceptions

Since World War II, private voluntary organizations (PVOs) have played a major role in U.S. efforts at international relief and development.[1] Prior to World War II, the United States did not actively engage in peacetime foreign assistance. With the reconstruction of Europe and the threat of Communism, the U.S. federal government rightfully perceived foreign aid as a critical dimension of American foreign policy. Since the terrorist attacks on the United States on September 11, 2001, foreign assistance has again become a topic of debate. In 2002, President George W. Bush designated international development as one of the three strategic pillars of U.S. national security (the other two are defense and diplomacy).[2] Clamors for aid reform are mounting, especially after the Bush administration announced in 2006 concerning what it calls *transformational diplomacy* or *transformational development* and the creation of a new position, director of foreign assistance.[3] This new director will serve also as administrator of the U.S. Agency for International Development (USAID) and oversee a newly created Bureau of Foreign Assistance.[4]

Transformational development calls for the United States to promote change within states on democratic governance. Political, social, and economic institutions are of primary concern to U.S. foreign policy as opposed to state-to-state relations.[5] Foreign aid, as part of transformational development, is meant to strengthen fragile states, provide humanitarian aid, support U.S. geostrategic goals, and ameliorate transnational diseases such as HIV/AIDS.

The Helping to Enhance the Livelihood of People, or HELP, Commission set up by Congress in 2004 was tasked with looking at the successes and failures of foreign aid. The HELP Commission's final report recommended new foreign aid legislation.[6] Think tanks, such as the Center for Global Development, the Brookings Institution, the Center for Strategic and International Studies, the Wye River Consensus Group, each came out with a set of recommendations for foreign assistance reform.[7] These studies are similar in that they recommend rewriting the current legislation and restructuring foreign aid programs to better address contemporary humanitarian, development, and security interests. At the same time, these studies emphasize bilateral aid and are curiously silent on a key group of implementers of foreign aid, the PVOs. This oversight is ironic given that PVOs work in countries with local populations as agents of change through their programs. Historically, the U.S. government has relied on PVOs to carry out humanitarian and development activities that complement U.S. foreign policy objectives.

This book focuses on PVOs and their phenomenal growth from 1939 to 2005 (fig. 1.1). The PVOs—the American Friends Service Committee, the Jewish Joint Distribution Committee, CARE, World Relief, and Catholic Relief Services, to name just a few—perform a vital function. They are the expression of human caring overseas, a compassion that was formalized during World War II and has continued to grow. This book explores the relationship between PVOs and the U.S. federal government, particularly through the lens of American foreign policy. This

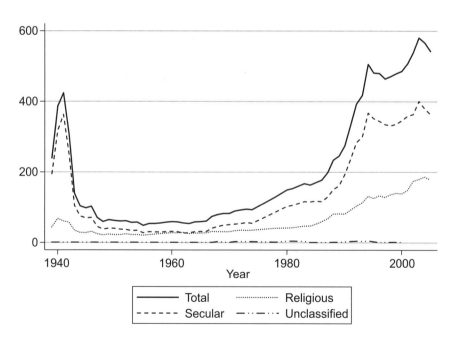

Figure 1.1. Numbers of PVOs, 1939–2005.
Source: McCleary Private Voluntary Organizations Data Set.
Note: Data missing for 1975–77, 1979, 1982.

nexus is a neglected, yet vital, connection between the American people and their government.

The public tends to focus on the accountability of PVOs: do our donations really go to the programs and people these agencies claim to serve on our behalf? Contributors have the right to question where their dollars are going and how they are being used and to receive information outlining the need for their dollars. Donors tend to give to organizations that are efficient (fulfilling their mandate through their programs) and represent the values of the donor. In other words, giving to a charity is a personal choice, partially a transaction of compassion but grounded in a factual assessment of the efficiency of the charity's work.

A growing number of watchdog groups serve the public and ensure that nonprofit organizations remain private and voluntary. In addition, the International Revenue Service (IRS), with the support of key congressional committees,[8] is reinstituting the commensurate test enacted into law in 1964. Over the years, legislators sought to regulate the activities of charitable organizations, particularly when gross violations came to the public's attention. Recent congressional focus on nonprofit organizations is due to the large endowments of universities. Congress would like to see nonprofit organizations distribute a minimum percentage of their funds annually. The commensurate test requires nonprofits to demonstrate that they are allotting significant amounts of their funds to charitable programs and not to administrative activities.

Yet, as contributors of volunteer time and money to PVOs, the general public has little understanding of the extent and nature of the federal support PVOs receive and how the federal government pressures and regulates these organizations. This relationship is important to examine. The PVOs carry out not only what we, as contributors, want done as an expression of our compassion but also what the federal government wants implemented as part of American foreign policy. In many global contexts, what PVOs do, be it building water wells in the Guatemalan highlands or sending emergency food to Pakistani earthquake victims, is often perceived as representing the donor's values and what the donor, as contributor to PVOs, stands for. The PVOs that accept U.S. federal support exist and work at the nexus of civil society and U.S. foreign policy.

The contribution of this book is to understand how PVOs represent civil society's humanitarian concerns while concurrently relating to the U.S. federal government. A significant aspect of the interaction between PVOs and government is economic. The PVOs accept federal assistance in the form of grants, contracts, subsidies (food commodities, excess government property), and shipping. Since 1939, PVO financial independence, or dependence on the federal government for assistance, has been a contentious issue. Financial independence of the PVOs is interrelated with types of federal funding mechanisms.

To find out how much federal assistance PVOs have received over time, I constructed a large data set on revenue and expenditures from 1939 to 2005 for all U.S.-based PVOs engaged in international assistance and registered with the federal government. The data set is new and the most comprehensive on U.S.-based PVOs. (The data set is available at http://ksghome.harvard.edu/~rmcclea/). This introduction describes the data and characterizes the main trends among religious and secular PVOs since 1939. What I mainly focus on in this book is the interplay between, on the one hand, revenue from the U.S. federal government, international organizations, and other governments and, on the other hand, private revenue, that is, funds PVOs raise from the general public. Do funds a PVO receives from the federal government, international organizations, and other governments serve as a magnet for subsequent private support? Or, once a PVO receives federal revenue, is it likely to continue to do so? Accepting federal aid raises concerns about whether PVOs were awarded funds based on their capability and willingness to fulfill U.S. priorities or whether PVO programs were inherently worthy of federal support.

Questions and Issues

This book focuses on the economic relationship between the U.S. federal government and PVOs. Using financial data from 1939 to 2005, I attempt to answer two sets of questions:

1. For PVOs that accept federal assistance, to what degree are they dependent on the federal government for their continuing existence? If PVOs, by accepting federal aid, become dependent on the government, what creates this dependency? Is it federal regulation? Is it PVO inertia? Are certain types of PVOs more independent of federal dollars than others?

2. The second set of questions has to do with PVOs as instruments of U.S. foreign policy. To what degree do PVOs that accept federal assistance view themselves as carrying out U.S. foreign policy? Given that U.S. foreign aid is shaped in some degree by foreign policy objectives, do PVOs lose programmatic independence from the government?

This study also assesses the extent to which international relief and development work is becoming a commercial activity. The term *commercial* has been used to designate two trends in government funding of relief and development projects. First, since the early 1970s, a substantial amount of development assistance has been channeled through commercial enterprises. In fiscal year 2005, USAID awarded 51% of total funds to for-profit entities,[9] an increase from 38% in fiscal year 2004. Furthermore, the for-profit firms receiving federal funding are increasingly fewer (tables 1.1 and 1.2) and are concentrated in the Washington, D.C., area, in geographic proximity to USAID.[10] By contrast, the headquarters of PVOs are geographically dispersed (for example, Catholic Relief Services is headquartered in Baltimore, Maryland; CARE in Atlanta, Georgia; Save the Children in Westport, Connecticut; and World Vision in Federal Way, Washington).

This study does not directly analyze the effects of for-profit firms competing with PVOs for USAID funding. However, a significant trend in the commercialization of foreign aid is occurring, with the for-profit share of USAID funds increasing and the PVO share decreasing.[11] From fiscal year 1996 to fiscal year 2005, USAID reported that the share of funds awarded to for-profit contractors rose from 33% to 58%.[12]

The second pattern of commercialization, evident since 1980, is the loss of preferred status PVOs enjoyed through set-aside funds. The PVOs are no longer the preferred constituency of USAID and must compete with

Table 1.1. Top ten recipients of USAID procurement funding (millions of 2005 dollars in awarded grants and contracts) in fiscal year 2000.

Name	Total amount	Organization type
Development Alternatives	$181	For-profit
Catholic Relief Services	$156	PVO
CARE	$155	PVO
Barents Group, LLC	$151	For-profit
Chemonics International	$119	For-profit
Save the Children	$71	PVO
World Vision	$65	PVO
Hagler Bailly Services	$58	For-profit
Johns Hopkins University	$53	Nonprofit
Mercy Corps International	$49	PVO

Source: Information obtained from the HELP Commission.

Table 1.2.   Top ten recipients of USAID procurement funding (millions of 2005 dollars in awarded grants and contracts) in fiscal year 2005.

Name	Total amount	Organization type
Development Alternatives, Inc.	$497.1	For-profit
Chemonics International, Inc.	$450.9	For-profit
John Snow, Inc., and nonprofit subsidiary	$242.4	For-profit
Research Triangle Institute	$234.7	Nonprofit
Family Health International	$216.6	Nonprofit
CARE	$172	PVO
Catholic Relief Services	$172	PVO
BearingPoint (formerly KPMG Consulting)	$141.4	For-profit
Louis Berger International Group	$113.4	For-profit
Consortium for Elections and Political Processes Strengthening	$101.8	Nonprofit

Source: Information obtained from the HELP Commission.

for-profit entities for contracts and grants. An example of the displacement of PVOs as the main implementers of U.S. foreign assistance is the Global Development Alliance, which primarily promotes government–private sector partnering.[13] The PVOs are a small part of this three-way partnership (government, private enterprise, PVO).

Historically, PVOs have functioned under the regulation of the federal government, viewing their activities as complementary to those of the federal government. In other words, PVOs historically have not tended to operate independently of the federal government. This long-term and at times heavy-handed regulation by the federal government, particularly during World War II, shaped the nature of the PVO sector today. Today, in attempts to circumvent government direction and regulation, PVOs act as an interest group. The PVOs accepting federal assistance lobby Congress to influence funding in both level and type and to ensure that the government does not increase regulation of PVOs. I find that the more federal funds a PVO receives, the more likely that PVO is to receive private funds. My estimate from statistical analysis is that for every federal dollar a PVO receives this year, that same agency will receive 30 cents more next year in private funds.[14] So it is understandable from the PVO perspective that continuing to have federal dollars available is a good thing, with a positive effect on a PVO receiving increased private funds.

Another hypothesis I wanted to test is if those PVOs dependent on federal funding tend to follow the U.S. government's policy direction.[15] In contrast, PVOs that remain financially independent can serve as pressure groups, urging the government to alter U.S. foreign policy focus. One way of testing this is to look at PVO-government relations during wartime. The time period of this book covers several U.S. wars: World War II, the Korean War, the Vietnam War, and the war in Iraq. I find that PVOs with minimal if any federal funds seek to remain independent of the government and the military. More importantly, PVOs that are not dependent upon federal dollars may have little reason to directly influence U.S. foreign policy. PVOs that heavily rely on the federal government for funds, such as Catholic Relief Services and CARE, have tended to cooperate with the U.S. government and military in wartime.

Overview of the Data Set

To identify the agencies in international relief and development, I went to the federal agencies responsible for overseeing their activities: USAID and its predecessor government agencies—the President's Committee on War Relief Agencies (1939–42), the War Relief Control Board (1942–46), the Committee on Voluntary Foreign Aid (1946–51), and the Foreign Operations Administration/International Cooperation Administration (1953–61). Recent data on registered agencies are available from USAID (1962–present).

The assembly of long-term information—especially before the 1980s—was challenging. Sources of data, aside from government agency reports, include PVO annual reports, U.S. State Department documents, and Internal Revenue Service (IRS) documents. I assembled data for 1939 to 2005, excluding a few budget years for which USAID reports were not prepared: 1975–77, 1979, and 1982.

The standard USAID statements break down PVO revenue into three broad categories: federal, international organizations and other governments, and private. For the full sample from 1939 to 2005, the average breakdown for revenue shares is 22.6% federal, 2.3% international organizations and other governments, and 75.2% private. When the information is available, federal receipts are distinguished by type of federal assistance: grants, contracts, freight, Public Law (P.L.) 480 food, and excess property (box 1.1).

Box 1.1. Scheme for data set on PVO revenue and expenditure

Revenue
Federal government
    USAID freight
    P.L. 480 freight
    P.L. 480 food
    USAID grants
    USAID contracts
    Other U.S. government grants
    Other U.S. government contracts
    U.S. government surplus property
International organizations and other government
Private
    In-kind contributions
    Private cash contributions
    Other private revenue

Expenditure
    International programs
    Domestic programs
    Administrative outlays
    Fund-raising expenses

Source: McCleary Private Voluntary Organizations Data Set.

Dollar values for in-kind programs, such as freight, P.L. 480 food, and excess property, are based on market values estimated by USAID and other government agencies. Revenue from international organizations and other governments is a composite of funding from multilateral organizations, such as the United Nations, along with receipts from state and local governments and foreign governments. I refer to this category as international organization (IO) revenue. Private revenue is divided among in-kind donations, cash donations, and other revenue.

On the expenditure side, there is the division of program outlay between foreign and U.S. operations. Two other spending categories are administration and fund-raising. Box 1.1, based on the system used in recent USAID reports, shows the categories of revenue and expenditure in which the data have been compiled. Earlier years have less disaggregation by category.

The data set includes information on 1,689 U.S.-based PVOs that registered with the U.S. federal government sometime between 1939 and

2005. The label *U.S. based* means that an agency received 501(c)(3) tax-exempt charitable status with the U.S. IRS. The organization might have been founded in another country; for example, the Save the Children Federation originated in England. However, the PVO must have a U.S. office. The PVOs were classified by date of founding; when this date could not be ascertained, a PVO was classified by the legal ruling year, which tends to be a few years after establishment. In a small number of cases, I was unable to designate a founding year.

I hope to dispel the widely held perception that PVOs are an undifferentiated amalgam of agencies. As the classifications of registered PVOs in the data set over decades show, the field of international relief and development has become increasingly heterogeneous, with diversity across subgroups as well as increasingly within groups (for example, within the group of secular PVOs). A classification scheme was created with 16 categories of PVOs: one secular, fourteen forms of religious, and one unclassified (see table 1.3). The secular PVOs were further classified into six types by sector activities (see table 1.4).[16] This information becomes

Table 1.3.   Classifications of PVOs.

Code number	Category
1	Mainline Protestant
2	Roman Catholic
3	Orthodox
4	Faith-founded Christian
5	Ecumenical Christian
6	Other Christian
7	Evangelical
8	Jewish
9	Muslim
10	Hindu
11	Buddhist
12	Jain
13	Interfaith
14	Other religion
15	Secular
16	Unclassified

Table 1.4. Classifications of secular PVOs.

Code number	Category
1	Economic growth, agricultural development, and trade
	a. Agricultural development
	b. Private sector, small enterprises
	c. Engineering and infrastructure
2	International relief and development
	a. Community/capacity building
	b. Ethnic unity/ethnic issues
	c. Human rights/international law/democracy
	d. Peace groups and conflict resolution
	e. Relief and development issues
	f. Gender issues and family planning
3	Education and training
	a. Children's basic education
	b. Higher learning (universities, research)
	c. Professional associations and societies
4	Natural resource management
	a. Environmental issues
	b. Animal rights and protection
5	Culture and society
	a. Cultural issues
	b. Society organizations
	c. Communication and media
	d. Foundations
6	Medicine and health issues
	a. Medicine and hospitals
	b. HIV/AIDS programs

Source: McCleary Private Voluntary Organizations Data Set.

relevant to the discussion when secular agencies began to dominate the field of international relief and development.

After extensive research—using PVO annual reports, InterAction membership data, and other sources—all but 26 PVOs were assigned to one of the 15 classified categories in table 1.3. The 26 unclassified organizations constitute a negligible part of total PVO revenue and expenditure. Each agency was classified by type at founding and in 2005 (or at the agency's final year of existence), thus creating a basis for tracking changes over time in the nature of each organization. Overall, I identified 67 cases of changed classification. Because these changes often involved a gradual transition, I do not isolate the particular year of change. Among the 67 changes, 49 constitute shifts from religious to secular, 17 among religion types, and 1 from secular to religious.

The largest PVOs to change classification were World Vision (evangelical to faith-founded Christian, 2005 revenue of $795 million), Food for the Poor (Catholic to faith-founded Christian, $760 million), Northwest Medical Teams (evangelical to faith-founded Christian, $242 million), Christian Children's Fund (mainline Protestant to secular, $186 million), Mercy Corps International (ecumenical Christian to secular, $184 million), and Cross International (Catholic to interfaith, $171 million).[17]

To classify registered PVOs, information was obtained from PVO annual reports, InterAction documents, and publications from other umbrella organizations and independent "watchdog" groups. However, many of these organizations rely on self-reporting by the PVOs. For example, InterAction—the largest umbrella organization for U.S.-based PVOs working in international relief and development—does not verify information submitted by member PVOs. Three Web sites—those for Guidestar, Charity Navigator, and Ministry Watch—check information submitted to them and have a rating scheme for PVOs. In addition, most PVOs have their own Web sites. I also used the annual membership directories of the National Council of Churches of Christ, USA; written histories of PVOs; and personal communications.[18]

Table 1.3 shows seven types of Christian PVOs: mainline Protestant, Roman Catholic (henceforth abbreviated as Catholic), orthodox, evangelical, faith-founded Christian (sometimes shortened to faith-founded), ecumenical Christian (sometimes abbreviated as ecumenical), and other Christian. For Protestant religions, I followed much of Brian Steensland and colleagues' classification scheme, which provides a useful framework because it distinguishes denominational organizations from newer nondenominational types.[19] I made a few departures from the Steensland Protestant typology. First, I classified black Protestant with mainline Protestant. Second, I coded the Unitarian Universal Association as mainline Protestant.[20] Third, Vineyard Church was classified as evangelical, although some of its congregations would be considered Pentecostal.

I chose not to use the entire Steensland classification because it is based on General Social Survey (GSS) religion categories.[21] To study U.S.-based PVOs, it is necessary to distinguish finer categories within Protestant Christianity. For example, Steensland has no ecumenical category. In addition, Steensland's classification of all nondenominational Protestants as evangelical elides the theological differences between nondenominational Protestants and evangelicals. Further, the faith-founded Christian category captures a recent change in the religion scene, namely, the rise of agencies that are neither evangelical nor denominational but that adhere to broad Christian values. My approach relies on sources within the field of international relief and development to create categories that reflect the faith statements of the agencies.

With regard to Catholic PVOs, I used the Catholic Network of Volunteer Service, the U.S. Catholic Conference of Bishops, and the *Official Catholic Directory*. Catholic Relief Services is the only Catholic PVO in the sample that received part of its funding directly from the U.S. Catholic Conference of Bishops through an annual national collection in the parishes.

Coding faith-founded Christian organizations was complicated. I define *faith-founded* organizations as those based on religious principles or values but with no formal affiliation with an organized religion. For organizations that identified their religious values as drawn from a particular organized religion, the agency was classified by the type of organized religion, mainline Protestant, for example. Christian organizations were identified as faith-founded Christian when they held that their religious values came from no particular denomination of a religion. Christian agencies based on at least two specific Protestant denominations are classified as ecumenical Christian. PVOs classified as *interfaith* are formed by at least two distinct major religious or spiritual traditions, not all Christian.

Evangelical PVOs are characterized by their doctrine, which emphasizes evangelicalism. As a group, they accept basic tenets: the inerrancy of the Bible and its authority as the sole source of God's word; the deity of Jesus as Christ and personal salvation through him; the sharing of the conversion experience with others; and pre- or postmillennium beliefs.[22] Evangelical PVOs can be humanitarian agencies of denominations (e.g., Adventist Development and Relief Agency), agencies of parachurches (e.g., International Association of Missions of the Vineyard Churches), or independent faith-founded evangelical agencies (e.g., World Vision in its initial structure). In classifying evangelical PVOs, membership directories were helpful, for example, those of the Association of Evangelical Relief and Development Organizations (AERDO), the National Association of

Evangelicals (NAE), the Evangelical Fellowship of Mission Agencies, the Intervarsity Web site for missions (www.urbana.org), the World Evangelical Alliance, and the Evangelism and Missions Information Service's biannual *Mission Handbook: U.S. and Canadian Christian Ministries.*

Non-Christian religions such as Jewish, Muslim, Hindu, and Jain (see table 1.3) represent a small fraction of the total number of registered PVOs. The Jewish agencies such as B'nai B'rith International, the Hebrew Immigrant Aid Society, Bellefaire Jewish Children's Bureau, and the National Council of Jewish Women were originally established as service organizations to the Jewish immigrant communities in the United States. Muslim organizations such as the Aga Khan Foundation and Grameen Foundation, among others, are guided by Islamic values and work worldwide. The only registered Buddhist organization—the Tibet Fund—serves the refugee and immigrant Tibetan communities around the world. The Tibet Fund is the humanitarian agency of the Dalai Lama's government in exile.

To enter the sample, a PVO must have registered with the relevant federal agency—USAID since the early 1960s. Since a key criterion for registration was orientation toward international relief and development, there is some correspondence between the sample universe and the research focus of this book. However, PVOs differ in the extent of their activities geared toward international programs. Most purely domestic PVOs do not register with USAID—and are therefore not in the sample—but some registered PVOs have international activities that comprise only a small part of their programs. For example, international program expenditures of the American National Red Cross total less than 1% of total program outlay in many years.

Data on international and domestic program expenditure gauge the extent of each PVO's international orientation. At present, these data exist for 1946–52 and 1967–2005 (excluding the years of missing reports: 1975–77, 1979, and 1982). The international fraction of activity (international program outlay divided by total program outlay) was calculated for each PVO and year with available data. Interpolation or extrapolation of the data for each individual PVO yielded estimates of international fractions for years of missing data. Each dollar item—for example, total revenue—was then adjusted by multiplying by the international fraction. This procedure gives estimates of the internationally oriented part of each dollar item, such as total revenue. Therefore, the data set can include, on a consistent basis, PVOs with very different degrees of international orientation. Division of each dollar item by the consumer price index or CPI (with a base of 2005 = 1.0) generates real values in units of 2005 dollars.

In many cases, existing PVOs merged to form a larger organization. The data set includes the dates of these mergers; my research has been extensive enough to compile a nearly complete list of mergers. Typically, the merged PVO is assigned the same code number as the organization that dominated beforehand in terms of revenue and expenditure. Usually, the name of the combined entity is the same as that of this dominant part. Splits or spin-offs of PVOs are much rarer than mergers.

Trends in PVOs, 1939–2005

Figures 1.1–1.6 display important features of the data. They first present a breakdown of total PVOs as secular, religious, and unclassified. Then they show an assessment of the breakdown of religious PVOs (14 types) in terms of the eight groups that comprise most of the activity by numbers and dollars: mainline Protestant, Roman Catholic, orthodox, faith-founded Christian, ecumenical, evangelical, Jewish, and Muslim.

Figure 1.1 shows numbers of PVOs from 1939 to 2005. The total number rose early in World War II from 240 in 1939 to 387 in 1940 and to 424 in 1941. Then the number plunged during the war because of the government's efforts to eliminate duplicate programs. This consolidation reduced the number of PVOs to 103 in 1946 and 60 in 1948. Subsequently, the number rose in most years, reaching 543 in 2005. Growth was especially rapid from 1986 to 1994, during which the number increased from 178 to 506.

The fraction of PVOs that were religious went from 18% in 1939 to a peak of 52% in 1962. Then the religious fraction fell, reaching 26% in 1994. Since then, the number of religious PVOs, especially of the evangelical type, has grown faster than the secular number. In 2005, the 179 religious PVOs were 33% of the total.

Figures 1.2 and 1.3 show the breakdown of religious PVOs into eight main types. In 1940, the composition was 40% Catholic, 22% Jewish, 15% mainline Protestant, 9% evangelical, and 6% faith-founded. During the war, the main change was the decline in the Catholic share. In 1946, the distribution was 38% Jewish, 19% mainline Protestant, 16% evangelical, 12% faith-founded, and 3% Catholic (with the single Catholic PVO the predecessor to Catholic Relief Services). In the post–World War II period, the most striking changes were the rise in evangelical and faith-founded Christian numbers and the relative decline in Jewish numbers. In 2005, the breakdown was 49% evangelical, 13% faith-founded, 8% Catholic, 7% mainline Protestant, 6% ecumenical, 5% Jewish, 2% Muslim, and 1% Orthodox, with 8% in other religions.

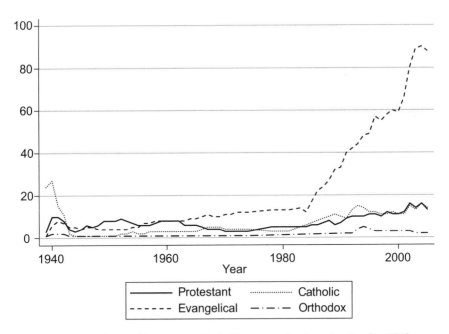

Figure 1.2. Numbers of Protestant, Catholic, evangelical, and orthodox PVOs.
Source: McCleary Private Voluntary Organizations Data Set.
Note: Data missing for 1975–77, 1979, 1982.

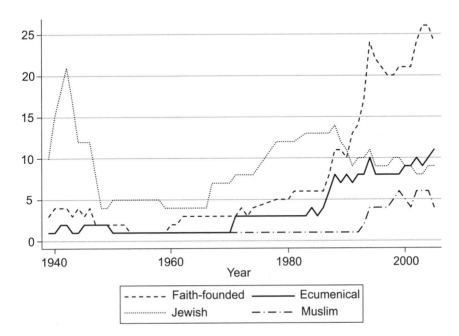

Figure 1.3. Numbers of faith-founded, ecumenical, Jewish, and Muslim PVOs.
Source: McCleary Private Voluntary Organizations Data Set.
Note: Data missing for 1975–77, 1979, 1982.

Table 1.5. Time pattern for founding and new registering of PVOs.

Time period	Number founded[a]	Number newly registered
Before 1900	85	—
1900–38	161	—
1939	221	240[b]
1940	132	178
1941	92	130
1942–49	77	81
1950–59	75	28
1960–69	104	50
1970–79	158	87
1980–89	238	188
1990–99	258	475
2000–5	47	232
Unknown founding year	41	—
Totals	1,689	1,689

Source: McCleary Private Voluntary Organizations Data Set.
[a] Numbers founded apply only to our universe of PVOs registered at some point between 1939 and 2005.
[b] Number for 1939 equals the number of all PVOs registered at that date.

Changes in numbers of registered PVOs involve large flows into and out of registered status. Although the largest number registered in a single year was 581 in 2003, the total number of PVOs registered at least once between 1939 and 2005 was 1,689. To register, a PVO must first be founded and then decide to register (and be accepted). I know founding dates only for PVOs that registered at least once between 1939 and 2005. The distribution of these founding dates appears in the second column of table 1.5.

Note that 246 PVOs have founding dates prior to the start of the sample, 1939. The large number of foundings, 445, between 1939 and 1941 reflects relief efforts related to World War II. Column 3 shows numbers of newly registered PVOs. The number 240 for 1939 is the full stock of PVOs registered at that date. The large number of new registrants, 308, for 1940–41 again reflects World War II.

Table 1.6 deals with outflows of PVOs. Column 2 shows, for each period, the number of PVOs in their final year of registration. However, PVOs not registered in 2005 but registered in at least one prior year may

Table 1.6. Timing of final registration year and losses from mergers.

Time period	Number in final registration year[a]	Number lost from mergers
1939	30	12
1940	92	3
1941	138	12
1942	173	64
1943	43	13
1944	15	0
1945–49	66	3
1950–59	27	2
1960–69	33	4
1970–79	31	1
1980–89	79	3
1990–99	251	4
2000–4	168	6
Totals	1,145	127

Source: McCleary Private Voluntary Organizations Data Set. Determined as of report for 2005, for which the number registered was 543.
[a] Determined as of Volag report for 2005, for which the number of registered agencies was 543.

eventually return to the sample. One finding in column 2 is the large number of PVOs, 433, that were in their final year of registration during the World War II period, 1939–42. Especially following the bulge of new registrants early in the war (1939–41 in table 1.5), the federal government forced many smaller PVOs to exit—especially from 1940 to 1942 (Table 1.6).

One channel through which smaller PVOs disappeared was mergers, amounting usually to takeovers by larger PVOs. Table 1.6, column 3, shows the number of PVOs that vanished due to mergers. The timing corresponds to that in column 2—for example, if a PVO ceased to exist because of a merger in 1943, then that PVO's last report will be for 1942. Hence, the merger applies in table 1.6 to 1942.

Overall, the identified mergers constituted 11% of overall PVO exit, that is, 11% of the number of PVOs in their final year of registration, as shown in column 2 of table 1.6. Merger activity, encouraged by the federal government, was particularly strong during World War II, with 89 PVOs vanishing between 1941 and 1943 because of mergers; 42 of these went into a single PVO, American Relief for Poland.

Figure 1.4 shows the evolution of total real revenue for all PVOs and for secular versus religious. During World War II, the pattern of real revenue for all PVOs differed from that for numbers of PVOs because—after 1941—rising real revenue was concentrated among a sharply diminishing number of organizations. For all PVOs, real revenue in 2005 dollars increased from $316 million in 1940 to $2.8 billion in 1945, fell to $1.4 billion in 1947 and a low point of $510 million in 1952, and then advanced to $15.9 billion in 2005. The average growth rate over 65 years (1940–2005) was 6.0% per year.

The fraction of PVO revenue going to religious agencies went from 18% in 1940 to a peak of 79% in 1952. Then the religious fraction fell, reaching 39% in 1995. Subsequently, this share recovered to 46% in 2005. Since religious PVOs in 2005 were only 33% by number, the size in terms of revenue of the typical religious PVO was larger than that of the typical secular PVO.[23]

Figures 1.5 and 1.6 describe the real revenue of eight major types of religious PVOs. The fraction for Jewish organizations was a remarkable

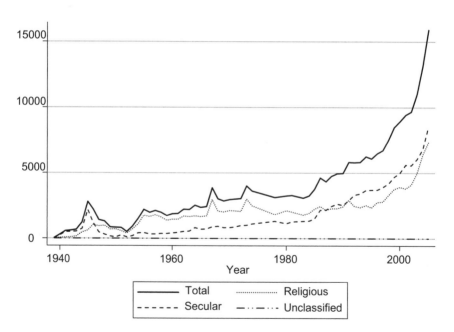

Figure 1.4. Revenues of PVOs (millions of 2005 dollars), 1939–2005.
Source: McCleary Private Voluntary Organizations Data Set.
Note: Real revenue is the dollar amount divided by the consumer price index (2005 base) and multiplied by the international fraction for programs. Data missing for 1975–77, 1979, 1982.

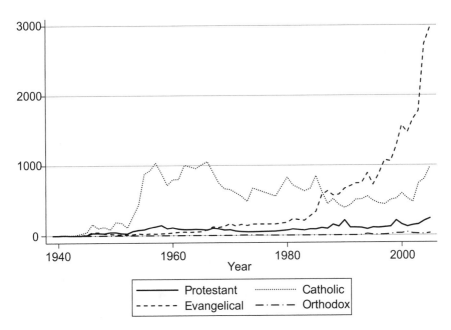

Figure 1.5. Revenues of religious PVOs (millions of 2005 dollars), 1939–2005.
Source: McCleary Private Voluntary Organizations Data Set.
Note: See note to figure 1.4.

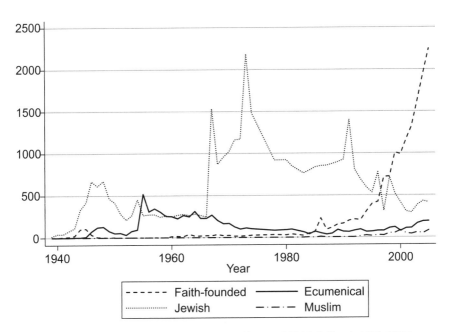

Figure 1.6. Revenues of religious PVOs (millions of 2005 dollars), 1939–2005.
Source: McCleary Private Voluntary Organizations Data Set.
Note: See note to figure 1.4.

72% in 1940, although Jewish PVOs were then only 22% by number. In 1946, the revenue shares were 64% Jewish, 16% Catholic, 7% ecumenical Christian, 5% evangelical, 4% mainline Protestant, and 3% faith-founded Christian, with less than 1% in other religions. The most striking changes thereafter were the decline in the Jewish share and the rises in the evangelical and faith-founded shares. In 2005, the percentages of total revenue were 40% evangelical, 31% faith-founded, 13% Catholic, 6% Jewish, 3% mainline Protestant, 3% ecumenical, and 1% Muslim, with 3% in other religions.

Figure 1.7 shows the evolution from 1939 to 2005 of the breakdown of total PVO revenue among its three main components—federal, private, and international organizations. Federal funding became significant only in 1950. For all PVOs, the shares of federal funding in total revenue averaged 23% from 1950 to 1954, 58% from 1955 to 1966, 39% from 1967 to 1986, 31% from 1987 to 1995, and 27% from 1996 to 2004 and then fell to 19% in 2005. Thus, the federal share reached a high point during the

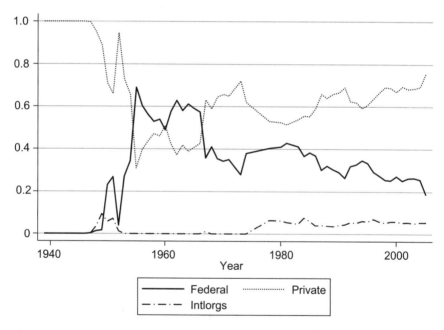

Figure 1.7. PVO revenue shares (federal, private, international organizations), 1939–2005.
Source: McCleary Private Voluntary Organizations Data Set.
Note: See note to figure 1.4. Revenue for each component is calculated as in figure 1.4.

Eisenhower-Kennedy-Johnson years (1955–66) and has since declined sharply. In contrast to federal funding, the share of revenue coming from international organizations has never been large.

After World War II, private contributions to PVOs dropped but then rose sharply to meet the humanitarian needs during and after the Korean War. Private revenue to PVOs continued to climb in contrast to the federal revenue trend. Federal revenue to PVOs spiked during the Korean War and dramatically rose as technical assistance programs became part of the cold war strategy. Since the late 1960s, when the Vietnam War escalated, the federal share of PVO revenue has consistently dropped. The share of revenue from international organizations spiked like other sources of funding during the Korean War. Funding from international organizations, reflecting the American "go-it-alone" attitude, has never been significant for U.S.-based PVOs.

Figure 1.8 highlights the evolution of the federal share since 1955 and indicates the pattern separately for religious and secular PVOs. For a few years in the 1950s, federal support favored religious PVOs in the sense

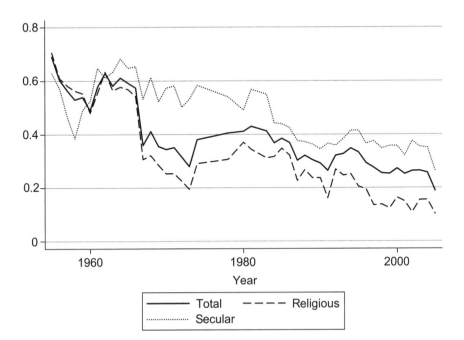

Figure 1.8. Federal share of total revenue (total, religious, secular), 1955–2005.
Source: McCleary Private Voluntary Organizations Data Set.
Note: See notes to figure 1.7.

that their share of revenue from federal sources was greater than that for secular PVOs. However, from 1955 to 1966 the federal shares for secular and religious PVOs became similar, with both averaging 58%. The federal share for religious PVOs fell sharply in 1967 and thereby became much smaller than that for secular PVOs. From 1967 to 1985, the federal share averaged 53% for secular PVOs and 29% for religious ones. The federal share for secular PVOs fell starting in the mid-1980s, and the share for religious PVOs continued to decline. Thus, from 1986 to 1995 the shares averaged 38% for secular and 24% for religious PVOs, and from 1996 to 2005, the shares averaged 35% for secular and only 14% for religious PVOs.

Another way to look at federal support is to consider the number of PVOs that received zero federal dollars. From 1953 to 2005, of PVO-year observations with positive total revenue 41% showed zero federal support (4,358 of 10,602). The overall percentage breaks down to 38% for secular PVOs versus 47% for religious. In 2005, of all PVOs with positive total revenue 46% reported zero federal dollars (248 of 542). The breakdown was 42% for secular and 54% for religious.

Looking at table 1.7, we see some circulation among the top ten agencies (ranked by revenue) registered with USAID over the decades. From 1950 to 2000, there were 60 spots to be filled in the top ten list over those six decades. Over that time period, 24 agencies appeared in those 60 slots at least once. Three agencies appeared in the top ten in all six decades: CARE, Catholic Relief Services, and American Jewish Joint Distribution Committee. World Vision and Save the Children also became enduring fixtures in the top ten.

As federal ad hoc mechanisms for funding humanitarian assistance became permanent programs, certain PVOs were in a position to garner significant federal dollars. We know this to be the case with Catholic Relief Services and CARE. Among religious PVOs, the shares of federal funding in total revenue varied a great deal over time and by religion. Catholic agencies usually had the largest share coming from federal sources, averaging 71% from 1955 to 1988 and 48% from 1989 to 2005. This funding is dominated by Catholic Relief Services, which effectively functions as a quasi-governmental agency—it maintained an average federal funding share of 69% from 1955 to 2005. CARE comes in a close second and has the largest federal share of secular agencies. Among the secular PVOs, from 1995 to 2005 CARE maintained a 66.4% average federal funding share.[24] Save the Children, also a secular agency, started receiving significant federal dollars in the mid-1980s. Save the Children became one of the top ten in revenue at this time and has remained there. Save the Children's average federal funding share from 1980 to 2005 was 43.4%. World Vision,

Table 1.7. Top ten lists for PVO total real revenue (millions of 2005 dollars).

PVO	Type	Total revenue	Federal %
	2005		
Americares Foundation	Secular	849	0.0
World Vision	Faith-founded	795	18.4
Food for the Poor	Faith-founded	760	5.7
GAVI Fund	Secular	747	8.6
Catholic Relief Services	Catholic	699	47.4
CARE	Secular	624	35.4
Feed the Children	Evangelical	543	4.5
Save the Children	Secular	392	31.4
MAP International	Evangelical	344	0.0
Samaritan's Purse	Evangelical	314	2.4
	2000		
CARE	Secular	506	54.2
World Vision	Faith-founded	452	16.1
Catholic Relief Services	Catholic	433	61.9
United Armenian Fund	Evangelical	276	0.0
Food for the Poor	Faith-founded	268	19.1
Americares Foundation	Secular	260	0.0
Feed the Children	Evangelical	244	0.8
Institute of International Education	Secular	168	64.3
American-Jewish Joint Distribution Committee	Jewish	150	0.0
Save the Children	Secular	149	47.2
	1990		
United Israel Appeal	Jewish	610	8.6
CARE	Secular	439	51.5
Catholic Relief Services	Catholic	329	72.6
Institute of International Education	Secular	210	33.1
Christian Children's Fund	Secular	147	0.0
Rotary Foundation	Secular	142	1.4

(*continued*)

Table 1.7. *(continued)*

PVO	Type	Total revenue	Federal %
American-Jewish Joint Distribution Committee	Jewish	138	27.1
Lutheran World Relief	Protestant	138	87.0
World Vision	Faith-founded	121	27.0
Save the Children	Secular	109	48.9
	1980		
Catholic Relief Services	Catholic	828	68.7
United Israel Appeal	Jewish	615	7.8
CARE	Secular	463	70.2
American-Jewish Joint Distribution Committee	Jewish	149	3.6
Institute of International Education	Secular	136	18.5
Church World Service	Ecumenical	86.8	43.7
Christian Children's Fund	Secular	84.9	0.0
Hadassah	Jewish	75.0	3.3
Summer Institute of Linguistics	Evangelical	54.0	2.0
Adventist Development and Relief	Evangelical	37.8	70.9
	1970		
United Israel Appeal	Jewish	760	0.1
Catholic Relief Services	Catholic	652	64.6
CARE	Secular	500	82.8
Church World Service	Ecumenical	167	34.3
American-Jewish Joint Distribution Committee	Jewish	120	4.5
Hadassah	Jewish	97.6	1.7
Christian Children's Fund	Secular	82.8	0.8
Lutheran World Relief	Protestant	65.1	39.3
Foster Parents Plan	Secular	57.4	0.2
MAP International	Evangelical	54.5	0.6

Table 1.7. *(continued)*

PVO	Type	Total revenue	Federal %
	1960		
Catholic Relief Services	Catholic	795	61.6
CARE	Secular	314	67.8
Church World Service	Ecumenical	252	55.2
American-Jewish Joint Distribution Committee	Jewish	168	3.8
Lutheran World Relief	Protestant	105	57.4
Hadassah	Jewish	57.0	0.7
Christian Children's Fund	Secular	25.6	0.0
Foster Parents Plan	Secular	25.4	7.9
Organization for Rehabilitation and Training	Jewish	16.4	0.0
Mennonite Central Committee	Evangelical	15.6	17.3
	1950		
American-Jewish Joint Distribution Committee	Jewish	247	2.5
Catholic Relief Services	Catholic	194	32.7
Hadassah	Jewish	155	61.9
CARE	Secular	54.1	11.3
Church World Service	Ecumenical	53.4	0.0
Lutheran World Relief	Protestant	42.6	33.8
Mennonite Central Committee	Evangelical	9.6	6.2
Organization for Rehabilitation and Training	Jewish	9.1	0.0
International Rescue and Relief Committee	Secular	8.8	53.4
Near East Foundation	Secular	8.2	2.4
	1945		
United National Clothing Collection	Secular	1220	0.0
American Society for Russian Relief	Secular	363	0.0

(continued)

Table 1.7. *(continued)*

PVO	Type	Total revenue	Federal %
American-Jewish Joint Distribution Committee	Jewish	187	0.0
United Israel Appeal	Jewish	156	0.0
United Service to China	Secular	129	0.0
American Relief for Italy	Secular	90.4	0.0
American National Red Cross	Secular	63.9	0.0
Young Men's Christian Association	Faith-founded	55.3	0.0
Catholic Relief Services	Catholic	51.5	0.0
War Prisoners' Aid	Faith-founded	46.8	0.0
	1940		
British War Relief Society	Secular	61.3	0.0
American National Red Cross	Secular	59.5	0.0
American-Jewish Joint Distribution Committee	Jewish	30.3	0.0
Bundles for Britain	Secular	12.8	0.0
British American Ambulance Corps	Secular	10.5	0.0
Fortra, Inc.	Secular	10.0	0.0
Hadassah	Jewish	9.39	0.0
American Relief for Poland	Secular	6.73	0.0
Commission for Polish Relief	Secular	6.09	0.0
American Relief for Norway	Secular	5.74	0.0

Source: McCleary Private Voluntary Organizations Data Set.
Note: Real revenue is in millions of 2005 dollars, and amounts have been multiplied by the share of international program expenditure in total program expenditure. The rightmost column shows the percentage of total revenue that came from federal sources.

also a persistent fixture in the top ten, had a 93% federal funding share in 1985 and 87% in 1986. World Vision's average federal funding share from 1980 to 2005 was 35.2%, not as high as Catholic Relief Services, CARE, and Save the Children.

From the mid-1960s to 2005, the ecumenical, mainline Protestant, and evangelical agencies experienced a decline in federal revenue. Ecumenical Christian agencies averaged 67% of their revenue from federal sources from 1955 to 1967 but only 18% from 1968 to 2005. The mainline Protestant group was also high in its federal share early on—averaging 53% from 1955 to 1965—but then fell to 18% from 1966 to 2005. If we look at evangelical agencies, they averaged 33% from 1955 to 1967 but only 11% from 1968 to 2005. The only religious type of agency to have an increase in federal revenue from the late 1970s to 2005 was faith-founded Christian. The federal share for Jewish PVOs averaged only 7% from 1955 to 2005. The Jewish agencies experienced a dramatic decline after WWII, with less than 1% share of federal revenue by the year 2005.

To summarize some of the patterns, during World War II U.S.-based PVOs were predominantly secular and oriented toward ethnically based relief efforts. Then, from the end of the war through the 1970s, religious PVOs became relatively more important (when gauged by revenue and expenditures). A great expansion of secular PVOs took place from the mid-1980s to the mid-1990s, resulting again in a paramount position for secular organizations. However, since 2002 religious PVOs have expanded faster, resulting in a nearly equal division of revenue between secular and religious organizations in 2004–5. These trends are discussed in relation to U.S. foreign policy in the coming chapters.

Points of Contention between PVOs and the Federal Government

Throughout the book, I discuss four primary points of contention between PVOs and the federal government: P.L. 480 food aid, PVO-military relations in wartime, PVO independence and federal funding mechanisms, and future PVO-government relations.

Food Aid

Food aid is a contentious issue in which everyone has a stake and an opinion. Begun in 1949, for feeding programs in Europe the U.S. secretary of agriculture channeled donated surplus farm products to PVOs registered with the federal government. In 1954, at the end of the Korean War, the food program was expanded to include a greater variety of agricultural products and the reimbursement of shipping costs to PVOs for transporting the commodities overseas. Indeed, real food aid peaked from the mid-1950s to the early 1960s and tended to decline thereafter (except for a spike in 2003–4).

The Food for Peace program, proposed by Senator Hubert Humphrey, sought to closely link food programs with economic development in Asia, Latin America, and Africa. In 1960, President John Kennedy made Humphrey's proposal a reality by creating the Food for Peace Office to coordinate food aid with development assistance. The result was a closer alignment of PVO work with foreign policy objects, particularly discouraging programs in countries of peripheral strategic importance to the United States and supporting programs in places like Vietnam, Latin America, and India. By the mid-1960s, half of the food aid was distributed by PVOs registered with the federal government.

The increasing reliance on food aid as part of U.S. foreign policy led to clashes between the federal government and PVOs. From October to December 1975, the U.S. government suspended availability of P.L. 480 food to PVOs. Through its bilateral program (country to country under P.L. 480, Title I), the U.S. government was selling surplus crops to Russia, China, and West Africa because of famines in those regions, thus leaving less surplus food available for established food programs in other parts of the world. The Protestant agencies objected to what they saw as the use of food commodities as an instrument of American foreign policy. To influence public policy, in 1975 Lutheran World Relief and Church World Service set up offices in Washington, D.C., to monitor legislative activity and engage in advocacy efforts in an effort to make the U.S. government more responsive to world hunger and poverty issues.

Differences of opinion on food aid and subsequent intense lobbying efforts were most noticeable with regard to the African famine in 2002–3, but they resurface from time to time as other food crises occur around the world. Similarly, trade policies are a contentious issue, featuring some of the same stakeholders involved in food aid. This is one area where the interests of the U.S. government and its constituents (most notably the agricultural lobby) often stand in direct opposition to PVO humanitarian concerns in the developing world.

Many PVOs have come to view advocacy as one of their core functions. A contradiction (potentially ethical) therefore emerges: How can PVOs accept federal funds and subsidies yet aggressively and publicly pressure to shape the U.S. foreign policy that drives the flow of federal funds to the PVOs? PVOs are generally unwilling to give up advocacy, and they often say that their advocacy work is funded by their private donations. In all fairness to PVOs, their advocacy efforts are neither better nor worse than the lobbying of any trade association whose members are receiving a corporate subsidy or have large government contracts. The core of the issue comes down to the federal government making a rational choice—instead of giving federal funds to an entity that is not carrying out U.S. policy and that uses its funding to lobby for more money, the U.S. government ought to award funds to an organization that will perform as desired, in other words, spend the funds on programs.

The Role of the Military in Humanitarian Aid

Perhaps the most contentious issue dividing the PVOs from post–World War II reconstruction up to the George W. Bush administration is the trend to promote the role of the military in relief and reconstruction efforts. During post–World War II relief efforts, PVOs distributed relief supplies and set up displaced persons camps under the authority of the Allied military command. The escalation of the Vietnam War in 1967 led to a restructuring of operations on the ground, with PVOs and USAID programs reporting to General Westmorland. In 1986, Congress authorized the humanitarian assistance activities by the Department of Defense. The role of the Department of Defense in humanitarian activities expanded in 1996, with Congress authorizing the deployment of military personnel specifically for humanitarian projects.[25] In 2002, the U.S. National Security Strategy subsumed development as an essential part of national security.[26] The responsibility of USAID fell under the rubric of addressing "the underlying conditions that terrorists seek to exploit" such as lack of economic opportunity, political participation, and social integration.[27] The fundamental idea is that political marginalization and lack of economic development are conditions driving conflict and threatening U.S. national security. This idea can be traced back to the Kennedy presidency and the founding of USAID, the Peace Corps, and the Alliance for Progress as mechanisms of economic change and creators of opportunity.[28]

In 2005, the Department of Defense released a directive spelling out the nature of stability operations, such as those in Afghanistan and Iraq.[29] The leap in funds allocated to the Department of Defense's Overseas Humanitarian, Disaster, and Civic Aid Office reflected the new emphasis on the role of the military in humanitarian activities (table 1.8).

The integration of PVO, private sector, and military reconstruction and humanitarian efforts on the ground now takes place under the aegis of the Department of Defense. The secretary of state, in coordination with the Department of Defense, is responsible for ensuring that the Foreign Assistance Act of 1961 is carried out.[30] The Department of

Table 1.8. Overseas humanitarian, disaster, and civic aid appropriation (in millions of 2005 dollars).

Fiscal year	Total funding	Supplemental funding
2004	$58.7	$35.5 Iraq and Afghanistan
2005	$175.8	$95 (tsunami), $22 emergency
2006	$60.8	
2007	$63.2	

Source: Prepared by Tom Smith, PGM-HDM, 601–3657, http://www.dsca.mil/programs/ha/new/OVERSEAS_HUMANITARIAN_DISASTER_AND_CIVIC_AID_b.pdf.

Defense directive clearly states that when civilian agencies cannot or will not perform humanitarian and reconstruction efforts, the Department of Defense will do so.

Following the conflict in Afghanistan and at the onset of the war in Iraq, members of the PVO community became increasingly vocal in their opposition to the practice of military personnel carrying out relief operations in these conflict zones. In some cases, the military personnel have even worn civilian clothing, blurring the line between combatant and relief worker and thus posing what the PVO community felt was an imminent threat to their safety. If hostiles could no longer distinguish between military personnel and those in the development community, many of whom work hard to maintain a neutral stance, then the latter would become a target for violent attack. In addition, InterAction, the umbrella organization for U.S.-based PVOs, argues that having the military carry out humanitarian tasks ignores the experience and expertise of relief workers, who have been doing it far longer. During the war in Iraq, InterAction has become increasingly vocal in its criticism of the Bush administration over this issue, making its case public in the media.

This point of conflict relates directly to another, namely, the role of USAID and the State Department within the administration and with outside stakeholders. As early as the post-Afghanistan reconstruction phase and related to the role of the military to a certain extent, an important question surfaced: which departments within the federal government will be responsible for, and therefore receive funding for, humanitarian work?

The Bush administration made the unprecedented move of funneling most of the funding through the Department of Defense (Strategic Partnership Office), thereby sidestepping the traditional role of USAID and the State Department. These actions were a serious blow to USAID and an indication that the agency's credibility had suffered. It is likely either a result or merely further evidence of then–Secretary of State Colin Powell's differences with Defense Secretary Donald H. Rumsfeld and the Pentagon. On these issues, the PVO community seems to be squarely on the side of USAID. While at times USAID is the face of the administration to PVOs, at other times the PVOs identify more with USAID in opposition to the policies of the larger administration. This is most apparent during the intense lobbying efforts surrounding the foreign affairs budget but is also notable in the case of shifting political alliances within the executive branch.

This trend became most apparent in the period following the Afghanistan conflict which has continued into the present. As time went on, the catch phrase of the administration became *transitional diplomacy*, referring to the need for democracy-building initiatives as part of the development process. In addition, Andrew S. Natsios, during his tenure as USAID administrator, introduced transformational development as the main focus of the agency.[31] *Transformational development* refers not only to addressing the traditional "core humanitarian accounts" or sector-based funding but also to effectively altering economic and political institutions in countries to sustain economic development and undermine conditions that foster terrorism.

Funding Priorities

There was and continues to be talk of a major overhaul in the way U.S. foreign aid is administered, namely, that poverty reduction will not be emphasized as much as democracy-building. So far, this transition is most evident in the 2006 creation of a new position of the director of foreign assistance at the State Department, which is now a dual role for the administrator of USAID. The director of foreign assistance is man-dated with "the transformation of the U.S. Government approach to foreign assistance," yet the director lacks the authority to carry out this mandate.[32] Within the State Department and USAID, the director only provides guidance to the Office of the Global AIDS coordinator rather than direct authority over the President's Emergency Plan for AIDS Relief (PEPFAR).

It should be noted that the major foreign aid initiatives created and her-alded by the Bush administration, namely, PEPFAR and the Millennium Challenge Account (MCA), are not funded primarily through USAID.

The MCA is funded by a newly created entity, the Millennium Challenge Corporation, and PEPFAR money is channeled mainly through the Health and Human Services budget, although some funds remain at USAID. The director of foreign assistance, as with PEPFAR, lacks direct authority over the MCA. This means that the director lacks not only policy authority but also financial authority in coordinating USAID programs with those of PEPFAR and MCA.

The MCA is based on promoting countries to practice good governance, economic freedom, civil rights, and health, with the promise of major grants for nations that meet certain eligibility criteria in the aforementioned areas. The central idea is that economic growth and good government are the keys to meaningful foreign aid and the best way to reduce poverty, improve lives, and protect America.[33] This approach accords with many empirical findings that traditional foreign aid has failed to promote economic growth or alleviate poverty.[34] Hence, targeting of aid money toward institutional improvement may in fact be the compassionate course. On the other hand, the Bush administration has not been successful in promoting institutional development, notably in Afghanistan and now Iraq.

Many in the PVO community are concerned that PEPFAR and MCA will divert money from what they deem to be the "core humanitarian accounts" or sector-based funding such as Child Survival, International Disaster Assistance, Migration and Refugee Assistance, Emergency Refugee and Migration Assistance, and International Organizations and Programs (the so-called 150 accounts). Momentum surrounding issues like microenterprise, gender equality, refugees, and food aid ebbs and flows. The PVOs see themselves in a watchdog role, guarding against the possibility that the MCA and PEPFAR not be merely publicity campaigns and disguised attempts to cut funding from sector-based funding of aid delivery. Recent developments seem to bear out PVO concerns, with the "core humanitarian accounts" taking a severe cut in the 2007 budget request after five years of remaining flat.

The Future of Foreign Aid

The only clear forces in the Bush administration are those seeking to make foreign aid more synonymous with economic development. Again, this may actually be the compassionate approach to take, but a conflict exists between sector-based funding, favored by the PVOs, and the country-based budgets built into the new funding process. This conflict will have to be resolved. Concerns were also raised that additional consolidation of

USAID within the Department of State would only further subordinate long-term development goals to short-term foreign policy objectives set by the president and his staff.

The process of integrating USAID into the State Department has produced some positive results. A more unified and streamlined budgeting process operates on a single, standardized lexicon and uniform management system. This permits a view of the larger picture of development assistance by region, country, and funding levels.

The relationship between the federal government and PVOs continues to evolve in the face of the ongoing transformational development efforts and the shifting role of the State Department, the Department of Defense, and USAID. Many PVOs draw a significant amount of support through USAID-funded grants and contracts, and if the agency is eventually dissolved, they will need to raise significant private funds or get government funding through a different channel. The larger issues in the field of relief and development—the commercialization of the delivery of aid and the increasing integration of humanitarian assistance into security objectives—require PVOs not only to rethink their role but also, more importantly, to engage in a public policy debate. Drawing from a diminishing share of federal dollars, PVOs are relying more on the general public for funds. PVOs have to rethink and educate the public on what their role is to be in this global scenario.

2

World War II

U.S. FEDERAL GOVERNMENT CONSOLIDATION
AND REGULATION OF HUMANITARIAN
ASSISTANCE, 1939–45

It is no little thing to make mine eyes to sweat compassion.
—William Shakespeare, *The Tragedy of Coriolanus*

A recurring theme of this book is that the U.S. government responds to a perceived security threat by restricting U.S. private and voluntary humanitarian activities overseas. One rationale is that the government understands these restrictions as promoting efficiency by preventing duplication of relief efforts overseas. One way of promoting efficiency is to subordinate private voluntary organizations (PVOs) to military command. The government also must ensure that basic needs at home are being met and that PVO foreign activities do not interfere with domestic war production and supply efforts.

Another theme of this book is that during peacetime PVOs come under the aegis of the federal civilian administration. However, this model has been severely tested since the terrorist attacks of 9/11 and the war in Iraq. During periods when the United States was actively engaged in foreign military operations, humanitarian aid to a war zone was regulated by the U.S. military in the field and in Washington, D.C. This role of the military has applied from the Mexican War (1846–48) to the war in Iraq (2003–present). After the U.S. entry into World War II, President Franklin D. Roosevelt initially delegated to the office of the Secretary of State oversight for all the economic, political, and fiscal aspects of humanitarian efforts in liberated zones of Europe and Africa. However, the civilian administration of humanitarian efforts failed to resolve jurisdictional disputes among civilian agencies as well as between the agencies and what was then known as the War Department. In 1943, President Roosevelt reacted to this impasse by giving the War Department final authority over civilian assistance in theaters of military operation. Within the International Division of the Armed Service Forces, a committee was created to oversee all humanitarian supplies. The military then oversaw all planning for and distribution of civilian supplies. In the field of operation, military authority was supreme. In Washington, D.C., the State Department continued to be the final arbiter of policy planning. This pattern, established during World War II, would initially continue after 9/11 and began to erode as the U.S. military operation in Iraq moved into stabilization and reconstruction efforts. It is clear that in a post-9/11 world, security and development issues are closely interlinked.

Increased government oversight during times of U.S. military engagement prima facie appears to be justified for several reasons. The military relates to one entity as opposed to many. The humanitarian work is coordinated with military operations and "made representative of the whole American people." Third, private humanitarian aid supplements government relief efforts.[1] A primary reason for subsuming PVO activities under military oversight is to eliminate competition among PVOs by focusing on collaboration with the federal government as the most effective means of carrying out operations efficiently. It appears that during World War II, the heavy regulation of PVOs did not hinder the humanitarian effort.

Another downside on the ground is the lack of freedom of movement to operate in a country. The "preserving of humanitarian space" that is free of military presence and authority has been a historical problem for PVOs engaged in humanitarian relief and reconstruction efforts.[2] Establishing humanitarian space where PVOs can provide assistance is difficult. To do so, the military must engage in public order and policing activities. The U.S. military in post–World War II Europe controlled the shipping and distribution of aid as well as the movement of aid workers, a trend that continued during the Korean and Vietnam Wars. The Iraq and Afghanistan postmilitary action situations, otherwise referred to as stability operations, have required close military-PVO collaboration, giving the military authority over civilian, including PVO, activities.[3]

This chapter is divided according to the chronology of events. As the United States became increasingly involved in World War II, more specific and targeted federal controls were implemented to manage the diverse agencies and volume of contributions. Government regulations of the various forms of voluntary humanitarian relief took place in three phases: (a) the neutral years (1939–41) with the Neutrality Act of 1939, the Lend-Lease Act of 1941, and the President's Committee on War Relief Agencies (1941); (b) U.S. entry into the war (1941–43) and the formation in 1942 of the President's War Relief Control Board; and (c) the consolidation of the war effort and victory (1943–45).

American Neutrality 1939–41

At the inception of World War II, the Neutrality Act of November 2, 1939, prohibited certain types of economic relations with European countries designated as "belligerent" by proclamation of the president.[4] This act limited various types of economic activities in the affected countries. By April 1941, the Neutrality Act covered 18 countries. Under this act, all U.S. voluntary agencies seeking to send aid to populations in the belligerent countries had to register with the federal government and submit monthly financial reports to the Department of State. As a consequence, PVOs that engaged in relief efforts were required to register with the Department of State. (Exceptions to this rule were the American Red Cross, which had its own charter with Congress, and religious organizations.) The Neutrality Act did not cover agencies collecting funds and shipping goods to China, the Soviet Union, and Finland, viewed as nonbelligerent countries, and to Spain, which had recently ended its civil war.

With the September 1939 invasion of Poland, 900 entities responded to a State Department questionnaire requesting information on public humanitarian assistance. Most of these entities were local fraternal organizations and clubs, which set up relief committees to collect goods and funds for Poland. In December 1939, Russia invaded Finland, and another surge in humanitarian response occurred. Herbert Hoover immediately founded the Finnish Relief Fund, initially collecting $400,000 for emergency relief efforts. Many smaller entities and individuals responded. However, the Finnish effort was spontaneous, quickly dwindling to insignificant sums. The Polish relief effort, by contrast, relied on existing social organizations that had established structures for raising funds and collecting goods.

By the end of 1939, of 240 total registered entities (including individuals such as Helena Rubinstein Titus, the cosmetics magnate), 195 were secular, 24 Roman Catholic, 10 Jewish, 3 mainline Protestant, 3 faith-founded, 1 evangelical, 1 ecumenical, and 1 Orthodox (see fig. 2.1). As countries entered the war, relief efforts in the United States mounted rapidly. Nationalistic and ethnic divisions were readily apparent in the names of the relief committees and organizations.

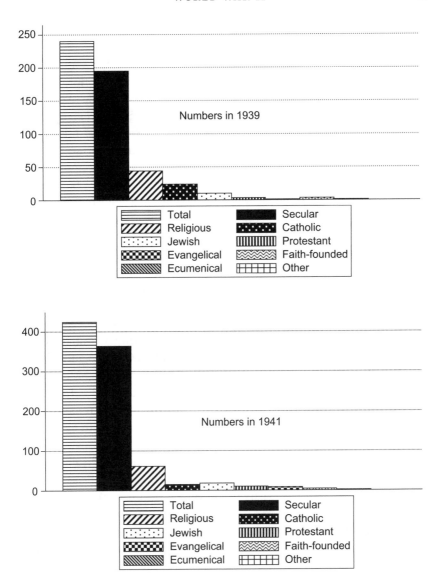

Figure 2.1. PVO numbers in 1939 and 1941.
Source: McCleary Private Voluntary Organizations Data Set.

In 1940, the establishment of the Selective Service prompted an increase in private appeals for goods for American inductees. As part of the larger war assistance effort embodied in the Lend-Lease Act (1941), PVOs were asked to raise funds for food, medicine, and comfort packages for prisoners of war. Also, under the Lend-Lease Act, China and the Soviet Union as war allies received humanitarian assistance.[5]

America at War 1941–43

With the bombing of Pearl Harbor in December 1941 and U.S. entry into the war, America's humanitarian response increased. The proliferation of charitable entities and their appeals for funds and goods became overwhelming. Shipping space for goods going overseas became scarce. Duplication of efforts, particularly with those of the American Red Cross, raised questions of the most effective means of addressing humanitarian concerns. New types of assistance were being created, such as setting up aid activities next to military camps established under the Selective Service Act. The President's Committee on War Relief Agencies was formed to oversee humanitarian efforts and to coordinate resources going to humanitarian entities, including the 300 agencies already registered under the Neutrality Act. The committee became the central coordinating body within the federal government for all humanitarian assistance public and private.

The formation of the committee meant increased federal intervention in humanitarian efforts. But, clearly, growing competition among entities meant duplication of efforts and proportionately more of an agency's resources allocated for fund-raising and overhead. The Community Chest, the United Service Organizations (USO), and the American Red Cross together in 1939 raised $160 million in nominal dollars, a sum amounting to $2.2 billion in 2005 dollars. By mid-1941, there were 545 agencies registered with the State Department, and by the end of 1941, there were 424 agencies remaining (see fig. 2.1). The majority of these agencies were secular (363), with 61 religious. In 1939, in terms of revenue, the secular and religious agencies were fairly close—$31 million for secular and $17 million for religious (in 2005 dollars; see fig. 2.2). By 1941, the secular agencies were raising six times as much funds as the religious ones ($496 million versus $77 million).

Problems might have been expected with several funding appeals taking place at once and the consequent occurrence of "donor fatigue." Yet, after three years of neutrality, the American public was not showing this fatigue. Rather, PVO real revenue increased from $573 million in 1941 to $2.8 billion in 1945 (fig. 2.3).

Federal officials were concerned over the reliability of agencies appealing for funds, the lack of control over agencies engaged in political propaganda activities, and the perception that corporations were being coerced into donating funds to agencies working in countries where they had business interests.[6] The committee required private agencies not previously registered with the federal government to submit monthly financial information similar to that submitted by registrants. The committee began coordinating activities of the various agencies, seeking to

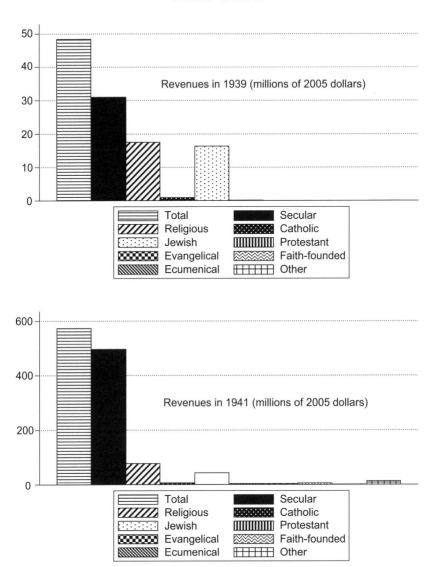

Figure 2.2. PVO real revenues in 1939 and 1941.
Source: McCleary Private Voluntary Organizations Data Set.

reduce duplication of overhead and other nonrelief expenses by negotiating mergers of agencies.

As an illustration of the duplication of effort, 308 PVOs were newly registered in 1940 and 1941 (table 1.5 in chapter 1), leading to a total registration of 424 by the end of 1941. Ninety agencies focused on British aid

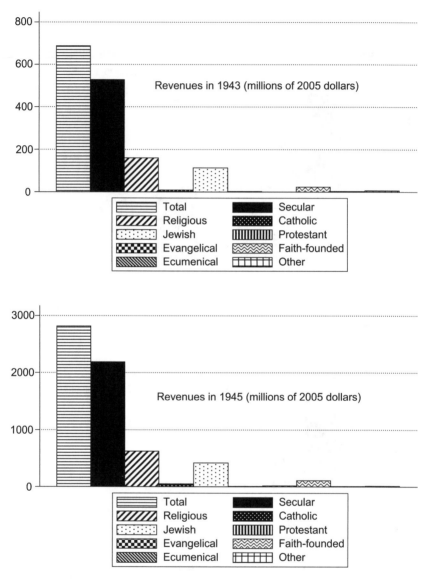

Figure 2.3. PVO real revenues in 1943 and 1945.
Source: McCleary Private Voluntary Organizations Data Set.

alone. In response, the federal government caused many of these PVOs
to merge (box 2.1) or otherwise leave the field. From 1940 to 1942, mostly
because of government action, 403 PVOs permanently left the list of
registered agencies (table 1.6 in chapter 1).

Box 2.1. Mergers of local agencies into national umbrella agencies during World War II (by date of merger)

American Friends Service Committee
      1944   LeSecours Francais

American Relief for Czechoslovakia
      7/44   United Czechoslovak Relief

American Relief for France, Inc.
      9/44   French Relief Fund, Inc.
           1944   Coordinating Council of French Relief Societies
                9/42   American Association for Assistance to French Artists, Inc.
                6/43   Federation of French Veterans of the Great War, Inc.
                4/43   French Committee for Relief in France, Michigan
                8/43   French Relief Association, Kansas City, Missouri
                7/43   French War Relief, Inc., Los Angeles, CA
                7/43   French War Relief Fund, San Francisco (Les Anciens Combattants Francais de la Gran Guerre)
           1941   French War Veterans of Los Angeles (Les Anciens Combatants)
                7/43   French War Veterans Association of Illinois
                7/43   Les Filles de France
                10/43   Relief for French Refugees in England/ Urgent Relief for France
           1944   Fighting French Relief Committee
                7/43   American-French War Relief, Inc.
                6/43   Franco-British Relief

American Relief for Holland, Inc.
  United Service to Holland
      Queen Wilhelmina Fund, Inc.

American Relief for Norway, Inc.
      1/44   American Relief for Norway
      9/44   Camp Little Norway Association
      9/44   Friends of Little Norway
      1/44   Norwegian Relief, Inc.
      9/44   Norwegian Seamen's Christmas and Relief, Inc.

(continued)

Box 2.1. (*Continued*)

American Relief for Poland
    Polish War Relief of the United States of America
        Polish American Council

6/43	Associated Polish Societies' Relief Committee of Worcester, MA
4/43	Association of Joint Polish-American Societies of Chelsea, MA
10/43	Federated Council of Polish Societies of Grand Rapids, MI
3/43	Humanitarian Work Committee, Glen Cove, NY
9/43	League of Polish Societies, New Kensington, Arnold, and Vicinity, PA
12/43	Legion of Young Polish Women, Chicago, IL
6/43	Polish Civic League of Mercer County, Trenton, NJ
9/43	Polish Naturalization Independent Club, Worcester, MA
8/43	Polish Relief, Carteret, NJ
2/43	Polish Relief Committee, Boston, MA
5/43	Polish Relief Committee, Brockton, MA
7/43	Polish Relief Committee, Cambridge, MA
6/43	Polish Relief Committee, Delaware, Wilmington, DE
12/42	Polish Relief Committee, Flint, MI
6/43	Polish Relief Committee, Holyoke, MA
3/43	Polish Relief Committee, Jackson, MI
7/43	Polish Relief Committee, North Dartmouth, MA
4/43	Polish Relief Committee, Philadelphia and Vicinity, PA
5/40	Polish Relief Committee, Rochester, NY
11/42	Polish Relief Committee, Taunton, MA
2/43	Polish Relief Committee of the Polish National Home Association Lowell, MA
3/43	Polish Relief Fund, Jewett, CT
9/43	Polish Relief Fund, Niagara Falls, NY
10/43	Polish Relief Fund, Palmer, MA
11/42	Polish Relief Fund, Syracuse and Vicinity, NY
6/43	Polish Relief Fund Committee, Milwaukee, WI
7/43	Polish Relief Fund Committee, Passaic and Bergen Counties, Passaic, NJ
10/43	Polish Relief Fund Committee, Los Angeles, CA
12/43	Polish Relief Fund Committee, Springfield and Vicinity, Springfield, MA

4/40	Polish War Sufferers Aid Committee, Cleveland, OH
7/43	Polish War Sufferers Relief Committee, Toledo, OH
6/43	Polish Welfare Council, Schenectady, NY
7/43	Polish Women's Fund to the Fatherland, Lawrence, MA
6/43	Polski Komitet Ratunkowy, Binghamton, NY
12/41	Relief Committee of the United Polish Societies, Chicopee, MA
3/42	Relief Fund for Sufferers in Poland Committee, Kenosha, WI
6/43	Toledo Committee for the Relief of War Victims, Toledo, OH
2/42	United Polish Committees, Racine, WI
7/43	United Polish Organizations, Salem, MA
4/40	United Polish Societies, Hartford, CT

Belgian War Relief Society

| 3/43 | Belgian War Relief Society, Inc. |
| 3/43 | Parcels for Belgian Prisoners |

British War Relief Society, Inc.

1946	*British War Relief Society, New York*
11/40	Allied Relief Fund, NY
1/42	Anzac War Relief Fund
2/43	American Friends of Britain, NY
6/43	American Hospital in Britain, Ltd., NY
2/43	American Seeds for British Soil, NY
2/46	British American Comfort League, Quincy, MA
6/43	British-American War Relief Association, Seattle
5/43	British Relief Society of Rhode Island, Pawtucket, and Blackstone Valley
6/43	British Sailors' Book and Relief Society, NY
6/43	British War Relief Association, Northern California
2/42	British War Relief Association, Southern California
4/43	British War Relief Society, Fall River, MA
9/41	Greater New Bedford British War Relief Corps, MA
6/43	Maple Leaf Fund, Inc., NY
1/40	Order of Scottish Clans, Boston, MA
4/43	Royal Air Force Benevolent Fund of USA, NY
7/43	The Silver Thimble Fund of America, New Orleans, LA

(*continued*)

Box 2.1. (*Continued*)

    5/43   Miss Heather Thatcher, Hollywood, CA
    4/43   Women's Auxiliary Board of Scots' Charitable Society, Inc., Dedham, MA

Greek War Relief Association
    3/44   Friends of Greece, Inc.
    11/43   Order of Ahepa
    11/43   Phalanx of Greek Veterans of America, Inc.

International Rescue and Relief Committee
    7/40   American Friends of German Freedom
    5/42   Emergency Rescue Committee

LaFayette Preventorium
    3/44   Committee of Mercy

Nowy-Dworer Ladies and United Relief Committee
    12/40   United Nowy Dworer Relief Committee
    12/40   Nowe-Dworer Ladies Benevolent Association

Polish Interorganization Council
    11/21/39   Polish Radio Programs Bureau

Polish National Council of New York
    1940   Centrala, Passaic, NJ

Polish Relief Fund
    10/30/42   Polish Relief Committee, Jersey City, NJ
    3/31   Polish Emergency Council, Essex County, NJ

United Yugoslav Relief Fund
(formerly American Friends of Yugoslavia)
    3/43   American Yugoslav Defense League
    4/43   Committee of Yugoslav War Relief, San Francisco
    5/43   Jugoslav Relief Fund Association, Chicago, IL
    4/43   Yugoslav War Relief Association of Southern California
    9/43   Yugoslav War Relief Association of State of Washington

War Relief Services–National Catholic Welfare Conference/
Catholic Relief Services–NCWC
    9/44   American Women's Unit for War Relief, Inc.

Source: McCleary Private Voluntary Organizations Data Set.

In addition to prompting a burgeoning of humanitarian groups, U.S. entry into World War II instigated rapid expansion of government measures to meet war relief and welfare needs. These measures meant streamlining private relief programs and bringing them into line with government war efforts. At the recommendation of the President's Committee on War Relief Agencies, a more permanent government entity, the President's War Relief Control Board, was formed in July 1942. It established regulations concerning the efficiency and economy of operation of agencies, including the power to revoke licenses should these requirements not be met.[7]

The President's War Relief Control Board had legal authority over domestic and foreign relief efforts, including the administration of the Neutrality Act as it pertained to humanitarian assistance. Unlike its predecessor agency, the President's War Relief Control Board regulated registration of all agencies engaged in foreign and domestic relief, including foreign agencies, refugee relief efforts, aid for the armed forces and their dependents, and all relief fund-raising efforts, including the transfer of funds as well as all types of relief efforts engaged in by agencies.[8] The only entities exempt from the board's oversight were the American Red Cross and religious entities not directly involved in war relief efforts.

At the recommendation of the President's Committee on War Relief, the board revoked the licenses of currently registered agencies and began a new registration process. In this manner, the board was able to force agencies out of business. At the same time, the board designated a single agency as the lead entity working in a country, with all others working through it (box 2.1). Agencies were pressured to merge with the designated lead agency. Measures were established by the board to ensure that agencies either merged or terminated. Due to stringent government efforts to eliminate duplication of efforts, the number of registered PVOs plunged during the war, reaching 98 in 1945 (see fig. 2.4). The reasons for heavy government regulation of PVOs were diverse.[9]

Duplications of local offices and staff were eliminated, and agencies were required to reduce their percentages of overhead costs. More important to the expansion of the field of international relief and development was the pressure by the President's War Relief Control Board on local relief organizations to consolidate into national agencies. Merger of 64 agencies into umbrella organizations designated to send assistance to specific countries in Europe occurred in 1942. In 1943, a second round of mergers consolidated the previous year's mergers into an umbrella national agency focused on a particular geographic region (box 2.1). Those agencies that refused to merge had their licenses revoked, thereby forcing them out of international relief activity. As countries were liberated by the Allied Forces, the President's

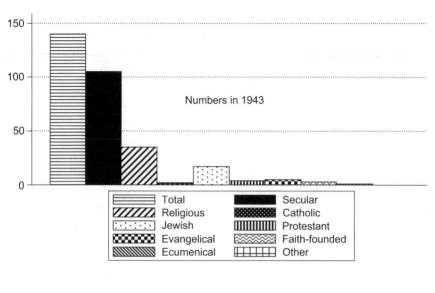

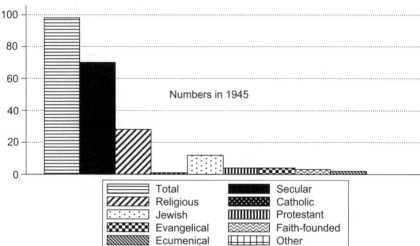

Figure 2.4. PVO numbers in 1943 and 1945.
Source: McCleary Private Voluntary Organizations Data Set.

War Relief Control Board either designated a lead agency through which to channel aid or simply created one. For example, in June of 1944 Rome was occupied by the Allied Military Force. The American Relief for Italy, Inc., was created at the request of the President's War Relief Control Board to receive all relief funds and goods coming from the United States. All other existing agencies working in Italy from this point had to coordinate with American Relief for Italy. The President's War Relief Control Board justified such a move on the grounds that it eliminated "factional disputes among organizations interested in aiding Italy" and as assurance to American donors and Italian recipients that the aid was "an impartial, non-partisan and non-political humanitarian effort."[10] The pragmatic reason for the creation of American Relief for Italy was control of coordination of relief efforts with the military theatre commander.

Critical to the formation of the national umbrella agencies was the role the War Relief Control Board played in resolving issues of organization, management, factional prejudice, and social differences. The board involved itself in resolving disputes among agencies, particularly those that had been forced to merge under one lead agency. The War Relief Control Board had authority over all relief efforts, domestic and foreign, including religious agencies, which were not required to register with the federal government. The board's regulatory and coordinating capacity was quite broad. It regulated the finances of relief agencies, coordinated relief appeals, and integrated their organizational policies, plans, and program procedures with those of the federal government, intergovernmental agencies, and the American Red Cross. The War Relief Control Board also had authority across the federal government. It was the single entry point for private agencies to the federal government. Through its authority, by forcing PVOs to apply to the War Relief Control Board for funding and to eliminate individual organizational appeals, the board consolidated and streamlined the field of humanitarian assistance.[11] The board was the federal government's singular institutional mechanism for controlling and regulating PVO activity.

The consolidation of private international relief efforts by the federal government seemed to have a positive effect. From 1941 to 1943, the number of registered agencies went down (figs. 2.1 and 2.4), but total revenue went up (figs. 2.2 and 2.3). Secular revenue did not increase as much as religious revenue. Religious revenue more than doubled from 1941 to 1943. Federal regulation of PVOs during World War II did not discourage humanitarian giving on the part of Americans because they were responding to war needs. Since PVOs were funded through public appeals and not government subsidies, they did not become financially dependent on the government for revenue. Perhaps for this reason, federal regulation of the PVOs' activities did not have a detrimental effect on their fund-raising.

Consolidating the War Relief Effort, 1943–45

In 1943, the President's War Relief Control Board initiated two further consolidating measures. The National War Fund was established to collaborate "with community chests in a united appeal for local charities and national war philanthropies, to organize a concurrent appeal in non-chest areas, and to distribute the resulting contributions to war-relief and welfare agencies approved by the President's War Relief Control Board."[12] In 1941, before the formation of the National War Fund, 632 Community Chests and councils raised funds locally. By 1945, the National War Fund Campaign included 798 participating Community Chests and councils with 3,035 USO clubs and 23 private umbrella agencies.[13] To avoid com-petition, the National War Fund campaign took place in October (last-ing until mid-November), and the American Red Cross raised funds in March. Funds raised through the annual countrywide campaign by the National War Fund went to 23 relief organizations as well as to the USOs, the United Seamen's Service, and the program of War Prisoners Aid, Inc. Funds were allocated to a single national private umbrella agency for each major war-welfare function and a single umbrella agency for each nation-ality (Polish, French, etc.).

The President's War Relief Control Board, which coordinated fund-raising efforts and the allocation of resources to PVOs, pooled funds earmarked for these agencies and had the final say in the allocation of resources.[14] Agencies that participated in the annual National War Fund could not conduct independent fund-raising activities. Rather, they had to affiliate with an umbrella agency. In addition to the National War Fund campaigns (1943, 1944, 1945), agencies could not solicit assistance from the public during the annual U.S. War Bond Sale in September, the U.S. Treasury War Loan Campaign held for one month (mid-January to mid-February), and the American Red Cross campaign in March. Therefore, for several months each year, agencies could not engage in public solicitations and fund-raising activities. An agency not included in any national fund-raising campaign had two difficult choices—either merge with a private umbrella agency on the National War Fund list or go out of existence.

The President's War Relief Control Board by the middle of 1943 was the single contact agency for any domestic and foreign entity in the United States seeking to engage in overseas relief assistance. The War Relief Control Board coordinated relief agencies' activities with the Office of Foreign Relief and Rehabilitation, the War Production Board, the State Department, and any other federal agency relevant to sending relief over-seas. Funds were released to agencies that provided the National War Fund with a budget that had been approved by the War Relief Control Board. Medical and agricultural supplies (seeds, food items, etc.) to be shipped had to be approved by the War Relief Control Board so that they did not hinder availability to American forces engaged in combat.

Shipping was tightly controlled to ensure steady troop supplies, including ambulances and food packages. Allied countries seeking American aid provided shipping to conserve American resources.

The second consolidation effort of 1943 was the creation of the American Council of Voluntary Agencies for Foreign Service (ACVAFS). Anticipating the need for increased humanitarian relief as the Allied military forces liberated areas of Europe, the Foreign Economic Administration was set up within the Office of Emergency Management of the Executive Office of the President. The Foreign Economic Administration coordinated the activities of various government war-related agencies, among them the Office of Foreign Relief and Rehabilitation Operations, which had oversight for the President's War Relief Board. ACVAFS was created in response to the U.S. government's need to have one civil society organization relating to the government on behalf of private voluntary relief agencies. From the perspective of the PVOs, ACVAFS was created in response to the government's intention to establish the Economic Cooperation Administration, which would direct and coordinate relief and reconstruction in liberated areas of North Africa and Europe. Initially, it was proposed that the Economic Cooperation Administration work only with the Red Cross. So they were not locked out by the government, the Catholic, Protestant, and Jewish agencies, at the recommendation of the President's War Relief Control Board, formed the ACVAFS.[15] ACVAFS gave them a unified voice vis-à-vis the government and some independence (leverage) even though their overseas activities were restricted by the government.[16] The ACVAFS was formed to coordinate the activities of PVOs with each other and the federal government, including especially PVOs with large-scale programs overseas. Unlike the United Jewish Appeal (UJA), the ACVAFS did not engage in centralized fund-raising or planning for its member agencies. Rather, ACVAFS was a coordinating umbrella organization with committees organized on specific issues relevant to its members and the federal government.

At the beginning, the ACVAFS resisted government pressure to coordinate PVOs, contending that it was coming dangerously close to "amalgamation." It argued that not only could smaller PVOs be just as efficient as large ones, but also the voluntary relationship among PVOs, their private donors, and recipients would be compromised if they were heavily regulated by the government. The War Relief Control Board continued to hold the view that information essential to humanitarian assistance was only obtainable through government channels. As a consequence, the federal government was in the best position to determine the allocation of resources to PVOs for humanitarian assistance overseas. This assumption was questioned by the ACVAFS, but it soon realized that it would have to work closely with the government, particularly the War Department.

Beginning in October 1943, the President's War Relief Control Board strongly urged PVOs to identify themselves as "American" in their name.[17] This provision carried over into their activities as an agency. Many PVOs provided aid because of ethnic, cultural, or kinship ties to peoples in Europe. The President's War Relief Control Board insisted that agencies involved in war humanitarian efforts be motivated as Americans in their efforts, thereby overcoming factional differences. By employing the principle of American-motivated humanitarian aid, the President's War Relief Control Board successfully oversaw the merging of agencies while allowing for diversity among the relief agencies. The War Relief Control Board also insisted that PVOs remain politically neutral and prohibited the comingling of relief contributions with political donations. The Control Board, along with the Department of Justice, prohibited political action and propaganda on the part of PVOs.

The federal government also controlled international monetary transactions, passports, and allocation of ocean freight through subsidy and licensing of commodity exports for humanitarian efforts. The President's War Relief Control Board served as the agency through which PVOs attained clearance for interactions with other federal agencies. PVOs were required to send to the President's War Relief Control Board quarterly estimates of export requirements.[18] The Control Board, in consultation with the Foreign Economic Administration, the War Food Administration, and the War Production Board, determined which agencies would receive export licenses and each agency's final allocation. The President's War Relief Control Board managed the licenses and monitored the allocation of commodities by agency. The advance reporting on the part of PVOs for estimated licenses and shipping was onerous, particularly for the smaller agencies.

The American Red Cross was a quasi-public organization that raised funds and supplies for the humanitarian efforts overseas. During the war, the American Red Cross worked with American Red Cross societies of the countries involved. Unlike other private agencies, the American Red Cross operated in occupied territories. The American Red Cross worked with governments in exile, government representatives, and in-country relief workers.

From the perspective of private agencies seeking to engage in humanitarian relief efforts in Europe, the federal government heavily regulated fund-raising activities through a network of local agencies, the pooling of funds raised, and funds distribution through one central Budget

Committee. The President's War Relief Control Board regulated competitive solicitation of contributions by requiring private agencies to suspend fund-raising activities during the National War Fund's annual campaigns, American Red Cross appeals, war bond drives, and solicitation of contributions in kind by the United National Clothing Collection.

The intrusive nature of federal regulation of PVOs and their activities did not produce homogeneity. PVOs remained diverse, with the religious agencies retaining their denominational brand. Furthermore, PVOs developed their own strategies for interacting with the federal government and in soliciting federal assistance. This situation is ironic given that such heavy government regulation resembled that of a socialist state and contrasted sharply with a model of competitive free enterprise. The government controlled not only PVOs during the war but also private enterprise through price controls and rationing.

Comparison of Religious and Secular Agencies

During the war years, the fraction of agencies that were secular peaked at 86% in 1941 and then declined to 71% in 1945 (see figs. 2.1 and 2.4, respectively). Correspondingly, the fraction of religious agencies rose from 14% in 1941 to 29% in 1945. In terms of total revenue, secular agencies garnered 87% of the total in 1941. Secular revenue was 61% of the total in 1944 and 78% in 1945. Correspondingly, religious agencies had 13% of total revenue in 1941, 39% in 1944, and 22% in 1945. The pattern is that religious total revenue increased particularly up to 1944, whereas secular revenue spiked in 1945 (see figs. 2.2 and 2.3).

Jewish Agencies

The UJA was a national private entity authorized by the President's War Relief Control Board to raise funds and distribute them to member relief agencies.[19] Unlike the National War Fund, which was a government fund-raising mechanism, the UJA was a loose federation (comprised of the Jewish Joint Distribution Committee [JDC], the United Palestine Appeal, and the National Coordinating Committee for Aid to Refugees and Emigrants Coming from Germany). Through centralized planning and allocation among the three organizations, Jewish agencies raised the majority of funds among all religious agencies (see figs. 2.2 and 2.3).

Once the United States entered the war in 1941, the JDC was prohibited, like other agencies, from sending funds to neutral countries because

these funds might be transferred to Nazi Europe. To circumvent the prohibition, the JDC asked their Swiss representative to submit a request to
the U.S. Treasury for a license to receive funds from JDC. Although the
sum requested was large, the U.S. Treasury approved the request. But,
again in 1942 and 1943, the U.S. Treasury would not permit the transfer
of JDC funds to Switzerland. The World Jewish Congress appealed to
use funds from blocked accounts in Switzerland and received the U.S.
Treasury Department's approval in mid-1943.

The success of Jewish humanitarian efforts during the war was due
to the leadership of wealthy, prominent men and the infrastructure of
the Jewish organizations. Joseph E. Davies, chairman of the President's
Committee on War Relief Agencies, commenting on a letter from
Edward M. Warburg, chair of the Jewish Joint Distribution Committee,
said "The striking feature of Warburg's method is that it is essentially
designed to reach the minority known to be able to contribute in size-
able amounts rather than to the mercurial, more or less irresponsible and
financially weak mass."[20] The person responsible for UJA's fund-raising
success was not Warburg but Henry Monitor, who introduced several
techniques, among them the "big gift" donors.[21] The generosity of a few
wealthy families (including that of John D. Rockefeller, Jr.) explains only
part of the significant amount of funds raised. The local Jewish Federations
and Welfare Funds, which in 1940 operated in 266 cities and reached an
estimated 97% of the American Jewish population, were headed up by
"competent paid executives and field men." In other words, the leadership
came from wealthy businessmen, who spearheaded the annual appeal by
donating large sums to the local fund.[22]

Each local Welfare Fund had an Allocations Committee that determined the amount of funds earmarked to each agency. Due to ideological
differences, the UJA did not operate in 1941, but the United Palestine Appeal
was allowed to engage in an independent fund-raising campaign.[23] Then,
starting in 1942, the UJA under the leadership of Monitor began to raise
significant funds. The UJA also sought to make its activities as ecumenical
and patriotic as possible.[24] In cooperation with the UJA, Nelson Rockefeller
and Eleanor Roosevelt organized a National Christian Committee of 80
prominent Americans, with Thomas Watson, the president of IBM, as its
national chair.[25] In 1945, consensus among the member agencies of UJA
was broken. Disputes arose over yearly allocation percentages and earmarking of funds. The President's War Relief Control Board responded to
a request by successfully arbitrating the dispute.[26] Then, in 1947, President
Truman, General Eisenhower, and Henry Morgenthau kicked off the
UJA annual campaign. The urgency to raise more funds through private

donations was due to the termination of the United National Relief and Rehabilitation Administration and its supplementary aid.

Protestant Agencies

Protestant denominational agencies were few during World War II. Prior to 1943, the American Friends Service Committee and the Unitarian Service Committee did not raise significant funds. Their budgets increased once they became beneficiaries of the National War Fund and affiliated with umbrella agencies such as the American Christian Committee for Refugees. Mainline Protestants did not form an umbrella relief organization during World War II for two reasons. First, Protestants were the majority in the United States, between 60% and 70% of the population.[27] By contrast, the Jews and Roman Catholics were religious minorities. To have a presence in the field of relief, the minority religions had to organize umbrella organizations.

Second, mainline Protestant denominations were focused on mission activities and channeled funds through those networks. In 1938, the ecumenical International Missionary Council met at Tambaram, Madras. The largest representative body of the council was the Foreign Missions Conference of North America, which consisted of close to 100 missionary boards of various denominations.[28] With an emphasis on creating Christian unity and evangelizing particularly in non-Christian countries, Protestants sent aid through the Foreign Missions Conference of North America, which channeled its funds through the ecumenical International Missionary Council.[29] The Foreign Missions Conference of North America was an ecumenical religious organization, not an agency, and as a consequence its funds were not reported to the President's War Relief Control Board.

During the war years (1939–45), significant funds flowed through the Foreign Missions Conference of North America. From 1939 to 1942, Protestant churches raised $19.8 million (in nominal dollars) for overseas missions. In 1944, the Foreign Missions Conference raised funds of $4.77 million and in 1945 $5.26 million.[30] (To convert to 2005 dollars, nominal amounts in 1944–45 have to be multiplied by around 11.) The struggle between missions and humanitarian service within the Protestant denominations would intensify after World War II with the creation of the ecumenical umbrella agency Church World Service.[31]

Another ecumenical organization—amounting to an agency rather than a religious body—was the American Christian Committee for

Refugees. The JDC gave funds to Protestant agencies—the American Christian Committee for Refugees, the American Friends Service Committee, and the Unitarian Service Committee—to keep these entities operating prior to the creation of the National War Fund.[32] Once these agencies affiliated with the National War Fund, they were able to function without Jewish assistance.

Roman Catholic Agencies

The Roman Catholic Church, in discussions with representatives of President Roosevelt, decided to consolidate the numerous individual Catholic charities into one agency, the War Relief Services of the National Catholic Welfare Conference.[33] In April 1943, War Relief Services became a registered agency with the National War Fund. It is unclear whether War Relief Services would have been able to function without funds from the National War Fund.[34] Without direct government intervention in the formation of War Relief Services and subsequent governmental assistance, the Catholic contribution to the war effort and its subsequent growth into the largest postwar PVO (Catholic Relief Services) would probably not have happened.

The national war effort, as organized by the President's War Relief Control Board, sought to be nonpartisan and inclusive of all religious faiths. To that end, the War Relief Control Board created agencies such as Refugee Relief Trustees and War Prisoners Aid, Inc., umbrella organizations that coordinated the activities of Catholic, Protestant, and evangelical agencies to be inclusive and to avoid duplication of relief efforts. The USOs, providing recreational and welfare services to the military troops, was made up of six independent agencies from across the American religious spectrum.[35]

The National Conference of Christians and Jews, formed in the 1920s, sought to promote an interfaith spirit in the United States. Fascist and anti-Semitic groups in the 1930s began using the term *Christian*, fostering anti-Semitism that spread and was widely acknowledged by 1938. To counter anti-Semitism, public figures openly spoke of the commonality of the two religions.[36] Leaders of the "three great faiths"—Judaism, Protestantism, and Roman Catholicism—participated in the National Conference of Christians and Jews, traveling together across the country. Eventually, Americans would refer to their religious heritage as "Judeo-Christian," partly as a result of these interfaith efforts.

In terms of total religious contributions to the war relief effort, the Protestant contribution was the smallest among the major religions (see table 2.1). When we add the amount raised by the Foreign Missions Society of North America, the Protestants contributed total revenue in nominal dollars of $8.77 million in 1944 and $14.5 million in 1945. The lack of Protestant giving is often attributed, in part, to the widely held view that the victims of Nazism were non-Christian.[37] The exception was the Lutheran denomination. One-third of the total funds of the International Missions Council from 1939 to 1945 was raised by the Lutheran World Convention and sent to missions in the Lutheran countries of Scandinavia and to the predominantly Lutheran country of Germany.[38]

The Roman Catholic hierarchy in the United States was aware of the persecution of Catholics in Germany. Yet weak Roman Catholic contribution was due to a fear of Communist refugees entering the country and taking jobs or becoming an economic burden on society. Widespread anti-Semitism and xenophobia were fueled in Catholic publications and by Father Coughlin's speeches and in his publication *Social Justice.*[39]

Table 2.1. Religious and secular agencies' contributions to foreign relief (millions of 2005 dollars), 1939–45.

Year	Protestant	Catholic	Jewish	Religious total	Secular	Grand total ecumenical
1939	1.4[a]	6.3	118.4	125.5	224.2	349.7
1940	8.9	40.3	298.8	412.8	1,835	2,252
1941	27.5	47.9	293.9	525.4	3,378	3,910
1942	23.0	28.6	491.5	654.5	3,094	3,748
1943	32.5	53.8	649.6	917.3	3,024	3,942
1944	97.3	164.3	1,898	2,742	4,229	16,306
1945	158.0	287.8	2,344	3,499	12,208	25,778

[a] For the Protestant category, from 1939 to 1943, the Foreign Missions Conference of North America raised $19.8 million in nominal dollars for overseas activities. Since there was no breakdown by year, their contribution is not included in the Protestant/ecumenical total for years 1939 through 1943. Data were compiled from the International Missionary Council, *The International Missionary Council and Continental Missions in the War of 1939–1945* (London: Morrison and Gibb, Ltd., 1946) and Joseph I. Parker (ed.), *Interpretative Statistical Survey of the World Mission of the Christian Church. Summary and Detailed Statistics of Churches and Missionary Societies, Interpretative Articles, and Indices.* (New York: International Missionary Council, 1938).

When considering total revenue of religious PVOs (shown in figs. 2.2 and 2.3), the Jewish effort was by far the greatest during World War II. The fraction Jewish was 94% in 1939, 56% in 1941, 72% in 1943, and 67% in 1945. The Roman Catholic share of total religious revenue was 5% in 1939, 9% in 1941, 6% in 1943, and 8% in 1945. The faith-founded fraction was 0 in 1939, 8% in 1941, 15% in 1943, and 17% in 1945. The bulk of the revenue for faith-founded agencies went to the YMCA and the YWCA. The mainline Protestant agencies had 1% in 1939, 5% in 1941, 2% in 1943, and 1% in 1945.

To explain why Protestant giving was the lowest of the three main faiths, we have to look at how fund-raising was conducted by each religious group during the war years. Protestant fund-raising was done through Protestant denominations. In other words, Protestant agencies and missions were raising funds from Protestants. By contrast, Roman Catholics, until 1943, were raising funds from parishes. In 1943, the Roman Catholic Bishops, under pressure from Winthrop Aldrich, formed Catholic Relief Services and became a registered member of the National War Fund. This structure meant that Catholic Relief Services beginning in 1943 was receiving funds not just from Catholics but a share of funds from the American public at large. This structure supported the doubling of Catholic spending on relief from 1942 to 1943 (figs. 2.2 and 2.3). The Jewish agencies had their own centralized fund-raising mechanism in the JDC and the UJA. Jews were the most generous of the three religious groups.

Secular Agencies

Initially, Americans responded by donating to existing ethnic associations and clubs. These entities created relief funds to aid Europeans of the same ethnic group. As the date of the mergers shows (box 2.1), ethnically oriented agencies sprung up so quickly that the President's War Relief Control Board actively sought to regulate their activities. The secular PVOs raised slightly less than triple the combined revenue of the religious PVOs (figs. 2.2 and 2.3). American Relief for Poland raised funds through Roman Catholic parishes, as did other agencies with a largely Catholic constituency. Many of the Protestant and Roman Catholic religious PVOs were just being formed, and as result the ethnically oriented agencies were natural recipients of donations (see discussion at beginning of chapter 3). Most of these agencies had offices in New York City, from whose ports they could ship clothing, food, and medical supplies. Agencies specified particular countries (over 22) as donation destinations.

From Relief to Reconstruction

Toward the end of the war, the President's War Relief Control Board began to engage increasingly in the administration of commodity shipping. The Foreign Economic Administration delegated to the War Relief Control Board the responsibility of covering the export requirements of all registered agencies. Agencies would request licensing for shipment of donated goods from the public, purchased commodities, and rationed government commodities. From the perspective of individual agencies and the government, coordination of relief supplies was a bureaucratic maze. The theater commander determined on-the-ground needs. The next step was identifying which humanitarian agencies could fill the need. In Washington, coordination among the War Food Administration, the War Production Board, the Foreign Economic Administration, and the State-War-Navy Coordinating Committee was required to approve the nature of the relief and its shipment. The President's War Relief Control Board, reporting to the Foreign Economic Administration, managed and oversaw the licensing and allocation for each agency.

During the war years, PVOs were restricted almost entirely to assistance behind the Allied front, mainly in Great Britain, Norway, Belgium, the Netherlands, France, and China. In addition, PVOs provided emergency humanitarian assistance to displaced populations and refugees. With the end of the war, the geographic scope of assistance was no longer limited to Western Europe but included Central and Eastern Europe, the Middle East, and Asia. The volume of humanitarian assistance provided by PVOs increased after the war, and the nature of the assistance expanded to include not only emergency relief assistance but also reconstruction or what was then called "welfare assistance."

With the end of the war, the President's War Relief Control Board terminated in March 1946. In its place, President Truman recommended the creation of the Advisory Committee on Voluntary Foreign Aid. Although PVOs were no longer required to register with the federal government, they had to register to be eligible for government commodities, shipping, and the exporting of commodities. By the end of 1946, there were 103 agencies voluntarily registered with the committee. Of those 103 agencies, 12 had never been registered with the federal government. With the formation of the committee, a new model of state-PVO relations was initiated, one favoring economies of scale and a close relationship with the federal government.

3

The Beginning of the Cold War and the Promotion of Economic Development, 1946–59

The democratic world is busy in a life-and-death struggle
to maintain its hard-won liberty.
—Edgar H. S. Chandler, *The High Tower of Refuge*

On March 12, 1947, President Harry S. Truman announced details to Congress of what eventually became known as the Truman Doctrine. In his speech, he pledged American support for "free peoples who are resisting attempted subjugation by armed minorities or by outside pressures."[1] This speech included a request for congressional approval of military and economic aid to the governments of Greece and Turkey.[2] Truman explained that he intended to send American military and economic advisers to countries whose political stability was threatened by Communism. A few months after Truman's speech, Secretary of State George Marshall announced a U.S. economic plan to work with European nations toward reconstruction. American policy toward Germany shifted from retribution to reconstruction. The destruction of European cultural values, political institutions, and economic systems represented the loss of the foundation of the United States. The purpose of U.S. assistance to Europe was one of "recovering" European society as it had been before the war.

Immediate postwar relief efforts focused on the needs of millions of displaced persons and refugees in Europe, the homeland of origin for the majority of Americans. Germany would continue to receive distinct treatment, but it would no longer be punitive.[3] Some programs begun during the postwar period, such as the feeding of children (which evolved into the school lunch program as part of the Public Law [P.L.] 480, Title II), would remain a permanent priority of American relief and development agencies. Yet it was not until Truman's Point Four Program, formulated in 1949, that private voluntary organizations (PVOs) and the assistance that they provided under the rubric of "foreign aid" would become a permanent tool of American foreign policy and would extend beyond Europe to "underdeveloped areas" of the world.[4]

The Rise and Fall of the Ethnically Oriented PVOs

The identification with Europe on the part of Americans was reflected in the ethnic relief agencies that quickly formed and became prominent during World War II. In terms of numbers, shown in figure 3.1, the ethnic agencies (all classed among the secular group) rose from 110 in 1939 (56% of the secular agencies and 46% of the total) to a peak of 194 in 1941 (53% of seculars and 46% of the total). Then the ethnic number fell sharply to 28 in 1945 (40% of seculars and 29% of the total). After the end of World War II, the number of ethnic PVOs experienced a gradual decline in absolute and relative terms, reaching 26% of seculars (14% of the total) in 1959.

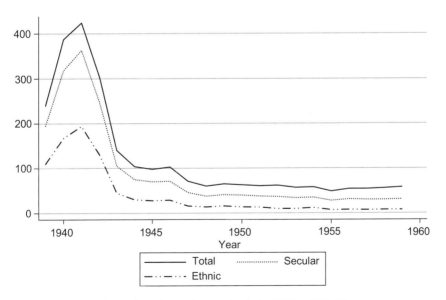

Figure 3.1. Numbers of total, secular, and ethnic PVOs, 1939–59.
Source: McCleary Private Voluntary Organizations Data Set.

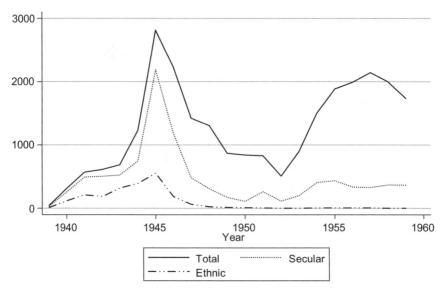

Figure 3.2. Real revenues (millions of 2005 dollars, adjusted for international share) for total, secular, and ethnic PVOs, 1939–59.
Source: McCleary Private Voluntary Organizations Data Set.

In terms of total real revenue, shown in figure 3.2, the ethnic group rose from $12.8 million in 1939 to $213 million in 1941, $323 million in 1943, and $556 million in 1945. Thus, as with other groups, the rising real revenue during World War II was accompanied by a sharp decline in the number of agencies. The revenue percentages for the ethnic agencies was 41% of seculars (26% of the total) in 1939, 43% of seculars (37% of the total) in 1941, 61% of seculars (47% of the total) in 1943, and 25% of seculars (20% of the total) in 1945. Thereafter, the ethnics experienced a gradual decline in real revenue in absolute and comparative terms. By 1959, the ethnics constituted only 0.6% of secular revenue (0.1% of the total).

Government-PVO Coordination and Cooperation, 1946–48

The Advisory Committee on Voluntary Foreign Aid was established as the successor agency to the President's War Relief Control Board in 1946. Registration with the Committee on Voluntary Foreign Aid was, as its name states, voluntary. The committee was a part of the State Department, with responsibility "to maintain a public record of the identity and activities of foreign relief organizations and the provision of necessary liaison and facilitating services."[5] In 1946, federal regulation and coordination of the solicitation of funds by PVOs was suspended. This setup meant that agencies had to spend more money on promotional materials, such as news stories, photographs, pamphlets, and radio publicity. For example, Church World Service spent less than 1% of its 1947 annual income on publicity, but in 1949 the amount spent rose to 3.25%.[6]

In 1947, Europe experienced extreme weather, leading to crop failure and further complication of relief efforts. The U.S. government was concerned that, in competition with each other, PVOs would not raise sufficient funds to carry out their programs on which the government relied. Through their umbrella organization, the American Council of Voluntary Agencies for Foreign Service (ACVAFS), PVOs coordinated with the United Nations (U.N.) Relief and Rehabilitation Administration (UNRRA), the Food and Agriculture Organization, the International Refugee Organization, and the U.N. Korea Relief Administration. However, the primary source of funds for PVOs was donations from the American public. And, the agencies had difficulty raising funds after the dissolution of the President's War Relief Control Board.

The U.N. Korea Relief Administration, as well as other U.N. entities, made direct appeals to the American public for funds. In 1947, the PVOs, through their umbrella organization, ACVAFS, argued that intergovernmental agencies such as the United Nations should receive funds from member governments and not by direct solicitation of the American public. The PVOs prevailed on this point. By 1960, U.N. entities could engage in direct appeals only through established U.S. committees and the United Nations itself through congressional allocation.[7]

In 1948, the U.S. government organized with the United Nations a national combined campaign, the American Overseas Aid-U.N. Appeal for Children.[8] Participation extended to 26 agencies, but funds garnered from the campaign were not sufficient to keep agencies operating without additional funds raised on their own. The agencies attributed the failure of the fund-raising campaign to confusion over being affiliated with a government entity, the United Nations. The inability to garner financial support from the American public forced agencies to close, and the total number of registered PVOs declined from 103 in 1946 to 62 in 1949 (see fig. 3.1).

It is not surprising that the number of registered agencies significantly dropped after World War II as they terminated their overseas efforts. Furthermore, since they were no longer required to register, the number of registered agencies would have fallen regardless. The decline in total number of agencies also showed up as a decline in total real revenue. In 1949, the total real revenue for the 60 registered PVOs was $872 million versus 103 registered PVOs with a total real revenue of $2.23 billion in 1946 (see fig. 3.2).

Registration with the Advisory Committee on Voluntary Foreign Aid offered PVOs eligibility to receive government subsidies on ocean freight (payment of transportation costs for surplus foods, clothing, medicines, hospital and school supplies and equipment, and tools). During the war years, the U.S. government had subsidized ocean freight for PVOs as part of the overall war effort. After World War II, Congress continued the practice but with the proviso that each PVO accepting free shipping be registered with the Advisory Committee on Voluntary Foreign Aid and be licensed to operate in certain geographic areas.[9] The government viewed the transportation subsidy as a means of controlling the overseas activities of PVOs.

Registered agencies also benefited from duty-free entry of supplies into a country and free transportation provided by the receiving country from port to distribution point.[10] Registered agencies were eligible for U.S. surplus foods from the Department of Agriculture. This program would become the P.L. 480 program in 1954 (under the name Agricultural Trade and Development Assistance Act of 1954). Registered agencies were qualified by the Department of Commerce for expedited exportation of certain materials.[11] Eventually, registered agencies would qualify to apply for excess government property, such as clothing, vehicles, and equipment.

Toward the end of World War II, the U.S. military command assessed the needs of liberated countries and occupied zones. Detailed lists of needed relief supplies were sent to the agencies.[12] Soon, the governments of liberated Europe were reestablished and by the end of 1947 were not as much in need of immediate humanitarian relief as the occupied zones of Germany.[13] However, in occupied areas, this assistance continued after the war in the form of P.L. 30 and 188, which regulated the exportation of certain foodstuffs.

The Advisory Committee on Voluntary Foreign Aid, working closely with the umbrella organization ACVAFS, coordinated PVO overseas activities with those of the U.S. government. The ACVAFS served as a coordinating body for agencies by holding regular meetings to avoid duplication of effort and to set priorities for the member agencies. The leaders of the various organizations knew each other through ACVAFS activities and became acquainted with each other's organizational activities, structure, and mission. This model of coordination and cooperation worked well in the post–World War II era, when security issues continued to be paramount. Several umbrella agencies were set up to coordinate PVO aid.[14] However, this structure (PVO cooperation) would begin to weaken in the late 1960s. The Vietnam War and U.S. military escalation altered PVO-state relations in many dimensions.[15]

In 1945, the Potsdam Agreement formalized what had been occurring since 1944. A mass exodus of refugees from Czechoslovakia, East Prussia, Pomerania, Upper and Lower Silesia, western provinces of Poland, and east of the Oder-Neisse line was taking place into Western Germany. Many refugees were "expellees," German ethnic peoples who, by the Potsdam Agreement, could be forcibly removed from Poland, Czechoslovakia, and Hungary back to Germany. By 1946, there were nine million refugees in the Western zones of Germany, and four million were in the Soviet Zone.[16] By the beginning of 1949, the PVOs shifted their operational focus from displaced persons to refugees. By the end of 1950, there were close to ten million refugees in West Germany, accounting for one-fifth of the total population. "Escapees" coming from Eastern Europe and Soviet-occupied East Berlin were estimated at over three million and would continue to move into West Germany until the Berlin Wall was finished in 1961.

Refugees from the partition of India and Pakistan in 1947, estimated at 17 million, and Arab refugees from the creation of the Israeli state in 1948, roughly 1 million, added to the need for assistance. From 1945 to 1949, the Jewish Joint Distribution Committee (renamed American Jewish Joint Distribution Committee [AJJDC]) focused its efforts on providing relief and transportation for displaced Jews to Palestine.

The UNRRA (November 1943–June 1947) was an international organization made up of 47 member governments for the purpose of giving relief and rehabilitation to people in liberated countries in Europe and the Far East. In March 1944, the U.S. Congress appropriated $1.35 billion for UNRRA. During UNRRA's existence, the United States provided 73% of the agency's total operating funds.[17] The UNRRA was the central distribution agency allocating funds and supplies to governments on a need basis. In December 1946, the United States ended its financial support of UNRRA after it was revealed that supplies were being sent to Yugoslavia while Communist forces were attacking U.S. aircraft.[18]

Relief and rehabilitation under UNRRA consisted of food, clothing, fuel, medicines, household supplies, seeds, fertilizers, raw materials, machinery, transportation, and public utilities as well as technical assistance.[19] There were also health and welfare services as well as repatriation of displaced persons who were citizens of member states of the United Nations. The purpose of UNRRA was to create a reservoir of emergency supplies and services for member nations that requested assistance and proved their need. The nations given aid were those that did not have adequate foreign exchange to do the relief-and-rehabilitation job themselves. Each member nation was asked to contribute at least 1% of its national income.

The PVOs were asked by the U.S. government to appeal to the American public to donate clothing and food supplies. Many agencies, such as the Jewish Joint Distribution Committee, were service organizations, with their personnel carrying out urgent programs in Europe to ensure the physical safety of Jews.[20] The request by President Truman for the agencies to focus exclusively on raising supplies meant a shift in organizational mandate and structure for many PVOs. To avoid becoming merely "supply" agencies, 22 PVOs joined to form CARE (originally Cooperative for American Remittances to Europe).[21] Cooperating and sharing the responsibility of food distribution were the most efficient and cost-effective for the PVOs to continue to remain service agencies.

From 1943 through August 1945, the Supreme Headquarters Allied Expeditionary Force (SHAEF) dictated the operation of humanitarian aid in Europe. The military supplied food, clothing, and shelter for displaced persons. Under the Trading with the Enemy Act, PVOs were not permitted to provide humanitarian assistance to Germany. After the war, Lutheran World Relief, Church World Service, the Mennonite Central Committee, and Catholic Relief Services were vocal in their opposition to the U.S. policy of retribution toward the German population.

The UNRRA mandate was to serve only agencies that entered into a contractual agreement with it and were approved by SHAEF. (However, there were agencies that the UNRRA refused to contract with and that the military permitted to operate in Europe.) The military command designated UNRRA as responsible for coordinating and overseeing PVO activity. The Western European member countries of UNRRA specifically requested to deal directly with Allied military authorities, not UNRRA. In all but Yugoslavia and Greece, the distribution of relief supplies was supervised by Allied military authorities.[22] The UNRRA personnel were incorporated into military personnel for the actual distribution of the supplies. After the military withdrew, each country undertook the responsibility for distribution of relief supplies with minimal UNRRA supervision.

Beginning in 1944, SHAEF requested from UNRRA teams of qualified personnel; in turn, PVO personnel were assigned to work directly for UNRRA.[23] The UNRRA staff and the PVO personnel took direct orders from the military. The PVOs continued to pay their personnel's salary, while UNRRA provided room and board, free medical care, and transportation. The majority of PVO personnel and UNRRA staff were working in displaced persons operations in Germany.[24] March 1946 marked the month with the highest number of reassigned PVO personnel working for UNRRA. By May 1946, UNRRA was caring for 715,000 displaced persons in Germany, and 1946 was a watershed year for displaced persons aid. The Harrison Report, commissioned by President Truman in the summer of 1945, criticized the military's treatment of Jewish displaced persons.[25] The UNRRA, in its efforts to address needs of Jewish displaced persons, in February 1946 set up a Council on Jewish Affairs to deal exclusively with these concerns.

Starting in 1945, UNRRA began soliciting PVO assistance for medical services and welfare programs to be carried out directly by PVOs in-country under UNRRA supervision. The PVOs were instrumental in providing clothing and food supplies.[26] Each U.S. agency operating in post–World War II Europe required the approval of the President's War Relief Board or the certification of the American Council of Voluntary Agencies in Foreign Assistance. In-country, UNRRA supervised the PVOs, with military oversight.[27] The UNRRA control over PVOs was limited when countries, such as Poland and Czechoslovakia, retained governmental authority over PVO activity. The largest contribution of PVOs was not in personnel but in relief supplies. In Germany, it is estimated that the relief supplies sent by foreign voluntary agencies exceeded the total provided by UNRRA. The largest donations came from the ethnic agencies (the most generous being the Greek War Relief Association).[28] A similar situation applied in Hungary and Finland. Most of the relief supplies donated and channeled through UNRRA were designated for distribution in named countries.

Table 3.1 shows the revenue of those agencies that contracted with UNRRA. The U.S. government was channeling funds to PVOs through

Table 3.1. Revenue of UNRRA members.

Year	UNRRA PVO revenue (millions 2005 $)	Total PVO revenue (millions 2005 $)	UNRRA %
1943	175	688	25.4
1944	401	1,230	32.6
1945	517	2,810	18.4
1946	1,100	2,230	49.3
1947	906	1,420	63.8

Source: Data were compiled from George Woodbridge, *UNRRA: The History of the United Nations Relief and Rehabilitation Administration*, 3 vol. (New York: Columbia University Press, 1950).

UNRRA. (Data on the percentage of revenue contracting PVOs received from UNRRA are not available.) The contracting agencies were financially benefiting from their arrangement with UNRRA because, as total PVO revenue was falling (column 3), PVOs contracting with UNRRA were garnering a higher percentage of revenue.

Relief supplies in the form of clothing were large, mostly because of national clothing drives organized in the United States, Canada, and New Zealand. In the United States, three national clothing drives were held (autumn 1944, spring 1945, and early 1946). The first clothing drive was organized by the "three great faiths"—Judaism, Roman Catholicism, and Protestantism. The religious organizations collected, bundled, warehoused, and transported the clothing to shipside. The UNRRA organized the shipping. The two subsequent U.S. clothing drives were made a quasi-governmental event, with President Roosevelt appointing a national chair and Eleanor Roosevelt giving her support. By the end of UNRRA's existence in 1947, U.S. PVOs had contributed $209,895,377 (in nominal dollars) to relief work, making up 6% of UNRRA's total contributions.

Figure 3.2 shows that total real PVO revenue went down from $2.23 billion in 1946 to $1.42 billion in 1947. Protestant revenue fell from $37.3 million to $35.6 million, Catholic declined from $169 million to $106 million, and ecumenical rose from $74.7 million to $122 million. Evangelical revenue went from $48.9 million to $47.4 million, and Jewish went from $670 million to $613 million. The biggest fall from 1946 to 1947 was for secular—from $1.19 billion to $486 million.

In April 1946, there were 11 U.S. agencies that began shipping food to Germany through the Council of Relief Agencies Licensed for Operation in Germany (CRALOG), a consortium they had formed as members of ACVAFS and with U.S. government approval.[29] The major reason for the formation of CRALOG was to ensure that relief work in Germany conformed to U.S. foreign policy. By channeling aid to Germany through CRALOG, the U.S. government deterred the formation of agencies by Germans in the United States who might seek to use relief aid for political ends.[30]

As with those agencies that contracted with UNRRA, member agencies of CRALOG received U.S. government funds channeled through CRALOG (table 3.2). Looking at the percentage of revenue (rightmost column, table 3.2.), CRALOG agencies had significant revenue, and it suggested that as overall revenue to PVOs was going down (column 2), the percentage of revenue of the CRALOG member agencies was also declining but not as rapidly. Several PVOs contracting with UNRRA were

Table 3.2. Revenue of CRALOG members.

Year	CRALOG PVO revenue (millions 2005 $)	Total PVO revenue (millions 2005 $)	CRALOG %
1946	914	2,230	41.0
1947	876	1,420	61.7
1948	909	1,310	69.4
1949	640	872	73.4
1950	582	843	69.0

Source: McCleary Private Voluntary Organizations Data Set.

also member agencies of CRALOG, for example, American Federation of Labor, Brethren Service Committee, and Lutheran World Relief (see notes 23 and 29 for membership lists of UNRRA and CRALOG, respectively). This meant that these agencies had secure sources of funding and were not as reliant on the American public for revenue as those PVOs that did not belong to either UNRRA or CRALOG.

The CRALOG representatives in Germany were under the authority of the U.S. military command, which was responsible for their welfare (room, board, and security). The CRALOG activities in Germany occurred in two stages. From March 1946 to May 1947, food and clothing were shipped. In May 1947, the U.S. military command allowed CRALOG agencies to bring work teams to Germany to address housing for displaced persons and refugees, construct neighborhood centers and homes for the civilian population, and provide medical service teams. Whereas food supplies sent by CRALOG members were collected by each agency, the clothing donations were raised through a drive of the United National Clothing Collection, the largest registered entity in 1945, that took place in 1945 (and annually thereafter through 1947). The agencies of CRALOG, like other PVOs, refrained from their own clothing drives to participate in the centralized campaign coordinated by UNRRA (which also provided ships for the transportation of the clothing overseas). The CRALOG agencies received a proportion of the clothing donated. The agencies operating in Europe continued their humanitarian work through 1949. However, realizing that four years after the humanitarian efforts they had to switch to a permanent solution, the U.S. Congress passed the Agricultural Act of 1949. This program would become known as the P.L. 480 food program administered by the Department of Agriculture. Surplus food commodities were allocated to agencies, which initially covered the cost of packing and trucking the goods to ports for shipment. The U.S. government provided shipping for the P.L. 480 goods (see figure 3.3). The CRALOG and UNRRA membership overlapped for 1946 and 1947, and as a result member agencies benefited from revenue coming from these two different sources for these two years.

Rather than working alone, CRALOG agencies developed relationships with the humanitarian agencies of the Roman Catholic Church (*Caritas Verband*) and the Evangelical Lutheran Church (Evangelical Aid Society). The agencies served not only West German civilian needs but also those of close to ten million displaced persons expelled from Communist-occupied territories and German former prisoners of war. By the end of 1947, CRALOG was operating in the three Western-occupied zones of Germany in coordination with Caritas, Evangelical Aid Society, Red Cross, Federation of Workers, welfare agencies, and the German Equity Welfare Union. Supplies were transferred to these agencies and distributed through their networks in Germany. The exception was insulin, which was distributed by CRALOG directly to the German Public Health Ministry.

Another regional umbrella agency, Licensed Agencies for Relief in Asia (LARA), again comprised of members of ACVAFS and registered with the Advisory Committee on Voluntary Foreign Aid, sent relief to occupied areas in Asia (Japan, Okinawa, and Korea).[31] The agency was the only one licensed to work with the Supreme Commander for the Allied Powers (SCAF) to send relief supplies to Asia. Like CRALOG, LARA relief supplies were based on a list provided by the Allied military command. Transportation of goods from the United States was provided by SCAF and distributed in-country by domestic agencies. Similar to CRALOG, all LARA operations and staff in Asia were under the authority of SCAF.[32]

The PVO CARE was another umbrella agency formed in 1945.[33] Whereas the majority of the member agencies of CRALOG and LARA were religious, the member agencies of CARE were primarily secular and ethnic. Unlike CRALOG and LARA, CARE was a conduit for individual Americans to send aid directly to individuals in European countries. In May 1946, CARE began shipping excess military food containers. These containers were sent to 17 European countries. Germany received twice as many containers as all the other countries combined. This pattern reflected the federal government's restrictions during the war on the formation of German ethnic relief groups in the United States. After the war, the government facilitated German humanitarian relief efforts through CRALOG and CARE.

With the dissolution of UNRRA in 1947, U.S. agricultural commodities continued to be shipped overseas. The government shipped goods through bilateral agreements such as the Philippine Rehabilitation Act of 1946, the program for Government Aid and Relief in Occupied Areas, the post-UNRRA Relief Program, the British Loan, the Greek-Turkish Aid Program, the Interim Aid Program of 1947, and finally the Economic Cooperation Administration (ECA) of 1948. The ECA specifically named the American Committee on Voluntary Foreign Aid as the agency through which PVOs qualified for surplus agricultural commodities and reimbursements on freight.

Coordinating Jewish Fund-Raising

In January 1939, the United Jewish Appeal (UJA), a fund-raising organization made up of the AJJDC, the United Palestine Appeal, and the National Coordinating Committee for Aid to Refugees and Emigrants Coming from Germany, was reconstituted.[34] The purpose of UJA was to minimize competition between the Zionist and non-Zionist groups for local donations and to coordinate nationally their fund-raising activities for European relief activities, assistance to Jewish displaced persons and refugees, and services for Jews seeking resettlement in the United States.[35] In December 1945, the UJA raised $100 million ($1.1 billion 2005 dollars), exceeding its combined efforts of the previous six years (1939–44). The success of the appeal, however, could not match the needs in Europe.

In 1946, the surviving European Jewry was estimated at 3.1 million, and close to 1 million Jews lived in increasingly hostile environments in Arab countries. In 1946, there were 175,000 Jewish displaced persons who returned to Poland and Romania from Russia, and 250,000 Jewish displaced persons were in camps in Germany and Austria. The AJJDC was working to address the immediate relief needs of 750,000 Jewish displaced persons and preparing to move 30,000 Jews, the largest number since 1939, to Palestine.[36] To meet the need, in 1946 the Jewish organizations coordinated and formalized their fund-raising efforts under UJA in a manner that had never been accomplished before.[37] By the end of 1946, the UJA had raised $130 million.

In 1947, several factors led to increasing tensions within the UJA. The UNRRA ceased operating, and the U.S. Army Displaced Persons feeding program ended as the military began pulling out of Europe. The International Relief Organization, successor to UNRRA, was much smaller in size in terms of staff and material resources. In November 1947, the United Nations passed a resolution on the partition of Palestine. Even given the unprecedented success of the UJA 1946 campaign, its constituency members—AJJDC, United Palestine Appeal, and the National Coordinating Committee for Aid to Refugees and Emigrants Coming from Germany—had been borrowing from American and Palestine banks to meet urgent needs in Europe. With Jews in Arab countries under persecution, the pressure to continue to raise unprecedented levels of funds placed stress on existing disagreements between Zionists and moderate Jewish groups. To ensure the success of continued Jewish support for Jewish causes overseas, a critical shift in fund-raising strategy was made that altered the focus of Jewish philanthropy in America for decades to come. Palestine, rather than being a refugee haven, was now promoted as a political entity, a Jewish state.[38] The majority of American Jewry was not ideologically driven but would financially support a Jewish state, dovetailing their interests with those of the Zionist groups.[39] This new focus resulted in a highly successful 1948 UJA campaign, with close to $150 million or $1.2 billion in 2005 dollars raised.

The AJJDC, after Israel attained its statehood in 1948, moved quickly to transport 167,000 Jewish refugees to Israel. This movement included the entire Jewish population of Yemen and the evacuation of the Jewish community beginning in 1947 before Libya, in 1951, gained its independence.[40]

In 1950, with European displaced persons camps closing and focus shifting to normalizing life at home, contributions to UJA dropped. Edward M. M. Warburg described the situation as donor fatigue.[41] Yet, during the first nine months of 1949, the AJJDC moved 198,436 Jews to Israel. The AJJDC, with initial funds of $10 million ($82 million 2005 dollars), entered into an agreement with the state of Israel to assist in resettling refugees. The agency also assisted 19,404 Jewish refugees admitted to the United States, and 8,863 Jewish refugees were settled in Canada and South America.[42] By 1950, the AJJDC experienced a significant drop in revenue (table 3.3). Jewish agencies would continue to serve the Jews who had repatriated to Europe, but the welfare and security of Israel would dominate the attention of the Jewish community and become a central part of American foreign policy for decades to come.

Also significant to note is that the Jewish agencies after World War II were focused on assisting Jewish displaced persons and refugees. This pattern would change over time, particularly as Israel became a mature state. By the 1970s, the dilution of Jewish giving to non-Jewish causes and the creation of new PVOs to address non-Jewish issues

Table 3.3. Expenditures (nominal dollars) of the Jewish Joint Distribution Committee on its Palestine (Israel) program, 1933–50.

Year	Expenditure
1933–39	$1,769,804 (exclusive of $860,000 expended on cultural activities)
1940–45	$6,510,779 (exclusive of $646,307 invested in the Palestine Economic Corporation)
1946	$2,333,700
1947	$6,879,500
1948	$15,458,100
1949	$24,081,900
1950	$19,642,500

Source: Samuel Halperin, "Ideology or Philanthropy? The Politics of Zionist Fund-Raising." *The Western Political Quarterly* 13, 4 (December 1960): 970, fn. 60.

(e.g., environment) would create a financial crisis for the established Jewish agencies.

Containment and Reconstruction: 1948–54

With the Communist takeover of Czechoslovakia in February 1948, the priorities of U.S. foreign policy shifted to the containment of Russia's political and military aggression. From 1948 to 1954, the ECA and its successor, the Mutual Security Agency (MSA), administered the bilateral programs of the European Recovery Program, popularly known as the Marshall Plan. Included in the ECA was shipment of U.S. farm products and ocean freight for PVOs registered with the Advisory Committee on Voluntary Foreign Aid.[43]

Congress was looking for ways to coordinate and oversee PVO activities overseas. A main reason for the return to governmental oversight was the security threat of Communism. The underlying raison d'être of government-PVO relationship, the implementation of U.S. foreign policy objectives, brought pressure to bear on PVOs to register with the U.S. government and to act in concert with government policies. Part of government oversight was security clearance for personnel of voluntary agencies operating technical assistance programs under U.S. government contracts. The American Friends Service Committee, a pacifist group, rejected such government oversight as well as the explicit linking of foreign assistance to military assistance and did not renew its contract. The focus of foreign aid was now on technical assistance and food aid, tools that could be used to build trust in the United States.[44]

In 1948, the PVOs again returned to collaborate on fund-raising as well as budget review by the Advisory Committee on Voluntary Foreign Aid. In 1948, Congress passed the Displaced Persons Act. Many agencies shifted their focus to helping settle refugees in the United States. Until the mid-1950s, refugee resettlement and later the Korean War (1950–53) were the humanitarian priorities of U.S. agencies.[45]

The 1948 Displaced Persons Act initially permitted the admission of 205,000 refugees who were fleeing persecution. Over the next two years, an allotment for 200,000 more refugees was instituted. In 1951, the United States passed the Internal Security Act as a means of establishing oversight over legal immigrants and giving the government the authority to deport political "subversives." In 1952, the Immigration and Nationality Act came into effect. This act reaffirmed the national origins quota system, limited immigration from the Eastern Hemisphere while leaving the Western Hemisphere unrestricted, established preferences for skilled workers and relatives of U.S. citizens and permanent resident aliens, and tightened security and screening standards and procedures. From 1950 to 1954, PVOs undertook the responsibility of resettling the refugees. In some cases, this resettlement was done with government funding through grants and loans.[46]

The Cold War and the Rise of Catholic Relief Services

The Korean War began a few days after the passing of the Point Four Program. The Korean War heightened U.S. concern over the spread of Communism, particularly to Southeast Asian countries (Korea, Indochina, Burma, Thailand, and Indonesia).

During the Korean War (1950–53), U.S. voluntary agencies contributed $22,364,062 to humanitarian aid to Korea.[47] The overwhelming majority of these agencies were Christian, and a significant number were involved in mission work.[48] The American Relief for Korea (Committee on Korea), made up of member agencies of the ACVAFS, functioned similarly to CRALOG and LARA. Once the war ended, similar to the structure of PVO-military relations after World War II, humanitarian agencies working in Korea were under the coordination of the Korean Association of Voluntary Agencies, which ensured that the agencies met the requirements set down by the U.S. military.

The centralization of PVO relations with the government's Advisory Committee on Voluntary Assistance was viewed as a positive development, reducing registration requirements and coordinating various departmental activities. (The Agriculture Act of 1949 made surplus commodities available to PVOs registered with the advisory committee.) Furthermore, with registration, PVOs became eligible for designated funds set aside solely for PVOs. Eventually, these PVO-designated accounts would total seven. Under the "set aside" funds for PVOs, only registered agencies could qualify. Set aside funds were for programs initiated by PVOs as opposed to U.S. government–initiated activities, which did not require PVO registration.

In 1949, Congress passed the Agricultural Act, of which section 416 permitted PVOs to ship at no cost perishable agricultural surplus commodities (dried eggs, butter, cheese, and dried milk) to Europe, Asia, and Latin America. The agency CARE, which had ceased to be a cooperative of agencies and had become a PVO in its own right, successfully lobbied the Senate to be included in the bill.[49] The motivation behind the act was to subsidize U.S. farmers and to find new markets for surplus U.S. agricultural products. During 1951, at the height of the Korean War, providing surplus agricultural commodities to PVOs was suspended. In 1953, at the end of the war, the surplus commodities under section 416 were renewed but in larger quantities, thereby creating the need for new legislation.

The P.L. 480 program, begun in 1949, shipped "surplus" food from the United States to 36 countries. Figure 3.3 shows the value in millions of 2005 dollars of the amounts of surplus food shipped abroad through this program. The amount was $195 million in 1950, then rose to a peak of $1.3 billion in 1955. After a dip, the program rebounded to another peak—at $1.2 billion—in 1964. Thereafter, the real dollar amounts fell fairly steadily, except for a brief rebound in 2003–4.

From its start in 1949, the P.L. 480 food program was heavily concentrated among a small number of PVOs. The number receiving this assistance was less than 20 in all years except for 1955 (when it equaled 36) and 1999 (when it was 22).

From 1950 through the mid-1980s, most of the P.L. 480 food outlays were channeled through eight PVOs—refereed to as the Big Eight in figure 3.3. (The eight are Catholic Relief Services, CARE, Hadassah, Lutheran World Relief, Church World Service, International Rescue and Relief, American Friends Service Committee, and AJJDC.) An average of 98% of the total value of food shipments went through these eight PVOs during the 1950s. Catholic Relief Services, by itself, received over half of P.L. 480 funds from 1953 to 1963.

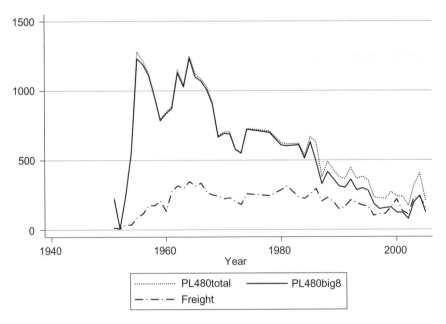

Figure 3.3. Real federal outlay (millions of 2005 dollars) for overall P.L. 480 food program, part channeled through Big Eight PVOs, and freight, 1950–2005.
Source: McCleary Private Voluntary Organizations Data Set.
Note: The Big Eight PVOs in the P.L. 480 surplus food program are Catholic Relief Services, CARE, Hadassah, Lutheran World Relief, Church World Service, International Rescue and Relief, American Friends Service Committee, and American-Jewish Joint Distribution Committee.

Figure 3.3 also shows real federal outlays for reimbursement of ocean freight. These outlays rose through the 1950s to reach $207 million in 1959. The amounts were between $200 million and $350 million going into the 1980s.

As the Marshall Plan was concluding, Congress considered ending ocean freight reimbursements to PVOs. Through their umbrella organization, ACVAFS, PVOs successfully lobbied Congress to continue subsidizing freight (albeit at a lower level). This subsidy was included in the 1951 Mutual Security Act (section 535) with a small but significant change in wording. The ECA stated that the U.S. government would reimburse freight costs to PVOs "recommended by the Advisory Committee on Voluntary Foreign Aid."[50] The 1951 Mutual Security Act read "approved" in place of "recommended." The PVOs had lobbied hard to avoid State Department efforts to assess the competence of each PVO to carry out foreign assistance activities.[51] The compromise was strong legislative language with no bureaucratic enforcement mechanism. From this moment, registration with the Advisory Committee on Voluntary Foreign Aid and its successor federal agencies would be viewed by PVOs as government endorsement of their activities, a seal of approval that PVOs could promote to the public and use to raise funds.[52]

The Mutual Security Act included contracts to PVOs to provide technical assistance to developing countries.[53] Technical assistance programs were concentrated in Latin America, Africa, and South Asia. But, unlike previous legislation, the 1951 Mutual Security Act explicitly linked humanitarian, economic development, and military aid. In contracting to operate technical assistance programs overseas, PVOs were careful to make clear that their humanitarian and religious motivations were integral to the national security interests of the United States.[54] The PVO personnel working on governmental technical assistance contracts had to obtain security clearances. Some Protestant PVOs objected to the language, but only the American Friends Service Committee withdrew.[55]

In 1953, the Foreign Operations Administration was established as an independent government agency outside the Department of State to consolidate economic and technical assistance on a worldwide basis. Its responsibilities were merged into the International Cooperation Administration (ICA) one year later (1953–61).

The ICA administered aid for economic, political, and social development purposes. Although the ICA's functions were vast and far reaching, unlike its successor, the U.S. Agency for International Development (USAID), ICA had many limitations placed on it. As a part of the Department of State, ICA did not have the level of autonomy its successor, USAID, would exercise. During the 1950s, multilateral institutions such as the United Nations and the Organization of American States were playing a large role in international humanitarian aid.[56] The PVOs understood their role to be that of providers of supplementary assistance, with the primary role for addressing relief needs overseas going to the U.S. government.[57]

The Mutual Security Act of 1954 reframed U.S. foreign assistance. Previously, the notion of humanitarian aid was defined as organized refugee, food, and relief efforts designed for immediate assistance. The Mutual Security Act called for technical assistance provided by PVOs that went hand-in-hand with military aid to developing countries as well as to European ones. The PVO activities were expanding beyond humanitarian aid for development. As former colonies in Asia and Africa began to gain their independence, American foreign policy shifted to one of enlightening the developing regions of the world by exporting Western democratic values, science, and technology. The umbrella organization, ACVAFS, actively cooperated with the U.S. government in carrying out this new foreign policy approach.

One difficulty was that the PVOs did not have personnel that were technically trained. With government funds, ACVAFS operated the Technical Assistance Information Clearing House to publish a listing of PVOs, their geographic presence around the world, and their programs. Some agencies viewed the Technical Assistance Information Clearing House as a governmental mechanism for obtaining information on PVOs and their overseas programs. Through individual contracts to agencies, the federal government sought to obtain information from the experience of PVOs with local communities in exchange for technical advice and equipment.[58] But, the Point Four technical assistance program remained an explicit tool of U.S. foreign policy.[59]

Under the Eisenhower administration (1953–61), the federal government increased funding to PVOs through contracts, ocean freight reimbursements, and P.L. 480 grants (Agricultural Trade Development and Assistance Act).[60] The P.L. 480 food distributed rose sharply from 1950 to 1956–57, then fell significantly through 1961 before rebounding (under Kennedy) for 1962–64 (see fig. 3.3). Freight rose from 1950 to a peak in 1955, was lower through 1960, rebounded in 1961–62, then remained fairly stable through the rest of the 1960s (again, see fig. 3.3). Starting in 1950, the federal government covered the costs of processing, packaging, and inland freight for routine agency shipments and surplus food commodities. In a 1955 amendment to the Agricultural Trade Development and Assistance Act (1954), the PVOs successfully gained two types of ocean freight reimbursement: one for regular agency supplies (covered by the Mutual Security Act of 1955) and the other for surplus food commodities (covered by the amendment).[61] Along with this concession, the PVOs obtained the ability to ship surplus commodities to more countries.[62] More important, the guaranteed federal coverage of all PVO ocean freight provided for increased demand on the part of PVOs for surplus food commodities. In addition, in 1955 the federal government added wheat, corn, rice, and beans to the P.L. 480 food program.

By the end of the 1950s, the Protestant PVOs were concerned that, with increasing federal subsidies (surplus food commodities, freight, and excess government property) and contracts, agencies would become politicized and less independent. Rather than implementing people-to-people projects, PVOs would become quasi-governmental agencies, carrying out U.S. foreign policy. The balance between accepting larger amounts of food aid along with ocean freight subsidy, while at the same time maintaining programmatic independence, was a continuing policy concern of PVOs. This issue often split along religious lines. Catholic Relief Services continually sought to increase federal assistance to PVOs, whereas the mainline Protestants—notably Lutheran World Relief and Church World Service—eventually elected to garner smaller amounts (table 3.4).[63] By the late 1950s, Church World Service made the decision to solicit government funds only for the resettlement of refugees in the United States.

In the mid-1950s, Catholic Relief Services stepped up its pressure on the executive and legislative branches of government to expand and increase supplies of commodities to PVOs. A split occurred among the PVOs along sectarian lines, with Catholic Relief Services and CARE pressing for increased federal assistance. On the other side were Lutheran World Relief and Church World Service. Lutheran World Relief exemplified one end of the spectrum and Catholic Relief Services the other. Lutheran World Relief advocated a form of international assistance that emphasized "volunteerism," which meant assisting people to become self-sufficient.[64] The volunteerism issue was part of a larger debate among the religious PVOs over church-state separation. The Protestant agencies

Table 3.4. P.L. 480 food and freight for Catholic Relief Services, Church World Service, and Lutheran World Relief, 1950–59.

	Catholic Relief Services		Church World Service		Lutheran World Relief	
Year	P.L. 480 food	Freight	P.L. 480 food	Freight	P.L. 480 food	Freight
1950	65.4	5.1	0	0	13.5	1.7
1951	35.0	7.4	0	0	7.4	1.8
1952	2.8	3.4	0	0	2.2	0.7
1953	143	18.0	31.7	6.7	30.7	3.6
1954	325	18.0	72.2	6.7	69.9	3.6
1955	720	39.2	141	9.4	62.2	3.8
1956	680	59.6	235	21.7	49.4	5.9
1957	614	106	240	35.1	94.6	10.8
1958	557	108	188	28.2	54.0	11.3
1959	427	103	136	37.9	50.9	11.9

Source: McCleary Private Voluntary Organizations Data Set.
Note: All amounts are in millions of 2005 dollars.

did not wish to be viewed as "agents" of the U.S. government. Historically, the Protestant agencies deliberately would not be recipients of significant federal funds.[65]

For its part, Catholic Relief Services advocated the principle of subsidiarity.[66] Subsidiarity provides a rationale for sustaining and strengthening overlapping objectives between private entities and the state. The principle was used by Catholic Relief Services to justify its role in state-sponsored activities. Catholic Relief Services, under the rationale of subsidiarity, saw garnering significant government commodities and revenue as a means of strengthening and broadening its presence in Latin America and parts of Africa where Roman Catholic missions had been set up. The lobbying pressure Catholic Relief Services brought to bear primarily on Congress would produce results by the mid-1960s.

In 1959, Senator Hubert Humphrey introduced what he called "using our abundance more wisely as a tool of international policy and international friendship."[67] The P.L. 480 program would now be called Food for Peace. Under President Kennedy (1960–63), the food program would be altered from a relief program to one of meeting development objectives. From 1953 to 1960, Catholic Relief Services and Church World Service garnered approximately 70% of the P.L. 480 commodities. Eight agencies (fig. 3.3) accounted for 98% of all P.L. 480 food commodities from 1953 to 1960.

In 1956, Congress authorized the packaging of surplus commodities in small containers and full freight reimbursement on surplus commodities. Catholic Relief Service from 1953 to 1960 garnered no less than 53% of its total revenue in the form of P.L. 480 food commodities.[68] After intense lobbying on the part of PVOs, oil seeds, edible oils, and fats were added to the list of agricultural products that could be shipped overseas.[69] The food continued to be donated as a gift from the American people even though PVOs sought to implement a "food-for-work" program and food grants.

Continuing the Pattern of Relief Aid

During the 1950s, American policy makers promoted foreign aid as economic development. The idea was that economic development would bring political stability and self-governance. This model of foreign assistance assumed that a target country had established political institutions and practices from which to draw upon and strengthen. Post–World War II Europe, with the economic assistance of the Marshall Plan, could rebuild their political systems and become functioning societies once again. The

Korean War and economic aid to Korea shifted the focus of the foreign assistance model. Economic development became a means of thwarting Communist influence. The political dimension of foreign aid—how to promote democratic institutions—was not clearly thought out. Policy makers simply understood economic development to lead naturally to democratic institutions.

Through their umbrella organization, the ACVAFS, PVOs successfully lobbied the executive and legislative branches to obtain concessions such as governmental regulation of U.N. appeals to the American public. The PVOs were also successful in permanently thwarting State Department efforts to assess the competence of each PVO to carry out foreign assistance activities.[70] With the introduction of the Point Four Program, the government sought contractual relations with "private, nonsectarian organizations with outstanding records of competence and experience" in technical assistance.[71] To make such a determination, the administration sought to increase its authority over PVOs by determining the "worthiness" of an organization and its programs and reporting those findings to the public.[72] The Point Four Program emphasized technical assistance, an institutional capability that traditional religious PVOs had not developed. As a result, when the government could not identify a qualified agency, it funded the establishment of agencies to carry out technical assistance, hence the term *volagency*.

Ultimately, those agencies engaged in humanitarian relief lost ground in their relations with the government. Governmental preference for volagencies marginalized the established religious PVOs who noted that they were having difficulty raising private funds for technical assistance programs, whereas the public generously gave for relief and humanitarian projects.[73] The most successful lobbying the ACVAFS engaged in on behalf of its member agencies was to secure ocean freight reimbursements for relief supplies and P.L. 480 surplus food commodities.

Also significant is that the Jewish PVOs were focused on assisting Jews and with good reason. This pattern would change over time, so that, by the 1970s, contributions to the traditional Israel-focused PVO declined, and younger Jews were focusing on poverty and the environment—humanitarian issues that were not Jewish specific. To address these broader concerns, new PVOs such as American Jewish World Service, Jewish Fund for Justice, and Mazon were created.

Until the Foreign Assistance Act of 1961 and the formation of USAID and the Peace Corps, it was implicitly accepted by the federal government that religious PVOs were best equipped to deliver humanitarian assistance (relief assistance, refugee assistance, and community-based technical assistance projects). After the election of John F. Kennedy, a Roman Catholic, it was decided that "church-related organizations would not receive contracts to administer programs overseas."[74] The ACVAFS representatives met with administration officials, and it was decided that religious PVOs could apply to be on the USAID list of organizations with which contracts could be negotiated if they submitted the required paperwork for registration. The upshot of the meeting was that religious PVOs would have to "sell" their services to program officers in the five contracting offices within USAID that had the authority to "negotiate, execute, amend and terminate contracts with individuals or organizations."[75] The profusion of contracting sources meant that PVOs not only had to market their projects to various sources but also would encounter different biases, requirements, forms, and procedures in applying for government assistance.

4

The Internationalization of American Aid

> If I am not for myself, who will be? If I am only for myself, what am I?
>
> —Hillel, *Pirkei Avot*

In the early 1960s, the approach of the Kennedy administration was to involve American civil society in the implementation of U.S. foreign policy through the creation of the Peace Corps and the Alliance for Progress. This trend was not new. Development assistance, as a vehicle of U.S. foreign policy, was being carried out through civil society organizations— private voluntary organizations (PVOs)—that gained entry into another country and access to its people.[1]

During the last two years of the Eisenhower administration, foreign assistance as technical development at the community level was increasingly viewed as a means of strengthening indigenous political institutions against Communism.

In the years from the end of World War II until the late 1960s, a shift in PVO overseas programs took place from relief to economic development projects. Beginning in the 1960s, the older social service and relief agencies, such as Catholic Relief Services (CRS), American Friends Service Committee, Church World Service, and American Jewish Joint Distribution Committee (AJJDC), had to confront a rise in secular PVOs. (See table 4.1.)

The established voluntary agencies were being overtaken by new PVOs in several dimensions. Whereas the traditional PVOs tended to be large and faith oriented, the newer secular PVOs tended to be small and specialized (microenterprise, community health programs, education projects). The large ethnic agencies formed during World War II were

Table 4.1. Numbers of registered PVOs, 1960–69.

Year	Number of PVOs	Number religious	Number secular
1960	60	28	32
1961	59	28	31
1962	56	29	27
1963	54	26	28
1964	59	27	31
1965	60	27	32
1966	61	28	32
1967	74	32	41
1968	80	31	46
1969	83	31	50

Source: McCleary Private Voluntary Organizations Data Set.

disbanded at the end of the war, whereas many of the religious agencies founded during that time continued to operate.

Working at the grassroots level with local partners, the new PVOs established networks and local expertise. The presence of these small, specialized PVOs (such as Volunteers in Technical Assistance, Education Development Center, Docare, and Pathfinder), with a small constituency base, challenged the traditional paradigm of the humanitarian agency (such as CRS, Church World Service, AJJDC, and CARE). Furthermore, these new agencies—referred to as *volagencies*—were focused on disseminating the application of American technical and scientific advances abroad. The newer PVOs applied recent innovations in agriculture, engineering, and medicine. These agencies valued relations with research institutions as well as corporations. The agencies that belonged to the American Council of Voluntary Agencies for Foreign Service (ACVAFS) were beginning to perceive correctly that the majority of government contracts were being awarded to cooperatives, universities, and firms.[2]

Breakdown of Secular PVOs by Subtype

The government foreign aid focus was on technical assistance and community development. Traditional PVOs had been stereotyped as relief agencies as they lacked the trained, professional staff and the organizational structure to engage in technical projects. In 1964, only 13 PVOs were administering 30 contracts of a total of 1,165 awarded.[3] Whereas the traditional PVOs had been actively courted and assisted by the federal government during and after World War II, these same agencies now found themselves outdated and outmaneuvered by the newer PVOs.

But, the reluctance to cooperate was not one-sided. The larger and more active PVOs were religious or faith-founded, with the exception of CARE. The election of the first Roman Catholic president raised questions about the separation of religion and state. Religious PVOs that historically had been recipients of federal largesse now found their legitimacy questioned. After some debate, the religious agencies were permitted to continue receiving federal assistance.[4] The test case for religious PVOs was the formation of the Peace Corps. Its director, Sargent Shriver, requested of collaborating organizations (which included universities) use of their overseas facilities. The Protestant agencies refused to permit the U.S. government to use their overseas facilities. By contrast, the Roman Catholic Church actively sought cooperation with the administration and agreed to Shriver's terms. The Protestant position forced Shriver to rule that the Peace Corps would work only with secular organizations so it would not appear to favor Roman Catholic organizations.[5]

The politicized nature of the relationship between religious PVOs and the federal government extended to technical assistance contracts (not surplus food and refugee assistance). The government ruled that contracts with "church-related agencies" would be determined on an ad hoc basis.[6] Religion was not the only reason for the lack of technical assistance contracts with religious PVOs (of which they had none in 1964). The perception existed within the federal government that religious PVOs were structured to deliver surplus food commodities and assist refugees. The U.S. Agency for International Development (USAID) officials questioned the institutional capacity of religious PVOs to carry out technical assistance projects.

Table 4.2 shows the breakdown of secular PVOs by function during the 1960s. The total number of secular PVOs grew over the decade from 32 to 50. In the 1960s, the largest share by type was in the category of international relief and development. This group comprised 22 PVOs (69% of seculars) in 1960 and 23 (46%) in 1969. The largest expansion over the decade occurred in the category of medicine and health planning—there were 6 of these (19%) in 1960 and 13 (26%) in 1969, the growth taking

Table 4.2. Numbers of secular PVOs by functional orientation, 1960–69.

Year	Total	Growth	Relief	Education	Environment	Culture	Health
				Numbers by type			
1960	32	1	22	4	0	1	4
1961	31	1	20	3	0	1	6
1962	27	1	17	2	0	2	5
1963	28	2	17	3	0	1	5
1964	31	2	18	3	0	2	6
1965	32	2	18	4	0	2	6
1966	32	2	19	3	0	2	6
1967	41	3	20	7	0	3	8
1968	46	4	22	6	0	3	11
1969	50	4	23	7	0	3	13

Source: McCleary Private Voluntary Organizations Data Set.
Note: "Growth" includes economic growth, agricultural development, and engineering and infrastructure; "relief" includes international relief and development; "education" includes education/higher learning and professional societies; "environment" includes conservation, animal protection, solar power, and so forth; "culture" includes communications, culture and society, and foundations; "health" includes medicine and health issues.

place in family-planning agencies. The PVOs oriented toward growth and development increased from one (3%) in 1960 to four (8%) in 1969.

Permanent Humanitarian Uses of Food

As a senator, John F. Kennedy actively supported the Food for Peace program. On becoming president, he created the Office of Director of Food for Peace; this director was directly under the president as a member of the White House staff.[7] The upward trend in expanding the Public Law (P.L.) 480 food programs began during the last two years of the Eisenhower administration. The increase was attributed to pilot projects of food for work and a large four-year feeding program in India.[8] In 1962, the Food for Work Program was formally implemented. The religious PVOs in particular had been actively lobbying since 1957 for this change in the P.L. 480 program.[9] The agencies took the position that donated goods were demeaning to the recipients.[10] Rather than fostering self-sufficiency, food donations encouraged dependency on handouts.

Another change in the surplus food program was a reorientation toward nutritional aspects of the feeding programs. Whereas previously only available surplus foods were allocated to the agencies, now agencies, through their umbrella organization the ACVAFS, requested foodstuffs that would balance out dietary needs.[11] A third change was introduced in the Food and Agricultural Act of 1962, which authorized school lunch programs. The lunch program continued to expand, particularly in Latin America with the Alliance for Progress.[12] In short, the programmatic focus was on community development projects and child nutrition programs. Not until the early 1970s would Congress and the agencies raise questions regarding the effectiveness of the feeding programs and whether they were "developmental" as opposed to relief measures.

As occurred during the Korean War, agricultural surplus commodities became scarce during 1965 and 1966 with the escalation of the Vietnam War. As PVOs experienced delays with the implementation of the food program, they successfully lobbied for changes in the Food for Peace (1966) legislation.[13] But, irrespective of the Vietnam War, U.S. agricultural surpluses were low by the mid-1960s. As a consequence, reference to "agricultural surpluses" was eliminated from the language of the Food for Peace legislation. Food aid was viewed by Congress as a "complement" to economic development and not a mechanism for disposing of surplus agricultural commodities. The Commodity Credit Corporation was now obligated to cover the costs for "enrichment, preservation, and fortification of commodities" made available to PVOs.[14]

In 1961, an amendment to the Mutual Security Act of 1954 made excess government property available to PVOs. Through their umbrella organization, ACVAFS, PVOs had been lobbying since 1952 for access to military excess property overseas. To maintain control over excess property, USAID required that a recipient agency be registered with USAID and that the PVO demonstrate that the excess property was needed and suitable to the agency's program. The amount and type of government excess property varied by year. In 1964, the ACVAFS secured from Congress ocean freight on excess property overseas.[15]

Amounts under excess property never became large compared to other sources of PVO revenue. In the 1960s (my data on excess property begin in 1964), the peak real value of excess property was $4.9 million in 1967, amounting to less than 1% of PVO total revenue. The largest recipients of excess property during the 1960s were International Human Assistance Programs (total receipts of $4.8 million), International Educational Development ($3.2 million), United Israel Appeal ($2.4 million), Church World Service ($2.0 million), and Organization for Rehabilitation and

Training (ORT; $1.7 million). The number of agencies receiving government excess property was three in 1964; this peaked at seven in 1968 and fell to five in 1969.

The Foreign Assistance Act of 1961 called for the creation of a new agency, USAID. The Foreign Assistance Act explicitly stated the purpose of foreign aid: "to strengthen friendly foreign countries by encouraging the development of their free economic institutions and productive capabilities."[16] The U.S. foreign aid emphasized the key interaction of political development with economic growth.

For the first time since the 1953 Mutual Security Act, a foreign assistance act did not contain earmarking of funds for the purchase of agricultural commodities. The creation of USAID brought coordination and streamlining to a plethora foreign assistance programs. (For a brief description of USAID's predecessors, see box 4.1.) In 1963, congressional support for foreign aid reached a nadir. President Kennedy appointed a committee, headed by General Lucius Clay, to review foreign aid assistance. The Clay report was negative, and Congress cut the foreign aid budget.[17]

During the 1960s, the ACVAFS worked with USAID officials to streamline and coordinate responses to disasters and emergencies overseas. The traditional pattern had been that agency personnel working in-country would alert the government to a disaster or emergency and propose a course of action. In 1964, the Foreign Disaster Relief office was established that would coordinate PVO and state agencies so that access to supplies was facilitated, information was shared, and studies were conducted on causes and prevention. The Office of Foreign Disaster also undertook studies of "disaster-prone" areas, distinguishing between "relief" and "reconstruction" phases. This issue would resurface as a point of contention between the State Department and the Department of Defense in the post-9/11 environment. (This point is discussed in chapter 7.)

Now, USAID had five contracting offices composed of four regional bureaus (Africa, Latin America, Near East, and Asia). Each office had considerable autonomy to negotiate, execute, amend and terminate contracts. The USAID missions had exclusive authority over contracts not exceeding $25,000. Furthermore, ambassadors in four Latin American countries and certain African nations had at their disposal funds of $25,000 with which to finance small activities without requiring Washington approval. The proliferation of authorizing offices in Washington, D.C., and in USAID missions meant that PVOs now relied on in-country staff to work with USAID missions.

Box 4.1. U.S. federal PVO oversight entities

President's Committee on War Relief Agencies (1941–42)	A presidential committee established in March 1941 to "examine the whole problem of foreign war relief in relation to local charities and to national defense welfare needs and to recommend measures that should be taken in the public interest" (Ringland 1954, 384). The members of the committee were Joseph E. Davies, Frederick P. Keppel, and Charles P. Taft.
President's War Relief Control Board (July 1942–March 1946)	The board established regulations "concerning the efficiency and economy of operation" (White House 1942, July 25, 1) of agencies and had the power to revoke licenses should these requirements not be met. Established by Executive Order No. 9205, July 25, 1942, taking over the functions of the President's Committee on War Relief Agencies.
Advisory Committee on Voluntary Foreign Aid (ACVFA) (1946–51)	PVO registration with the ACVFA initially was voluntary, and its focus was on short-term humanitarian aid. In 1948, PVOs were required to register to receive freight subsidy and eventually excess government property. Today, the ACVFA serves as the liaison between the federal government and PVOs. The committee is made up of private citizens. Reflecting the shift from relief to development, the Office of Private Voluntary Cooperation (PVC) was set up in 1971 within USAID to communicate federal policies to PVOs and to register those agencies interested in federal assistance. As part of restructuring of USAID, PVC was terminated by the George W. Bush administration in 2006.
Foreign Operations Administration (1953)	Established as an independent government agency outside the Department of State. Its function was to consolidate economic and technical assistance on a worldwide basis. Its responsibilities were merged into the International Cooperation Administration (ICA) less than a year later.

(continued)

Box 4.1. (*Continued*)

International Cooperation Administration (1953–61)	The ICA administered aid for economic, political, and social development objectives of U.S. foreign policy. Although the ICA's functions were vast and far reaching, unlike its successor, USAID, ICA had many limitations placed on it. As a part of the Department of State, ICA did not have the level of autonomy USAID currently maintains. At the time ICA was in existence, multilateral donors (such as those affiliated with the United Nations and the Organization of American States) were playing a greater role in foreign assistance.
U.S. Agency for International Development (1961–present)	In 1961, USAID was created with the passage of the Foreign Assistance Act, which reorganized U.S. foreign assistance programs, including the separation of military and nonmilitary aid. The agency unified already existing U.S. aid efforts, combining the economic and technical assistance operations of the ICA, the loan activities of the Development Loan Fund, the local currency functions of the Export-Import Bank, and the agricultural surplus distribution activities of the Food for Peace program of the Department of Agriculture.

Sources: National Archives and Records Administration, U.S. government, and USAID.

Population Control and Food Production

In 1966, Title IX, an amendment to the Foreign Assistance Act of 1961, focused on the promotion of democracy in civil society and governmental institutions. From that point, a central aspect of foreign aid would be participation at the local level through "cooperatives, labor unions, trade and related associations, community action groups, and other organizations which provide the training ground for leadership and democratic processes,"[18] In addition, at the end of 1966, the Johnson administration stated that foreign aid would focus on funding projects to lower population growth. For the first time, USAID permitted contraceptives as part of federally funded family-planning programs.[19] Participatory development became the official modus operandi. However, the amendment simply stated what already was the case. The PVOs had been shifting since the late 1950s into development or "service" work and away from relief activities. This pattern shows up the amount of P.L. 480 commodities awarded to PVOs during the 1960s. The number of PVOs receiving P.L. 480 food commodities fell from 19 in 1960 to 10 in 1969.

In 1967, the Foreign Assistance Act was altered to define in more detail what participatory development meant.[20] The PVOs viewed successful development as occurring at the microlevel. For PVOs to work at the grassroots level, USAID had to build into its structure funding flexibility.[21] Contracts, which were introduced in 1948, were used for the express purpose of procuring goods and services for specific USAID purposes and programs (P.L. 480 food, ocean freight, U.S. government excess property). Contracts were regulated by procurement regulations of USAID and the federal government, thereby ensuring significant government oversight. Contracts had also been used for technical assistance programs. However, the government had found that, for the most part, PVOs were welfare agencies motivated by humanitarian and religious values. The PVOs were not sufficiently staffed with qualified personnel to carry out technical assistance programs. The technical programs involving PVOs tended to be educational (teachers) and medical (medical personnel and supplies). Thus, as shown in table 4.2, there was some movement during the 1960s among secular PVOs toward education, health, and cultural areas instead of traditional relief activities. The government, even though it had a mandate to increase the role of PVOs in foreign aid, found many PVOs to be ill-equipped, focusing on meeting immediate basic human needs. Consequently, USAID turned to nonregistered professional associations, cooperative organizations, and public sector contractors to carry out foreign assistance.

By 1965, the problem of declining surplus food was noticeable. A combination of factors contributed to the decline. Increased domestic consumption, higher-than-average commercial farm exports to Europe, and reduced agricultural outputs contributed to the decline in agricultural goods. In addition to reduced quantities of foodstuffs in the aggregate, the variety was diminishing as well—for example, dried nonfat milk was eliminated from the P.L. 480 program in 1973. In 1965, President Johnson moved the Office of Director of Food for Peace to the State Department to coordinate it with other types of USAID programs. A shift in food policy occurred, with an emphasis on assisting developing countries to increase their agricultural production. Johnson continued to centralize foreign aid in the State Department by creating an Office of Special Assistant to the

Secretary of State for Refugee and Migration Affairs. In 1967, the Office of War on Hunger was set up within USAID.

By the mid-1960s, registration with USAID had become a "good house-keeping" seal of approval. The irony was that USAID officials did not monitor PVO overseas activities unless the agency was a recipient of food commodities, ocean freight, or excess property. By 1967, USAID dropped the requirement that any registered agency had to have one active "relief" project with the federal government. In practice, government oversight of PVOs was negligible.[22]

PVO Neutrality and the Vietnam War

The model for U.S. government–PVO relations in Vietnam was similar to that during and after World War II. The PVOs viewed their role as supplementing the operations of the U.S. government.[23] The religious PVOs—Protestant and Catholic—functioned initially in Vietnam as they had during World War II and the Korean War, as subsidiaries of the U.S. military and government. In 1954, voluntary agencies willingly accepted their complementary role to the U.S. presence in Vietnam to assist northern refugees fleeing to the south. However, a fundamental philosophical difference existed between the Protestant agencies on the one hand and CRS and CARE on the other hand. Whereas the Protestant agencies intentionally viewed themselves as engaging in neutral, nonpolitical work, CRS and to a lesser extent CARE viewed their activities as supporting the position of the U.S. government. More important, unlike the Protestant agencies, which initially did not take a political stance, CRS and CARE interpreted their work as part of the overall U.S. policy against Communism.

In 1965, President Johnson invited PVOs to work in Vietnam. At the invitation of USAID, ACVAFS sponsored a high-level PVO delegation to Saigon. Following the visit, Church World Service, Lutheran World Relief, and the Mennonite Central Committee joined to organize the Vietnam Christian Service.[24] From the beginning, Vietnam Christian Service viewed its work in South Vietnam as supplemental to that of the U.S. government's efforts to rebuild Vietnamese society. In Vietnam, each agency sponsored personnel both foreigners and Vietnamese. The Mennonites had the longest presence in South Vietnam (since the mid-1950s). As the war increased in intensity, the work and staff of voluntary agencies became targets of guerrillas. The PVO staff was killed and supplies confiscated. To be able to continue to operate, the voluntary agencies relied increasingly on U.S. military personnel for transportation, delivery of supplies, commissary privileges, postal service, and security.

International Voluntary Services (IVS), an ecumenical effort of the Mennonite, Brethren, and Quaker denominations, was founded in 1953 in response to President Truman's Point Four Program.[25] Focusing on community development, IVS was staffed by volunteers and funded by the federal government. In 1957, with the approval of the U.S. Overseas Mission in Saigon, IVS agricultural volunteers began working with refugees in South Vietnam. The success of IVS occurred because it remained small (a total of 400 volunteers over 15 years) and focused on rural agricultural development projects. By the mid-1960s, IVS expanded into educational projects in urban as well as rural areas. It remained a grassroots organization even when the U.S. Overseas Mission in Saigon sought to persuade IVS to change direction.[26]

In 1954, CRS began operating in Vietnam.[27] Prior to that, in 1952, CRS sent relief supplies at the request of the Vietnamese Catholic bishops. The defeat of the French forces and the signing of a peace accord created a large refugee population. In South Vietnam, 800,000 refugees with 80% Roman Catholic adherence created a problem for the newly elected Diem and his government. Diem, a devout Catholic, solicited assistance from CRS. It is estimated that CRS garnered 50% of U.S. humanitarian food commodities and other materials going to Vietnam. It came under criticism for assisting the Popular Forces militia starting in late 1966. Coming under intense public criticism for its partisanship in the Vietnam War, CRS in 1968 ended its Popular Forces program.[28]

Like CRS, since 1954 CARE had operated in Vietnam.[29] Like CRS, many of CARE's activities were indistinguishable from those of the U.S. government and its South Vietnamese allies. Both agencies played a role in carrying out U.S. policy in Vietnam. Like CRS, CARE executives shared the U.S. position that the Communists had to be defeated. As the war escalated, CARE became dependent on the U.S. military for security outside Saigon. The agency increasingly relied on government security forces to assist in the distribution of supplies. Like the other PVOs in Vietnam, the escalation of the war brought an end to their community development projects and shifted their efforts into humanitarian relief work.

By 1967, the entire presence of U.S.-based PVOs in South Vietnam was streamlined under a new organizational structure called Civilian Operations Revolutionary Development Support (CORDS), with General Westmoreland in charge.[30] USAID became the main vehicle for channeling assistance for development projects in Vietnam. By 1968, there were 39 PVOs (cooperatives, labor organizations, medical associations, educational organizations, and relief and development agencies) operating in South Vietnam.[31] Twenty of the 39 PVOs began operations in Vietnam from 1965. Once in the country, PVOs were pressured to support U.S.

policy in Vietnam. This position was particularly difficult for agencies like the Mennonite Central Committee.

A major and legitimate concern of the U.S. government was that PVOs were aiding the Viet Cong. The Protestant agencies understood their mission to be impartial and to serve both sides of the armed conflict. The increasing difficulty for Protestant agencies was how to remain neutral, not to become politicized, as U.S. military involvement escalated. The U.S. military controlled where the PVOs could work in the countryside. If an agency decided to work in areas near the Viet Cong, security became an issue. Agencies were also continually engaged in refugee relief work. As the fighting intensified, agencies found it difficult to mount long-term development programs. By 1967, with the war nearing its peak, the Protestant PVOs began to question U.S. policy in Vietnam. Whereas the Protestant agencies had tried to remain independent of U.S. policy and military operations, CRS was openly partial and supportive of U.S. foreign policy and military presence in Vietnam, leaving the agency vulnerable to sharp criticism for supporting U.S. policy and feeding militia in the South.

The military buildup in Vietnam reached its peak in 1969. At that time, 50 PVOs were operating in Vietnam. By 1971, the Mennonites broke off from Vietnam Christian Services. By 1974, Vietnam Christian Services had moved away from relief aid to development projects. Vietnamese were trained to operate agricultural projects, and U.S. PVO personnel left Vietnam. A $5 million project to distribute aid packages was offered by USAID, but Vietnam Christian Services turned it down because the agency was shutting down operations.

Being nonpolitical or neutral in wars, particularly where the United States is militarily committed, is an ethereal objective. The Vietnam War, unlike World War II and the Korean War, raised questions over the legitimacy of the military role of the United States in a foreign civil war. The PVOs, for the first time, were politicized in the sense that their activities in Vietnam could not be divorced from domestic politics in the United States. To their constituencies back home, the PVOs were viewed as accomplices in U.S. foreign policy, either willingly, as in the case of CRS and CARE, or as naïve pawns, as in the case of the Protestant PVOs.

Protestant PVOs and the Rise of the Evangelicals

Any discussion of evangelicals in international relief and development work must include World Vision (WV). While in my data set its classification has now shifted to faith-founded Christian, it is precisely this shift that makes it an important case study for understanding this cultural terrain.[32] In many ways, the story of WV parallels that of evangelical humanitarian work in the 20th century. It was born out of the classic missionary impulses of Bob Pierce, an evangelist with Youth for Christ. Originally focused on China and Korea, it was and still remains a child sponsorship initiative. Pierce would return from his travels in Asia and appeal to North American donors to "adopt" an impoverished child. In this way, in 1950 WV was born. Eventually, it would evolve from a child sponsorship organization to one of the largest and most influential development agencies in the world, one that is substantially funded by private donors. This reliance on private support contrasts with its counterparts CRS and CARE, two other large PVOs that continue to rely heavily on federal funds but have yet to successfully develop a strategy for attracting substantial private revenue. For example, from 1961 to 2005 the average revenue shares from federal and private sources, respectively, were 0.27 and 0.72 for WV, 0.70 and 0.28 for CRS, and 0.66 and 0.20 for CARE. (The missing share in each case corresponds to international organizations and other governments.)

By the late 1960s, WV was making inroads in the area of government funding. Founder Pierce and his executive vice president and chief operating officer Ted Engstrom went to Washington, D.C., to make contact with USAID to find out how to receive gifts-in-kind and other federal assistance. In 1975, WV received its first Development Program Grant from USAID. In its relationship with the federal government, WV took the approach that it wanted to learn from the government bureaucracy. The organization wanted to be taken seriously by the federal government and to become a player; it wanted to learn procedures for reporting and accountability. The organization wanted to do it right from the beginning to gain integrity within the community and to become a better organization.

An example of a denominational evangelical PVO is the Adventist Development and Relief Agency (ADRA). Founded in 1956, ADRA was originally known as Seventh-Day Adventist Welfare Service. The name was changed to Seventh-Day Adventist World Service in 1973. During the 1970s, the group began to expand from its original focus on disaster relief into long-term development projects. This shift reflected the larger trend in foreign assistance, a shift away from relief into community development.

Table 4.3 shows evangelical PVOs ranked in the top 20 in terms of total real revenue among all PVOs in selected years: 1940, 1945 (none present), 1950, 1960, 1970, 1980, 1990, 2000, and 2005. (These years are the ones used for the top 10 lists in table 1.7 of chapter 1.) World Vision is included here

Table 4.3. High-ranking evangelical PVOs.

PVO	Year	Rank	Total real revenue	Real federal revenue
Salvation Army	1940	17	3.5	0.0
Mennonite Central Committee	1950	7	9.6	0.7
	1960	10	15.6	2.7
	1970	12	32.3	1.3
	1980	15	27.6	0.5
Brethren Service Commission	1950	14	4.7	0.0
Adventist Development and Relief	1960	12	11.3	3.3
	1970	16	23.3	8.5
	1980	10	37.8	26.8
World Relief Corporation	1960	16	4.9	2.6
MAP International	1970	10	54.5	0.3
	1980	13	31.7	0.6
	2000	20	115	0.3
	2005	9	344	0.0
Summer Institute of Linguistics	1970	13	30.5	0.6
	1980	9	54.0	1.1
	1990	12	105	0.0
	2000	19	123	0.0
World Vision	1970	18	15.0	1.3
	1990	9	121	32.7
	2000	2	452	72.8
	2005	2	795	146
Brother's Brother Foundation	1990	14	78.0	0.2
	2005	12	275	0.2
Compassion International	1990	19	59.0	0.0

Table 4.3.   *(continued)*

PVO	Year	Rank	Total real revenue	Real federal revenue
Feed the Children	1990	20	58.4	0.1
	2000	7	244	1.9
	2005	7	543	24.5
United Armenian Fund	2000	4	276	0.0
Samaritan's Purse	2000	12	143	4.2
	2005	10	314	7.5
Operation Blessing International	2005	16	210	0.4

Source: McCleary Private Voluntary Organizations Data Set.
Note: This table lists evangelical PVOs ranked in the top 20 for total real revenue among all PVOs in the years 1940, 1945 (none present), 1950, 1960, 1970, 1980, 1990, 2000, and 2005. Real revenue is in millions of 2005 dollars. World Vision, founded as evangelical, is included although it subsequently changed type to faith-founded Christian.

because it was founded as evangelical, although it subsequently changed type to faith-founded Christian.

Traditional evangelical PVOs that ranked high in revenue in some years were Salvation Army (17 in 1940); Brethren Service Committee (14 in 1950); Adventist Development and Relief Agency (12 in 1960, 16 in 1970, and 10 in 1980); Mennonite Central Committee (7 in 1950, 10 in 1960, 12 in 1970, and 15 in 1980); and World Relief Corporation (16 in 1960). Summer Institute of Linguistics was 13 in 1970, 9 in 1980, 12 in 1990, and 19 in 2000, and MAP International was 10 in 1970, 13 in 1980, 20 in 2000, and 9 in 2005.

Among more recent types, Feed the Children was 20 in 1990, 7 in 2000, and 7 in 2005. Samaritan's Purse was 12 in 2000 and 10 in 2005; Brother's Brother was 14 in 1990 and 12 in 2005; Operation Blessing International was 16 in 2005; United Armenian Fund was 4 in 2000; and Compassion International was 19 in 1990. In 1970, WV was 18; it was 9 in 1990, 2 in 2000, and 2 in 2005. Traditional evangelical PVOs—such as Mennonite Central Committee, Brethren Service Commission, World Relief, and Adventist Development and Relief Agency—are similar to mainline Protestant PVOs in denominational structure. In contrast, recently formed evangelical PVOs—such as Feed the Children, Samaritan's Purse, and WV (which we classified as shifting later from evangelical to faith-founded Christian)— tend to have a flat structure, involving relations with parachurches.[33] This structure cuts across denominational loyalties and allows for fund-raising from a broad base of adherents.[34] In effect, these new organizational forms may have been a technological innovation that facilitated PVO fund-raising. This change may account for the growth of revenue for evangelical PVOs (and some faith-founded Christian PVOs) compared to revenue of PVOs affiliated with the traditional faiths (mainline Protestant, Catholic, ecumenical Christian, and Jewish).

Some evangelical PVOs, like Adventist Development and Relief Agency in 1960, 1970, and 1980 and WV in 1990, 2000, and 2005, have been big recipients of federal money, both for programs in the field and for developing their infrastructure as organizations. Others, such as Samaritan's Purse, have been tempted by the efforts of the George W. Bush administration to relax the restrictions put on religious groups seeking federal dollars but were not yet major recipients of federal money up to 2005 (see table 1.7 in chapter 1).

The Security of Israel and Jewish PVOs

Israel was the principal fund-raising issue of the Jewish fund-raising federation. Whenever Israel was attacked or under threat, the United Jewish Appeal (UJA), as well as other Jewish organizations, experienced a spike in donations. The Six-Day War in June 1967 marked a reinvigoration of Jewish-American identification with Israel.[35] As one UJA official expressed it, "In the '67 War the UJA didn't raise money, it took it in."[36]

In terms of the data, the share of Jewish revenue in the overall revenue of religious PVOs averaged 16% from 1960 to 1966, then spiked upward to 52% in 1967. This share remained between 42% and 57% through 1972, then spiked upward again to 73% with the 1973 Yom Kippur war. After that, the share steadily declined, reaching 43% in 1980, 38% in 1990, 10% in 2000, and only 6% in 2005.

In the 1960s, up to 1966, the largest Jewish PVOs by real revenue were AJJDC, Hadassah, ORT, and United Hebrew Immigrant Aid Society (HIAS). For example, in 1960, AJJDC had total real revenue of $168 million, Hadassah had $57 million, ORT had $16 million, and HIAS had $8 million. Beginning with the 1967 war, the largest Jewish PVO became the joint effort embodied in UJA. This agency was by far the largest revenue raiser among Jewish PVOs from 1967 to 1996. For example, in 1967 UJA secured real revenue of $1.3 billion, and in 1973, it got $1.9 billion. The final year of operation for UJA was 1999, when its revenue fell just short of that raised by AJJDC.[37]

The tension between American secularism and Judaism broke out in a confrontation in 1969 at the General Assembly in Boston, the annual gathering of the local federations. Younger Jews attending the assembly demanded rechanneling of funds from nonsectarian causes, such as hospitals and social service agencies, to Jewish institutions offering educational, religious, and cultural services. Young Jews sought to have funds invested in education on Jewish heritage and religion.

In the 1960s, younger Jews began the *Havurah* movement, which focused on Jewish community and spirituality.[38] Similar to the evangelical focus on personal aspects of religion, the *Havurah* movement emphasized individual engagement in religious activities. This movement shared characteristics with the liberation theology segment of the Roman Catholic Church. *Havurah* promoted living one's religious values and advocating radical change through them. Out of this movement, new Jewish PVOs emerged, such as the New Israel Fund, Mazon, Jewish Fund for Justice, and the American Jewish World Service.[39]

PVOs and the Secularizing of American Society

By the 1960s, the Roman Catholic Church in the United States had the largest religious network of welfare and educational institutions.[40] The 1960s marked a watershed, with the second Vatican Council and the liberalization of social mores combining to decrease the religious participation of parishioners and trigger a dramatic decline in the number of women becoming religious sisters.[41] The Catholic institutions lost a main source of their low-cost workforce, a blow that caused many agencies to fold.

Real revenue of Catholic PVOs peaked at around $1 billion in 1957 and again reached this mark in 1965–66. After that, revenue fell, although remaining between $400 million and $800 million through 2004 (rising to $980 million in 2005). Throughout the 1960s and even up to the early 1980s, Catholic revenues were concentrated almost entirely (by around 99%) in a single agency, CRS.

Most of the welfare and educational institutions set up by Catholics were sustained financially by "the army of lifetime volunteers," that is, the religious sisters. These women not only worked hard in the service of the poor but also often had to raise the funds with which to carry out their work. The rapid decline in religious vocations from the 1960s onward has been described as a substantial crisis for Catholic institutions.[42]

The cultural backdrop of the late 1960s of a renewed emphasis on personal experience and belief took precedence over institutional loyalties, be they religious, social, or political. Churches, associations, and PVOs were increasingly seen as groups of individuals free to come and go voluntarily. For evangelicals, the Jewish *Havurah* movement, and the Roman Catholic liberation theology movement, emphasis was placed on a radical interpretation of scripture. The interpreter was no longer an institutional authority but an individual interacting with the text itself. Religious revivalism was taking place across the United States, focusing on individual engagement. This lack of hierarchical structure, or the rejection of it, meant that informal, egalitarian forms of social organization were favored. Movements became "cross denominational" in the sense that evangelicalism applied across established Christian denominations, and *Havurah* applied across established Jewish movements (Reformed, Orthodox, and Conservative). Another option was to participate in social movements, such as those concerned with civil rights, the environment (with landmark legislation occurring in the 1960s), women's issues, and poverty issues.[43]

In the 1960s and into the 1970s, a new type of agency—the volagency—was established with USAID funds. This new type of agency was secular and technically specialized in its activities. Some of the agencies were founded by former Peace Corps workers, who returned to the United States seeking to continue working in development. (Other Peace Corps volunteers joined USAID.[44]) Another distinctive feature of the volagency was that it lacked a constituency from which it could raise private funds. As a result of having been established with significant government money, its continued existence depended on government largesse.

The traditional PVOs, members of the umbrella organization ACVAFS, were reluctant to open up their membership to newer PVOs, such as WV and the volagencies. These newer agencies joined to form Private Agencies in International Development (PAID).[45] Several of the traditional PVOs joined PAID while retaining their affiliation with ACVAFS. The PAID members focused on development and tended to be the smaller and specialized agencies. Many of these PVOs were working on issues related to the U.N. agenda. Whereas ACVAFS worked with the federal government, PAID members were advocacy oriented, independent of the federal bureaucracy. While ACVAFS had its headquarters in New York City, PAID opened its doors in Washington, D.C.

Until the Vietnam War, the PVOs were willing to view their work as complementary to that of the government. During the war, PVOs realized that their work had become politicized, particularly for those agencies that had sought to remain neutral. And, the PVOs' constituencies in the United States were engaged in the domestic debate on the war, bringing into question the nature of the work of the PVOs. At this time, the Protestant PVOs began distancing themselves from the U.S. government. However, at the same time, small, technically oriented PVOs were beginning to operate. By the mid-1970s, the volagency came into being, established with USAID funds and lacking a constituency base.

As a result of the changing international demands and the widespread presence of PVOs in countries throughout the world, USAID went through restructuring. There was one other change occurring in the field of international development. To acquire professional expertise, USAID had been contracting with universities, foundations, think tanks, and firms. By 1972, these groups rose from 1% of total registered agencies in 1960 to 3% in 1969.

The 1969 Tax Reform Act Section 170(e) reduced the in-kind contributions to voluntary agencies. (Companies could no longer donate in-kind inventory at market value but rather at cost value.) Some agencies reported a drop by up to 50% in their in-kind donations (table 4.4).[46] As a share of private revenue, in-kind donations for all PVOs constituted 39% in 1966. This share fell to a low point of 9% in 1973. Tax changes in 1976 (and, much later, in 2005) made in-kind giving more attractive again.[47] Partly in response to these changes, the share of in-kind donations in private revenue moved up starting in the mid-1970s, reaching 37% in 1994, 48% in 2003, 51% in 2004, and 47% in 2005.

If we look at shares of gifts in-kind revenue for agencies starting in 1950 (table 4.4), evangelical PVOs have consistently and increasingly relied over time on this type of income more so than other types of agencies. Secular agencies are least likely to garner gifts-in-kind. The overall trend, primarily due to favorable legislation, is for increasing revenue share from

Table 4.4. Shares of in-kind revenue in private revenue.

Period	All PVOs	Secular	Religious	Evangelical
1950–59	0.31	0.23	0.32	0.47
1960–69	0.31	0.14	0.36	0.53
1970–79	0.14	0.12	0.14	0.38
1980–89	0.17	0.21	0.15	0.38
1990–99	0.33	0.31	0.34	0.55
2000–5	0.45	0.34	0.55	0.66

Source: McCleary Private Voluntary Organizations Data Set.
Note: Each cell shows the average share of in-kind revenue in the total of private revenue for the indicated group of PVOs over the indicated time period.

gifts-in-kind for all three types of PVOs (secular, religious, evangelical). However, the largest PVO in 2005, Americares Foundation, was a secular agency that primarily relies on donations of medical supplies and medicines (table 1.7 in chapter 1). Americares Foundation, Feed the Children, Samaritan's Purse, and Food for the Poor are newer agencies that have benefited from changes in the tax gifts-in-kind rules.

During the 1960s, as American society was secularizing, religious PVOs in terms of real revenue continued to dominate. Total real private revenue for all PVOs went up from $959 million in 1960 to peak at $2.44 billion in 1967 and then to $1.85 billion in 1969. The religious part of this private revenue was $615 million in 1960, $2.06 billion in 1967, and $1.45 billion in 1969. The secular part of private revenue was $196 million in 1960, $378 million in 1967, and $396 million in 1969.

By the end of the 1960s, PVOs were beginning to diversify their governmental sources of funding to include multinational organizations and other governments. Diversification did not prove profitable. U.S.-based PVOs did not receive significant funds from the U.N. system or other governments The share of total PVO revenue from these sources in 1967 was only 1% but then rose to between 4% and 8% from 1978 to 2005. U.S.-based PVOs remained dependent on federal support, particularly in the form of P.L. 480 commodities and secondarily on ocean freight. This was a relationship the PVOs had actively advocated for and the consequence of which was the creation of a cartel of just a few agencies.

5

The Golden Age of PVO-State Relations

Development *is* politics...
—John Somner, *Beyond Charity*

The 1973 Foreign Assistance Act, known as "New Directions," formalized, strengthened, and enlarged what had been an ad hoc relationship between private voluntary organizations (PVOs) and the federal government. The trend of emphasizing funding for PVOs would continue with congressional support through the 1980s. Under the New Directions legislation, U.S. foreign aid broadened from American technology and large infrastructure projects to include local, culturally embedded community development programs.[1] As the religious agencies pointed out, the government was entering the traditional domain of PVOs by addressing local needs.[2] The New Directions legislation would be the only successful reform to the 1961 Foreign Assistance Act.

The PVOs recognized that the White House was playing to their strengths and advocated for funding mechanisms that gave them operational flexibility. The federal government formally introduced grants under the New Directions legislation. The PVOs actively participated with the U.S. Agency for International Development (USAID) in drawing up guidelines, formats, and procedures.[3] The emphasis on PVO-state relations prior to the New Directions legislation had been on contracts (purchasing of goods).[4] The new emphasis on grants was to help agencies that were primarily relief agencies to become development organizations.[5]

The other rationale for the shift to grants was to encourage U.S. agencies that worked domestically to become international to encourage them to apply their skills in developing countries.[6] Table 5.1 shows grants as the favored funding mechanism at the time the New Directions legislation was implemented in 1973. The number of PVOs getting grants

103

Table 5.1. Grants and contracts for PVOs, 1967–81.

Year	Number of PVOs with grants	Real amount of grants (millions 2005 $)	Number of PVOs with contracts	Real amount of contracts (millions 2005 $)
1967	27	97	—	—
1968	25	89	—	—
1969	30	110	—	—
1970	34	106	—	—
1971	36	121	—	—
1972	39	184	—	—
1973	38	403	—	—
1974	39	404	—	—
1978	70	283	30	97.4
1980	94	348	35	201
1981	105	462	38	196

Source: McCleary Private Voluntary Organizations Data Set.
Note: The data on grants begin in 1967, and the data on contracts begin in 1978. No data are available for 1975–77.

significantly increased from 1973 to 1981, from 38 to 105 PVOs receiving grants in my data. From 1974 to 1978, the number of PVOs receiving grants doubled. Real dollar amount of grants behaved differently, increasing fourfold from 1971 to 1973. Real revenue fell from $403 million in 1973 to $283 million in 1978, before rising to $462 million in 1981.

The number of PVOs getting contracts did not change a lot from 1978 (first year of my data for contracts) to 1981. The dollar amount jumped—from $97 million in 1978 to $201 million in 1980 and $196 million in 1981. When comparing contracts to grants, in 1981 the ratio of grant revenue to contact revenue was 2.4. For the same year, the ratio of numbers of recipient PVOs receiving grants as opposed to contracts was 2.8. The trend over time has been for USAID to favor grants over contracts.

The federal government encouraged the growth of PVOs through grants to extend its presence via the agencies into countries where there were no USAID missions. And, as missions were closed, the presence of PVOs in-country would permit USAID to transfer programs to them. Clearly, PVOs were increasingly valued for their ability to work at the local level in a way that the U.S. government could not. From the perspective of the federal government, grants as a funding mechanism were administratively easier, requiring minimal USAID staff oversight. The trend of awarding grants to a larger number of PVOs (not in terms of dollars) over contracts would persist over time.

Until the New Directions legislation in 1973, the established PVOs (Lutheran World Relief [LWR], Catholic Relief Services, CARE, Church World Service) were primarily relief agencies, relying on federal government contracts for the procurement of commodities and subsidized freight. The staffs of the established PVOs were committed individuals, many volunteers. Volunteers with appropriate skills, including language abilities and adaptability to living conditions in countries, continued to be instrumental to the work of PVOs. Grants were instituted by USAID to educate PVOs on how to engage in development work and build up their professional staff.

The PVO-State Partnership

Two types of grants were implemented: Development Program grants (DPGs) and Operational Program Grants (OPGs).[7] The DPGs were institutional support grants for three years. They were awarded on a first-come, first-served basis at the initiative of the PVOs. Small and large PVOs received DPGs. USAID did not have experience with institutional sustainability and how long it would take to get an organization to the point at which it could engage in development work. Between 1973 and 1979, around 40 DPGs were awarded. From these grants, a new type of PVO was created, secular and technical in nature yet closely affiliated with USAID (e.g., International Executive Service Corps [IESC]). Small PVOs on specialized issues such as race (Africare), gender (Overseas Education Fund), and microfinance (Acción) were favored.[8]

With regard to the OPGs, only registered PVOs that had the organizational capacity to carry out a program in-country were qualified to receive this type of funding.[9] Those organizations that applied and received OPGs had a counterpart contribution of 25% in either cash or in-kind contributions.[10] Since the OPGs were field oriented, USAID mission directors determined what kinds of programs they thought were needed and that fulfilled their mission's strategic objectives. All PVO field projects had to conform to USAID country objectives approved at headquarters in Washington, D.C.[11] Each USAID mission had the flexibility to interpret the OPG guidelines and regulations given country needs and context. However, the final approval for OPGs remained with USAID in Washington.[12] Organizations that received OPGs tended to have field staff in-country (for example, Volunteers in Technical Assistance [VITA]). Small agencies awarded OPGs were geographically specialized (for example, African Medical and Research Foundation); otherwise, they simply were not competitive.

Operating mission-led grants raised the administrative costs for PVOs, something they had not encountered with centrally administered funding out of Washington, which only provided for direct costs. Because of the financial burden to agencies, USAID introduced overhead into their budget allocations to PVOs.[13]

In 1979, Matching Grants were introduced as a form of cofinancing project. The PVO had to contribute 50% of the funding (with cash or in-kind contributions). Matching grants were unique in that they continued institutional support to a PVO at the same time strengthening the PVO's capacity to carry out in-country activities.[14] The PVOs awarded matching grants engaged in institution-building projects in the field and linked them to the overall work of the agency. At this point, U.S. PVOs worked with local community partners, usually local PVOs, as part of their in-country network, but funding local PVOs was not part of the intended purpose of matching grants. Matching grants provided multi-year (three years for new grantees and five years for renewing agencies) funding and could be used in several countries. The first matching grants were awarded to Save the Children, TechnoServe, and LWR.

The matching fund requirement (50%) of matching grants discriminated against smaller PVOs that could not raise the cash. Since all of the funding from a matching grant went into programs (and not to strengthen the organization per se), smaller PVOs lacked the financial ability to qualify. Small PVOs did not have the institutional capacity to compete with larger PVOs that had sizable headquarters staff to apply for grants. Small PVOs were disadvantaged in terms of economies of scale in their relations with USAID and their ability to raise private funds. Competing with the large, established PVOs for federal funds was becoming increasingly difficult as the federal government through the matching requirement favored the larger PVO.

The matching grants cut both ways. The larger PVOs, such as CARE and TechnoServe, praised the grant and the contribution the funds made to their work. Within the PVO community, receiving a matching grant meant the agency had successfully completed a lengthy application and review process. The awarded agency also had successfully competed against other PVOs to win the grant. Yet matching grants had one major weakness regardless of the size of the PVO. Coordination between PVOs and USAID missions remained cumbersome, with many local PVOs reluctant to work directly with a PVO that received funds from the U.S. government.

Congress began to question the matching grants program, viewing it as funding large PVOs rather than going directly to in-country development projects. Many of the large PVOs receiving matching grants had been in existence since 1945 with large budgets. Congress increasingly viewed matching grants as a cash cow for the PVOs.

Increasingly, USAID was becoming decentralized in the grant-awarding process. More grant decisions were being made by USAID missions. The specifics of the grants were tied into the decision-making process in-country. In addition, various offices and bureaus at USAID headquarters were awarding grants to PVOs. The decentralization of the grant-making process meant that it was difficult for USAID's Office of Private and Voluntary Cooperation (PVC) to track how much funding was going to PVOs. From the perspective of PVOs, the decentralization of the grant-making process meant that they had to have the resources to apply to different offices. By 1976, the administrative decentralization had created a complex bureaucratic anarchy resulting in what a General Accounting Office (GAO) report called "considerable confusion and annoyance to PVOs, which contend that their limited staffs must spend an inordinate amount of time complying with AID requests for information and program management requirements."[15]

While the grant-awarding process was decentralizing, the nature of the grants themselves was becoming more contractual.[16] The USAID missions and bureaus were increasing their substantive involvement in programmatic issues. Cooperative agreements continued this trend to its logical end.[17] Regarding strategic planning of the grant, USAID sought more substantive involvement by approving key staff, the budget, and an explicit evaluation plan; USAID designed the strategy for the cooperative grant and ensured that the project's work plan was on target with the USAID mission plan. Cooperative agreements were technically grants but had a larger role for USAID management over key decisions of the grant. Since the cost-sharing component could be waived, a PVO could receive 100% funding from USAID and be totally dependent on the federal government.[18]

By 1978, the Senate Appropriations Committee issued a warning to USAID to provide no more than 50% of a PVO's annual revenue. The PVOs had been debating this issue among themselves, with many contending that accepting significant federal funds inhibited private fund-raising and brought into question the "privateness" of the agency.[19] The PVOs were also cognizant that local partners in-country, particularly in

Latin America, opposed involvement with the U.S. government, thereby handicapping the PVO's ability to promote locally sustainable development projects.[20]

Ironically, the case that triggered congressional concern over "privateness" was a General Support grant (not one of the newer grants) to the Asia Foundation.[21] In 1975, USAID had awarded 15 General Support grants worth $11.2 million (in nominal value), with 80% of the funding going to three agencies: the Asia Foundation, IESC, and Opportunities Industrialization Centers International. The Asia Foundation had a history of cooperating with the Central Intelligence Agency (CIA), and as a result, USAID argued that the large grant to the Asia Foundation served U.S. foreign policy interests. Congress rejected USAID's argument, questioning the classification of the Asia Foundation as a PVO and characterizing the awarding of the grant as "a misdirection of United States assistance to PVOs."[22] The two other agencies, IESC and Opportunities Industrialization Centers International, were volagencies, both founded with USAID money. Congress criticized continued USAID support of IESC for the reason that the agency's programs were not addressing poverty alleviation. In contrast, Opportunities Industrialization Centers International was faulted for mismanagement of funds. Congress put USAID on notice that, from this point, public-private revenue ratios would become relevant for assessing further approval of funding to an agency. The era of volagencies had ended.

By 1977, a PVO's affiliation with USAID hampered its ability to implement the intent of the New Directions legislation. The complex, decentralized structure of USAID, with agencies required to work through in-country missions, politicized local projects.[23] In 1978, the federal shares of revenue were 87% for the Asia Foundation, 99% for Opportunities Industrialization Centers International, and 39% for International Executives. In 1978, in total, 35 PVOs had more than 50% of their total revenue coming from federal sources.

Table 5.2 shows that the number of registered PVOs rose from 83 in 1970 to 154 in 1981. Total real revenue of PVOs did not rise much over this period, going from $3.0 billion in 1970 to $3.3 billion in 1981. However, the federal part of PVO revenue rose by 39%, going from $1.0 billion in 1970 to $1.4 billion in 1981.

Not only had the number of PVOs substantially increased during the 1970s, but also the agencies had become more sophisticated in accessing federal agencies and sources of funding.[24] The culmination of PVO-USAID discussions and government reports led, in 1979, to the creation of the International Development Cooperation Agency (IDCA), which

Table 5.2.   PVO revenue 1970–81.

Year	Number of PVOs	Total revenue (millions 2005 $)	Federal revenue (millions 2005 $)
1970	83	2,968	1,018
1971	90	3,009	1,055
1972	93	3,058	960
1973	95	4,021	1,123
1974	94	3,621	1,377
1978	130	3,139	1,270
1980	150	3,261	1,341
1981	154	3,309	1,420

Source: McCleary Private Voluntary Organizations Data Set.
Note: USAID did not issue annual reports on PVOs in 1975, 1976, 1977, and 1979.

coordinated U.S. economic assistance programs and advised the president on development issues.[25]

The IDCA was given direct oversight for USAID as well as the Overseas Private Investment Corporation. The rationale was to depoliticize foreign aid by removing it from the State Department yet, in so doing, strengthen USAID's ability to make development policy. However, since the IDCA director continued to report to the secretary of state, this change in structure had little consequence for PVO funding and U.S. foreign policy.

The Ethiopian Famine and the Maturation of the PVOs

In 1972, world grain production fell due to drought conditions. The volume of agricultural commodities for export under Public Law (P.L.) 480 dropped to its lowest level in 1973 and 1974. The 1973–74 Ethiopian famine and the lack of political and humanitarian response jolted PVOs into a new realization. Famines and mass starvation were an international disaster, not a national one.[26] As one aid worker in Ethiopia expressed it, "Unfortunately, the central priority of many public and private expatriate donors is the development and preservation of the harmonious relationship with the host government rather than taking the necessary and often politically sensitive steps of getting the relief job done. Consequently, for many expatriate donors, on an operations level, a disaster does not occur until the host government officially says it occurs."[27] The U.S. PVOs

learned from the Ethiopian famine that they had to engage in public policy advocacy and education to further their agenda and avoid becoming
bogged down in diplomatic concerns.

The interconnection among management of land, farming techniques,
and natural cycles demonstrated to the PVO community the need to focus
on the multifaceted causes of poverty and hunger. With the International
Development and Food Assistance Act of 1975, Congress further affirmed
the humanitarian use of food, requiring a minimum of 1.3 million metric
tons of agricultural commodities to be distributed through PVOs and the
U.N. World Food Program.[28] In 1977, the International Development and
Food Assistance Act was amended to increase the levels to 1.6 million
metric tons.

In 1975, LWR and Church World Service opened a Washington, D.C.,
office in response to the federal government's suspension of P.L. 480 food
for PVOs from October to December 1974. The United States was selling
surplus crops to Russia, China, and West Africa, which were experiencing
famines. In this environment, bilateral aid was taking precedence over
humanitarian aid, and less surplus food was available for PVO humanitarian assistance.[29] Arguing that food should not be an instrument of
politics, LWR objected. The American Council of Voluntary Agencies for
Foreign Service (ACVAFS) was headquartered in New York City, and the
umbrella organization, Private Agencies in Development (PAID), had yet
to be formed. The Protestant agencies sought to monitor U.S. legislative
activity and to influence public policy to pressure the U.S. government to
be more responsive to poverty issues.

In a conscious decision to accept less federal funding, the Protestant
PVOs moved to increase their private revenue. This trend is shown in
table 5.3. Private real revenue of Protestant PVOs rose from $42 million in
1974 to $79 million in 1981.

PVOs as Policy Advocates

The PVOs had been working through their umbrella organization,
ACVAFS, with the U.N. system since the end of World War II.[30] Agencies
involved in relief and refugee work had collaborated with the U.N. Relief
and Rehabilitation Administration (UNRRA); the International Refugee
Organization and its successor, the U.N. High Commissioner for Refugees;
and the Food and Agriculture Organization. Without PVO participation,
the activities of the United Nations could not have been carried out. Yet
PVO-U.N. collaboration was not strong.

Table 5.3.   Protestant real revenue, 1970–81.

Year	Protestant PVOs real revenue (millions of 2005 dollars)		
	Total	Private	Federal
1970	81.6	55.4	26.3
1971	62.8	44.0	18.7
1972	54.4	43.7	10.8
1973	51.7	42.1	9.6
1974	50.8	41.6	9.2
1978	60.7	54.0	6.7
1980	75.6	65.7	9.4
1981	88.1	79.0	9.1

Source: McCleary Private Voluntary Organizations Data Set.
Note: USAID did not issue annual reports on PVOs in 1975, 1976, 1977, and 1979.

As the U.N. system expanded to include other specialized agencies, such as the U.N. International Children's Fund, U.N. Development Program, the World Health Organization, and the U.N. Disaster Relief Coordinator, collaboration with PVOs did not improve. Instead, competition for public funds created tensions between PVOs and U.N. agencies.[31] The U.N. system remained focused on governmental approaches to development. Not until 1975 did the United Nations organizationally begin to understand the collaborative value of working with PVOs.[32] The U.N. conferences on environment (1972), human habitat (1972), population (1974), food (1974), and women's issues (1975) raised public awareness of specific development problems. These conferences spurred a new growth in PVOs.

In 1980, the ACVAFS held a symposium with the World Bank. It was the first significant meeting between PVOs and the World Bank.[33] This nascent collaboration between PVOs and multilateral organizations was dampened by the Carter administration (1977–81), which did not view multilateral channels as conducive to furthering U.S. foreign policy objectives.[34] The share of international organization funding in total PVO revenue during the Carter presidency was 6.4% in 1978 and 1980 and 5.5% in 1981. Under President Ronald Reagan, funding from international entities to PVOs started low at 4.8% in 1983, then increased to 7.6% in 1984 and 6.2% in 1985. In July 1985, the third U.N.-sponsored World Women's Conference was held. The U.S. delegation viewed it as not only self-serving to the United Nations but also serving "the political purposes of a few countries."[35] Funding to PVOs from international sources dropped to 4.0% in 1986, 4.1% in 1987, 3.9% in 1988, and 3.6% in 1989. In other words, during the Carter and Reagan presidencies, U.S. relations with multilateral institutions, particularly the United Nations, were not highly valued.

Beginning in 1974, Congress passed a series of laws linking human rights performance with foreign assistance.[36] Congress, in a bipartisan manner, acted to make public the dissemination of human rights abuses by requiring the State Department to engage in an annual human rights review of foreign aid recipients. Secretary of State Henry Kissinger failed to carry out the congressional mandate. Kissinger's stalling tactics prompted the deputy coordinator for human rights in the State Department to visit informally Amnesty International's headquarters in London. In a classic example of what is known as the boomerang effect, based on information obtained from a senior U.S. official, Amnesty International collected through its global network documentation of human rights abuses and presented it to sympathetic congressional representatives.[37] With the election of President Jimmy Carter, the State Department actively moved to promote human rights. In 1978, the State Department released its first report on human rights.

In 1978, the secretary general of the United Nations issued an appeal for food aid to be sent to Vietnam. This proposal was unanimously approved by the General Assembly. Vietnam was experiencing four years of harvest failure due to droughts and floods. Cambodian refugees were fleeing into Vietnam as tensions between the Khmer Rouge and Vietnam escalated into heavy fighting.[38] In 1975, after U.S. military withdrawal and the fall of Saigon to the Communist North Vietnamese, the State, Treasury, and Commerce Departments imposed sanctions on Vietnam.[39] Humanitarian assistance would be considered on a case-by-case basis. Friendshipment, a consortium formed by the Mennonite Central Committee, LWR, Bach Mai, and Church World Service, legally shipped commodities to Vietnam on a case-by-case basis.

Church World Service, the relief agency of the National Council of Churches, represents 35 Protestant, Orthodox, and Anglican denominations. In 1978, consensus was reached within Church World Service to approve a food shipment to Vietnam. This shipment combined with a coalition of senators, farmers' cooperatives, and unions to create a boomerang effect that began with the appeal of the U.N. secretary general.

In 1978, Church World Service requested State Department permission for an emergency relief food shipment but was denied. Church World Service's decision to go it alone was a statement in favor of normalizing relations between the United States and Vietnam.[40] Unlike the previously mentioned Amnesty International case, the Church World Service shipment to Vietnam did not achieve its political objective—to pressure the U.S. government to withdraw the embargo on Vietnam.[41] Working with senators from wheat-producing states, Church World Service successfully obtained donations through farmers' cooperatives. The Teamsters Union agreed to transport the wheat to the port of Houston. Church World Service covered the shipping costs from Houston to Saigon. Even though the shipment reached Saigon, the United States continued its embargo on Vietnam.

The late 1970s were a period of political maturation for U.S. PVOs. They began to work more closely with Congress and developed a sophisticated understanding of how the legislative process worked. Congress historically has been sympathetic to PVOs and acted to further their causes. The PVOs, by learning how to effectively leverage Congress, gained a strategic ally vis-à-vis the executive branch.

PVOs as Transnational Agencies

A significant aspect of the political mobilization of PVOs was their evolution from being identified with one country ("American") to becoming a transnational structure in the form of a federation, consortium, council, or alliance.[42] The term *transnational* means that the PVO has national headquarters in countries other than the country of its origin. These country headquarters retain some type of affiliation with each other that may be in name only or more structurally significant. The formal evolution for many PVOs occurred over decades. For some agencies, such as CARE, Save the Children, and World Vision (WV), that process began in the late 1970s; for others such as Médecins sans Frontières and Oxfam, their organizational evolution began in the 1980s, culminating in a global structure by the mid-1990s.[43]

The growth of PVOs during the late 1960s and early 1970s occurred at a time when the U.S. military withdrawal from Vietnam raised questions about American global dominance. The late 1960s was accentuated by the social unrest accompanying the civil rights movement, violent protests against U.S. military involvement in Vietnam, and political disturbances such as the assassinations of John F. Kennedy, Martin Luther King, Jr., and Robert Kennedy in the United States. Public confidence in the government waned, and public consensus regarding what constituted fundamental American values and policy was fractured. Internationally, developing countries were challenging industrialized nations and calling for a new international economic order. African colonies were acquiring independence, and cold war security concerns were heightened for the United States in Latin America.[44]

Table 5.4 shows the classification of secular PVOs by program activity. Secular agencies had a broad range of activities; many were specialized in one particular area such as medicine, microfinance, environment, or

Table 5.4. Classifications of secular PVOs.

Code number	Category
1	Economic growth, agricultural development, and trade
	a. Agricultural development
	b. Private sector, small enterprises
	c. Engineering and infrastructure
2	International relief and development
	a. Community/capacity building
	b. Ethnic unity/ethnic issues
	c. Human rights/international law/democracy
	d. Peace groups and conflict resolution
	e. Relief and development issues
	f. Gender issues and family planning
3	Education and training
	a. Children's basic education
	b. higher learning (universities, research)
	c. Professional associations and societies
4	Natural resource management
	a. Environmental issues
	b. Animal rights and protection
5	Culture and society
	a. Cultural issues
	b. Society organizations
	c. Communication and media
	d. Foundations
6	Medicine and health issues
	a. Medicine and hospitals
	b. HIV/AIDS programs

Source: McCleary Private Voluntary Organizations Data Set.

technology. In tables 5.5 and 5.6, only the code numbers one through six are used to make analysis simpler.

The number of secular agencies registering with the federal government expanded rapidly starting in the late 1970s (see table 5.5).

The secular PVOs specialized particularly in education, health, and international relief and development issues. By the end of the 1970s, PVOs in the relief category began focusing on community development, refugees, and gender issues (table 5.6). Human rights gained in popularity only later, during the 1980s, which fits with the increasing influence of Amnesty International in the United States, establishing an office in Washington, D.C. in 1976.

Table 5.5. Numbers of secular PVOs by functional orientation, 1970–89.

Year	Numbers by type						
	Total	Growth	Relief	Education	Environment	Culture	Health
1970	51	4	24	8	0	3	12
1971	53	4	26	9	0	3	11
1972	54	4	25	11	0	3	11
1973	57	4	27	11	0	3	12
1974	55	4	25	11	0	3	12
1978	87	13	35	18	2	3	15
1980	103	12	43	25	2	2	18
1981	106	13	44	26	2	3	17
1983	117	14	47	26	5	4	20
1984	116	16	46	25	5	4	19
1985	118	17	47	24	6	4	19
1986	117	17	50	21	4	3	21
1987	130	18	54	24	6	3	24
1988	151	20	58	29	11	4	28
1989	162	23	55	33	16	2	31

Source: McCleary Private Voluntary Organizations Data Set.
Note: Data for the 1960s are in the comparable table 4.1 in chapter 4. "Growth" includes economic growth, agricultural development, and engineering and infrastructure; "relief" includes international relief and development and human rights; "education" includes education/higher learning and professional societies; "environment" includes conservation, animal protection, solar power, and so forth; "culture" includes communications, culture and society, and foundations; "health" includes medicine and health issues. No data available for 1975–77, 1979, or 1982.

Table 5.6. Breakdown of secular relief and development PVOs by type, 1960–81.

Year	Relief and development	Community development	Ethnic	Human rights	Peace	Refugees	Gender issues
1960	22	0	9	0	0	11	2
1961	20	0	9	0	0	10	1
1962	17	0	7	0	0	9	1
1963	17	0	7	0	0	9	1
1964	18	1	7	0	0	9	1
1965	18	2	6	0	0	9	1
1966	19	2	5	0	0	11	1
1967	20	4	4	0	0	11	1
1968	22	5	5	0	0	11	1
1969	23	5	5	0	0	12	1
1970	24	6	4	0	0	13	1
1971	26	6	4	0	0	15	1
1972	25	6	4	0	0	14	1
1973	27	6	4	0	0	14	3
1974	25	5	3	0	0	14	3
1978	35	14	2	0	0	13	6
1980	43	15	3	1	0	14	10
1981	44	16	3	1	0	14	10

Source: McCleary Private Voluntary Organizations Data Set.
Note: The first column shows the total number of registered secular PVOs in the broad category of "relief and development" (corresponding to the label "relief" in table 5.5). The next six columns show the breakdown of this total into six subcategories: community development and capacity building; ethnic unity and ethnic issues; human rights, international law, and democracy; peace groups and conflict resolution; refugees/emergency food, clothing, and housing/training/and so forth; gender issues and family planning.

Becoming transnational was a logical progression for PVOs. The growth of WV into one of the largest private and voluntary agencies in international relief and development today (by revenue) is a good example of the globalization process.[45] For WV, this process began at the request of Australia, Canada, and New Zealand for WV representatives. Increasingly, WV Australia, WV Canada, and WV New Zealand were contributing to WV without representation. They were concerned that the organization was an American entity and not international. For their part, WV staff recognized that profound anti-American feelings in Latin America and elsewhere meant that for WV to be perceived as an American agency was not conducive to carrying out its work. The creation of World Vision International (WVI) in 1978 was an attempt to create an entity that was truly transnational, in this sense similar to the International Red Cross, rather than a U.S.-based PVO. The shift was to globalize the organization while making it one entity with one voice.

As its purpose, WVI was created to raise funds and establish a network in various countries around the world. In 1978, when WVI was formed, World Vision U.S. (WVUS) was also created (analogous to WV Australia, WV New Zealand). Since WVUS was raising the largest proportion of the total funds, a unique weighing system of membership on the WVI board of directors was put into place. (Four WVUS officers, two Canadian, two Australian, one from New Zealand, and six to eight members at large were voted onto the board.) This weighted system allowed WVUS to maintain a decisive voting bloc. With regard to certain key issues, the weighted representation made a difference. One key issue was leadership positions at WVI.

Although the U.S. entity contributed more funds overall, the other partners contributed more funds per citizen. New Zealand raised NZ$4 for every citizen (when the New Zealand dollar was worth US$.0.96 in 1978). Australia had a huge membership base and therefore made a significant financial contribution. The support offices worldwide (Canada, United States, Australia, New Zealand, later the United Kingdom, Germany, and Taiwan) engaged in fund-raising. The field offices carried out the actual program operations.

In its approach to policy issues, WVUS was conservative, evangelical Christian. Australia was politically to the left of center, more progressive than WVUS. The Australians were geographically literate, more globally knowledgeable, and aware of Asian history. The Australian perspective was key in international program decisions.

The structure WVI used to internationalize itself was cumbersome. At times, tensions existed, but differences were worked out so that WVI always spoke publicly with a single voice.

Each national WVI office did not function independently to formulate policy positions separate from those of the international council. The WVI Council provided a forum for the views of board members of the various WV national entities to be expressed internally, while maintaining WV's single public voice on relief and development issues—including the Ethiopian famine, Sudan, women's issues, and development practices. The internal debate took place within the structure of the council and board of directors. For example, the debate to move beyond child sponsorship

occurred within the international structure. The concept of child sponsorship was viewed as a marketing term and was considered inappropriate
for use in the field. The evolution of WVI into a development organization was a contentious and lengthy process among factions within the
organization.

Religious Agencies

The Continued Growth of Evangelical Agencies

Beginning in the mid-1970s, a debate was taking place within the evangelical community regarding whether evangelicals should be engaging in
development and social ministry. Many within the evangelical churches
believed that social ministry was diversion from the evangelizing mission
of the Gospel.[46] At that time, WVI referred to itself as holding the naïve
view that Christian witness was something one incorporates into development work. During the 1970s, WV began to use television marketing.[47]
Private contributions helped WVI to grow; it began seeing a substantial
increase in private funds in the mid- to late 1980s. The WVI Child Survival
grants were matched by the federal government. The federal government,
for its part, was intrigued by the private resources the organization was
leveraging.

In 1978, an evangelical umbrella organization, the Association of
Evangelical Relief and Development Organizations (AERDO), was formed
by small evangelical agencies; it was a forum for chief executive officers
of these small agencies to advise each other and to engage in spiritual
renewal and fellowship.[48] In the 1980s, AERDO would evolve into a quasi-
professional organization bound together by theological unity. Annual
conferences held with plenary speakers focused on international relief
and development issues of concern to the small evangelical PVO. The primary mechanism of program assistance was gifts-in-kind. These evangelical agencies functioned as distributors of material goods to religious
networks overseas.[49]

The increase in the size of evangelical PVOs, compared especially
to mainline Protestant PVOs, may reflect differences in organizational
structures (see table 1.7 of chapter 1 on the expansion of evangelical PVOs
into the top ten lists by decade). In terms of fund-raising, denominational
PVOs are not permitted to solicit funds from congregations. Instead, relief
and development offices of denominations raise funds from local congregations and contribute a portion of these funds to the denomination's

humanitarian agencies. Thus, the hierarchical structure of mainline Protestant denominations defines the nature of fund-raising and the designation of funds.[50] Several studies conducted on congregational giving found that the decline in denominational tithing was due to congregants viewing the required apportionment as a tax rather than a ministry and resenting denominational control over funding priorities.[51]

Neither of the two new types of PVOs—volagency and parachurch—fit the model of the traditional PVO: a large, denominationally affiliated relief-assistance agency. Furthermore, ACVAFS was exclusive, refusing to accept the emerging PVOs as members. The ACVAFS membership was failing to recognize the growth in nontraditional PVOs. To bring together the new PVOs, both quasi-voluntary and parachurch, which were focused on working directly with local communities in foreign countries, PAID was formed. It was clearly understood by ACVAFS that PAID member agencies were "development oriented," whereas members of ACVAFS were primarily focused on emergency humanitarian aid and P.L. 480 commodities. For example, ACVAFS was the institutional contact for the U.S. government and PVOs on the issue of resettling refugees. With federal funds, ACVAFS handled the initial processing of refugees and then allocated them to agencies with resettlement programs. Also, ACVAFS maintained a close collaboration with the U.S. government departments and understood its institutional role as mediator/facilitator between the PVOs and the federal government.[52] It viewed the establishment of PAID as "duplicating and fragmenting" its activities. Some agencies were members of both ACVAFS and PAID, undermining ACVAFS's aim for exclusive representation of the PVO community.[53]

As mentioned, the topic of evangelism divided religious PVOs. Since its inception, ACVAFS's constitution required its members not to engage in "propagandistic" or proselytizing behavior.[54] The same has been true historically of contractual agreements between PVOs and the federal government. Even though the Salvation Army and the Mennonite Central Committee belonged to ACVAFS, they, like the mainline denominational agencies, were engaged in social ministry activities and not proselytizing. Evangelical PVOs such as WV were viewed by the established PVOs as failing to distinguish between Christian religious and missionary services on the one hand and relief and development work on the other hand.[55]

With growing diversity among the PVOs in their approaches to international relief and development programs, USAID increasingly managed its relationship with PVOs in an ad hoc manner. By the mid-1970s, serious issues arose over federal funding of PVOs, the independence of PVOs to carry out their programs, and PVOs as agents of U.S. foreign policy.[56]

Congress, seeking to continue to support PVO activities, directed USAID in 1977 to establish a registry of PVOs that included any agency requesting assistance from USAID. The idea was to begin to centralize the initial point of contact between PVO and USAID.

The Decline of Jewish PVOs

Real revenue of Jewish PVOs has declined in absolute terms and especially in relative terms since the mid-1970s. Numbers from the General Social Survey (GSS) indicate reasonable stability in the share of the U.S. population that self-identified as Jewish—around 2%—from 1984 to 2002. Thus, changes in numbers of U.S. Jews are likely not the key to changes in Jewish PVO revenue.

It is apparent from figure 1.6 in chapter 1 that some of the variations in the revenue of Jewish PVOs relate to conditions that affect Jewish refugees and the state of Israel. During and after World War II, giving for refugees and the new Israeli state were critical. Later, there were sharp peaks in Jewish PVO revenue associated with the Six-Day War in 1967 (real revenue jumped from $246 million in 1966 to $1.5 billion in 1967), the Yom Kippur war in 1973 (revenue rose from $1.2 billion in 1972 to $2.2 billion in 1973), and the Gulf War in 1991 (revenue increased from $928 million in 1990 to $1.4 billion in 1991). After each of these crises, real revenue of Jewish PVOs declined.

The longer-term decline in real revenue of Jewish PVOs also relates to changes in the type of giving by U.S. Jews. The United Jewish Communities reported in 2004 that 62% of American Jews engaged in philanthropy donated more to non-Jewish causes than to Jewish federations and causes.[57] Attributing the decline in Jewish philanthropy to assimilation and its impact on Jewish identity is too simplistic.[58] However, the political and philanthropic choices of a younger generation of Jews that grew up with the existence of the Israeli state are relevant issues.[59] As the Israeli state became economically developed, donations from American Jewry waned. Although the 1991 Gulf War and the beginning of peace negotiations with the Palestinians (Madrid Conference in 1991) spurred a spike in private giving, contributions fell off subsequently. Moreover, in response to the changed international scene, Jewish federations allocated a smaller percentage of their funds to overseas activities.

Another shift in Jewish charitable giving is from established federations to a more individualistic style of donating. (Jewish Funders Network has a membership of over 900 donors with combined assets over \$14 billion.[60]) A pattern of "a general sense of tzedakah and commitment to giving" among Jews explains their giving to non-Jewish causes.[61] Jews tend to be generous as a group and value philanthropic activity. Linking all three explanations—the maturity of the state of Israel, the shift to individualistic donating, and generalized giving—private charitable giving by U.S. Jews has not declined but has shifted away from federations and become more diluted (spread out among Jewish and non-Jewish causes).[62]

From Relief to Development

By the end of the 1970s, with significant grant funds from USAID, PVOs were shifting away from relief work to development. The model was one of "institution building," that is, transferring human skills and technology to countries to foster and facilitate indigenous-led development. Appropriate technology and business models were transferred to countries and implemented with local staff. The field of international development was changing, with opportunities for PVOs to be pioneers, rather than "complements" to U.S. policy. For the traditional PVOs, the focus was on family planning, P.L. 480 food, employment, and education. The "indigenization" of PVO work extended to P.L. 480 regulations, which required PVOs to have a U.S. citizen in-country to direct the distribution of food commodities. The issue for PVOs became twofold: seeking greater flexibility in appointing its own staff in-country and relying on in-country personnel.

Accompanying the shift from humanitarian relief to development was the burgeoning number of secular entities working in different aspects of international development (tables 5.5 and 5.6). By the end of the 1970s, a second generation of leaders and practitioners was directing agencies and formulating development strategies. These leaders introduced an entrepreneurial approach to engaging in international development. They were transforming agencies and making them more sophisticated in their relations with Congress and the American public.

Tensions over how to manage the delicate balance of carrying out U.S. foreign policy objectives and remain independent entities with their own mission and mandate would be a continuing debate. The federal share of revenue for all PVOs peaked at 63% in 1962, then fell to 34% by 1970. Dependency of PVOs on federal support subsequently stayed below 50%, although the revenue share rose to 38% in 1974, 40% in 1978, and 41% in 1980. What is significant is, with the government change in regulation of

PVO-state relations, namely, the introduction of grants as a favored funding mechanism in the 1970s, PVOs were less concerned about the balance of "privateness" over dependency on federal assistance. The reason is that grants, in contrast to contracts, gave PVOs considerable freedom in operating overseas. As a consequence, federal assistance to PVOs did not automatically translate into less independence for these agencies. Such was the case during the golden age of grants during the 1970s in PVO-state relations.

6

Federal Decentralization and the Militarization of Foreign Humanitarian Aid

Building on soft ground teaches you to rely on multiple supports.
—Kevin Healy, "From Field to Factory: Vertical Integration in Bolivia"

During the Carter administration (1977–80), political realities drove foreign aid, shifting focus away from humanitarian issues to security ones. This trend continued with the Reagan administration beginning in 1981. Both presidents deemphasized multilateral development assistance, favoring bilateral economic and development assistance. Carter favored food aid but not Economic Support Funds. By contrast, Reagan's administration increased Economic Support Funds and PVO involvement in development over bilateral aid. Reagan's foreign aid was defined by four pillars: policy dialogue and reform, technology transfer, private sector development, and institutional development. The Carter administration's foreign policy focused on the Middle East and Latin America. The Reagan administration continued these regional foci but increased foreign aid to Central America.

Shift in Foreign Aid Trends

Starting with the 1973 New Directions legislation, development funding favored private voluntary organizations (PVOs) and the role they played in promoting U.S. humanitarian interests abroad. The New Directions legislation embodied the view that the engine for development was the "basic needs" approach (health, nutrition, literacy, and education). For long-term beneficial effects, addressing the needs of the poorest sectors of a society and the poorest countries was fundamental. By the early 1980s, the basic needs approach came under attack. Scholars and political leaders of developing countries criticized the basic needs approach, arguing that it simply created more dependency on donors. What was required for long-term successful development were market-oriented strategies that fostered a vibrant private sector and strong agricultural promotion. The focus now turned to export-oriented growth and trade.

In 1980, Congress amended the Foreign Assistance Act to allow PVOs to continue working in countries after a prohibition had been placed as long as the U.S. national interest was not violated. Congress also favored PVOs by approving the exemption of their overseas personnel from income tax payments.[1] In 1980, the Biden-Pell Amendment to the International Security and Development Cooperation Act created grants to support PVO public education activities on world hunger and poverty.[2] The U.S. Agency for International Development (USAID) administered the grants, beginning in 1982, through a newly created Development Education Program. Like other grants, the Biden-Pell grants required PVO cost-sharing, in this case 15% (cash or in-kind contribution).[3] For the PVOs, these grants had a multiplier effect. As agencies were engaged in educating the public on hunger and poverty issues, they were able to cultivate new constituencies and potential donors.[4]

In 1981, Congress passed amendments to the Foreign Assistance Act mandating a fixed percentage (12%–16%) of development and disaster assistance funding to be channeled through PVOs.[5] A major review of its relationship with PVOs was conducted by USAID, and it circulated a policy paper with several recommendations.[6] Among them were increased program integration and emphasis on field programs, taking measures through the "privateness" rule to discourage PVO reliance on federal funds, simplify management and administrative procedures, and ensure that USAID funds were within "USAID-determined parameters." The response of the PVO community, as represented by its two umbrella organizations American Council of Voluntary Agencies for Foreign Service (ACVAFS) and Private Agencies in International Development (PAID), was negative. The criticisms of PAID were particularly direct, referring to the Reagan administration's new orientation on international development as promoting strategic and political interests.[7] The PVO umbrella organization, PAID, stated that if the "PVO community cannot achieve policy flexibility through dialogue with the Executive Branch, we will need to seek legislative assistance."[8]

The debate in the late 1970s over the privateness of PVOs resulted in new guidelines. By the 1980s, legislation was passed requiring agencies to obtain at least 20% of their annual revenue from non–U.S. government sources.[9] The majority of PVOs argued against the privateness rule on the grounds that it introduced financial inflexibility. By their nature, PVOs have difficulties raising funds for administrative costs. The public expects its donations to PVOs to reach the intended recipients. The privateness rule also discriminated against smaller and newer agencies, favoring larger and more established PVOs, which have financial flexibility. As a result, smaller innovative agencies trying out new technologies might financially struggle to survive.

A transition phase was built into the legislation (from 1982 to December 31, 1984), giving PVOs, particularly large ones like Catholic Relief Services and CARE, the opportunity to wean themselves from federal funds. The 1985 legislation stated that a minimum of 20% of a PVO's revenue (including cash resources) had to come from nongovernment sources. Table 6.1 provides one indicator of this dependence by showing the PVOs that ranked at the top in Public Law (P.L.) 480 commodities from 1970 to 1989. The dominance of Catholic Relief Services and CARE on this dependence is clear from the table.

Table 6.1.   Top PVO recipients of P.L. 480 funds, 1970–89.

	Number of times ranked				
PVO	1	2	3	4	5
Catholic Relief Services	8	7	0	0	0
CARE	7	8	0	0	0
Adventist Development and Relief	0	0	6	5	3
Church World Service	0	0	5	4	0
Lutheran World Relief	0	0	0	4	7
Save the Children	0	0	2	1	1
World Vision	0	0	2	0	1
Food for the Hungry	0	0	0	1	1
World Relief	0	0	0	0	1
American-Jewish Joint Distribution Committee	0	0	0	0	1

Source: McCleary Private Voluntary Organizations Data Set.

In reality, PVOs that accepted over 80% of their funds from the government could continue to receive USAID funding but not in the form of large, long-term grants (Operational Program, matching, and institutional support).[10] This requirement did not count as federal support the value of commodities (including in-kind contributions, donated goods and services, and freight) and the value of contracts and grants that were for USAID-initiated activities that the PVO was carrying out. If the P.L. 480 support had been included as federal funds, Catholic Relief Services and CARE would have had difficulty meeting the privateness rule. Taking all their federal income into account, Catholic Relief Services and CARE are major recipients of federal dollars.

In 1985, Congressman Lewis called for an increase in the privateness requirement from 20% to 25%. Unlike the previous privateness test, which applied only to set-aside funds for PVOs and their cash resources, the Lewis Amendment covered all USAID funding awarded to PVOs.[11] The Lewis Amendment proposed that meeting the privateness test would serve as a precondition for receiving government funding. If a PVO did not meet the new privateness test, then the organization was disqualified from future funding. However, the Lewis Amendment was never enacted. Rather, the 20% privateness rule that came into effect in 1985 and described in this section remained intact.[12]

Table 6.2 shows which of the PVOs in the top ten revenue lists from 1980 to 1984 would have been most likely to be affected by the Lewis privateness rule. The only ones with federal shares of revenue above 40% in the same year were Catholic Relief Services, CARE, Church World Service, Adventist Relief and Development, and Planned Parenthood. The table also illustrates the persistence of PVOs in the top ten lists. The same agencies keep reappearing over time, independently of the PVO classification as secular or religious.

A March 1987, a USAID audit of its programs found, in the words of the USAID administrator, "Management controls within AID'S Office of Private Voluntary Cooperation [PVC] were not sufficient to ensure private and voluntary organization compliance with their agreed upon cost-sharing responsibilities. Grantees were not making their required contributions and some in-kind contributions were overvalued or were not verifiable. Action was not taken by USAID when recipients failed to fulfill their cost-sharing obligations."[13] The fundamental issue was that USAID, from its inception, was not set up to review and police PVO financial arrangements. The arrangement was one of good faith that the PVOs would handle their own accounting accurately. However, congressional

Table 6.2. Largest PVOs by revenue: 1980, 1981, 1983, 1984.

PVO	Type	Real revenue (millions 2005 $)	Federal share
	1980		
Catholic Relief Services	Catholic	828	0.69
United Israel Appeal	Jewish	615	0.08
CARE	Secular	463	0.70
American-Jewish Joint Distribution Committee	Jewish	149	0.36
Institute of International Education	Secular	136	0.18
Church World Service	Ecumenical	86.8	0.44
Christian Children's Fund	Secular	84.9	0
Hadassah	Jewish	75.0	0.03
Summer Institute of Linguistics	Evangelical	54.0	0.02
Adventist Development and Relief	Evangelical	37.8	0.71
	1981		
Catholic Relief Services	Catholic	718	0.69
United Israel Appeal	Jewish	609	0.10
CARE	Secular	569	0.78
American-Jewish Joint Distribution Committee	Jewish	112	0.25
Church World Service	Ecumenical	93.5	0.43
Christian Children's Fund	Secular	86.3	0
Institute of International Education	Secular	77.2	0.27
Hadassah	Jewish	71.2	0.02
MAP International	Evangelical	59.9	0.01
Summer Institute of Linguistics	Evangelical	58.5	0.02
	1983		
Catholic Relief Services	Catholic	635	0.70

(continued)

Table 6.2. *(continued)*

PVO	Type	Real revenue (millions 2005 $)	Federal share
United Israel Appeal	Jewish	563	0.07
CARE	Secular	555	0.76
Christian Children's Fund	Secular	89.0	0
American-Jewish Joint Distribution Committee	Jewish	84.0	0.03
Hadassah	Jewish	73.0	0.02
Institute of International Education	Secular	70.4	0.27
Church World Service	Ecumenical	61.9	0.24
Summer Institute of Linguistics	Evangelical	59.0	0.01
Planned Parenthood	Secular	50.3	0.59
	1984		
Catholic Relief Services	Catholic	643	0.77
United Israel Appeal	Jewish	559	0.05
CARE	Secular	480	0.56
Christian Children's Fund	Secular	105	0
American-Jewish Joint Distribution Committee	Jewish	90.4	0.01
Institute of International Education	Secular	85.3	0.28
Hadassah	Jewish	84.4	0.03
Summer Institute of Linguistics	Evangelical	64.2	0.01
Save the Children	Secular	47.7	0.39
Mennonite Central Committee	Evangelical	44.5	0.01

Source: McCleary Private Voluntary Organizations Data Set.
Note: Data unavailable for 1975–77, 1979, 1982. Grants data start in 1967. Contracts data start in 1978 (except for 1951–52).

members were threatening to institute legislation if PVOs did not take concrete steps to engage in self-policing.

InterAction, the PVO umbrella organization, after a six-year vetting process, established PVO standards in the areas of governance, financial reporting, fund-raising, public relations, management practices, human resources, public policy, and program services. The Gifts-in-Kind (GIK) Standard of the Association of Evangelical Relief and Development Organizations (AERDO) was developed in response to fraud and abuse of resources on the part of member agencies.[14] Building on AERDO's Gifts-in-Kind Standard, InterAction created guidelines for its member agencies. This was one of the few instances in which broad consensus was reached on PVO standards.[15]

The formation of the Evangelical Council for Financial Accountability (ECFA) avoided the need for legislative regulation.[16] Ten years after its founding in 1979, ECFA continued to confront the possibility of legislative action on the part of Congress. The council's membership had grown from 31 to 490 members in ten years. Yet, as a mechanism for self-policing, ECFA was having difficulty enforcing standards on its membership. Financial and moral misconduct on the part of leading evangelists, as well as failure on the part of ECFA members to comply with ECFA standards, highlighted the weaknesses of self-policing procedures.[17] The threat of congressional action again forced PVOs to comply with developed standards.

Along with the privateness requirement, Congress mandated a shift from institution-building grants to funding actual programs in-country.[18] As part of this change in focus, USAID headquarters in Washington, D.C., deemphasized centrally funded grants in favor of mission and regional decision making on grants. Along with the decentralization came a streamlining of the policy process within USAID. Previously, mission and country directors had the freedom to award Operational Program grants (OPGs), and country directors gave approval for matching grants. Now, they were required to integrate their country development objectives into USAID's overall policy objectives.

Whereas centrally funded grants from USAID headquarters supported projects independent of country sector priorities, PVOs objected that they were now required to operate their USAID-funded programs in the same sectors and geographic regions as USAID missions. Clearly, PVOs operating in-country with USAID-funded programs had to closely coordinate with USAID country strategy. Furthermore, PVOs with USAID-funded activities could operate only in USAID recipient countries. This meant that PVO programs were potentially competing with USAID bilateral programs.

The coordination between USAID missions and PVOs increasingly took the form of cooperative agreements instead of grants.[19] Cooperative agreements involved USAID in the decision making of PVO projects, with close USAID oversight characteristic of a contract. The PVOs viewed cooperative agreements as adversely affecting their autonomy. Yet this funding mechanism was increasingly employed by USAID.

Senator Hubert Humphrey sought toward the end of President Carter's administration to depoliticize foreign aid by pushing for the International Development Cooperation Agency (IDCA) and giving this new agency oversight for USAID.[20] In actuality, President Carter did not support IDCA and USAID programs. Even though IDCA came into existence in 1979, USAID programs were not immediately transferred from the State Department to IDCA. The end result was that the State Department co-opted IDCA.

The administration of Ronald Reagan (1981–89) reversed Carter's decision by relocating IDCA along with USAID in the Department of State.[21] The Reagan administration, from its inception, held that economic development was best fostered by following a free-market approach to foreign assistance, with a stress on private sector initiative.[22] This theme would play out in the Reagan administration's approach to multilateral and bilateral aid. Firms in the United States were the primary vehicles of promoting open markets and strengthening private enterprise in foreign countries. The PVOs became part of this new trend in foreign aid but were not viewed as central actors.[23]

Within USAID, the Bureau of Private Enterprise primarily funded agricultural projects and worked through USAID regional bureaus. The USAID-funded Center for Privatization focused on intermediate-size financial institutions. With regard to PVO involvement in private sector initiatives, USAID was promoting PVO-private sector collaboration. Many PVOs had no experience with U.S. corporations. The chair of the International Institute for Trade and Development described the collaboration as articulating development needs from a diverse perspective, no longer the one held by PVOs.[24]

The Reagan administration advocated for a small government, including the outsourcing of public services to the private sector and public sector contractors. The public sector contractor was a hybrid organization, one driven by market-oriented principles but with a social commitment.[25] The promotion of outsourcing for public services was effected through contracts to small, minority-owned businesses, public services contractors and secondarily to nonprofits (large PVOs, small indigenous PVOs, nonprofit consulting firms, universities, research centers, and international organizations). Many PVOs realized the trend was moving toward more contracting, but PVOs were structurally unable to compete for contracts.

The principal purpose of a contract is to acquire services, and the contractor is an agent of USAID performing an explicit set of agreed-on functions. By contrast, a grant is viewed as an assistance relationship to implement a program of the recipient organization. Starting in 1967 (see tables 5.1 and 6.3), USAID-PVO relations have been implemented through assistance relationships, that is, grants. Unlike grants, contracts are publicly competitive. Obtaining information on requests for proposals (RFPs) for contracts requires staff and knowledge of the contracting process, something unfamiliar to the PVOs.[26] In gaining information on solicitations for contract bids, USAID recognized that organizations with Washington, D.C., offices would have an advantage.[27]

Table 6.3. Grants and contracts for PVOs, 1978–94.

Year	Number of PVOs with grants	Real amount of grants (millions 2005 $)	Number of PVOs with contracts	Real amount of contracts (millions 2005 $)
1978	70	283	30	97.4
1980	94	348	35	201
1981	105	462	38	196
1983	106	454	32	120
1984	100	403	41	133
1985	97	444	40	158
1986	103	732	40	123
1987	119	728	39	130
1988	129	801	39	129
1989	138	876	43	158
1990	151	884	44	227
1991	181	860	52	333
1992	201	1,160	57	291
1993	229	1,380	55	308
1994	239	1,510	72	471

Source: McCleary Private Voluntary Organizations Data Set.
Note: Data unavailable for 1975–77, 1979, 1982. Grants data start in 1967. Contracts data start in 1978 (except for 1951–52).

From the PVO perspective, contracts were too demanding and binding. Contracts required professional financial and staff resources to keep up with the RFPs and bidding process. The PVOs historically preferred grants, which gave the agencies more independence.

The Political Maturation of PVOs

The early to mid-1980s were characterized by a steady increase in foreign policy spending. The Reagan administration successfully obtained funding for U.S. security programs in Central America and the Middle East, as well as countries that granted military bases to the United States. Continued budgetary increases for security assistance raised the 1985 foreign policy budget to its highest level since the Korean War.

On October 24, 1984, the British Broadcasting Corporation on its evening news program showed a film of victims of the sub-Saharan African famine.[28] One hundred fifty million people were severely affected. The U.S. public response was spontaneous and generous. During that same year, the ACVAFS and PAID decided to merge into one organization, InterAction. InterAction sought to come up with an organizational mechanism for distributing public donations among its member agencies. This would be the first and last time that InterAction would accept donations from the American public for a humanitarian crisis.[29]

Civil armed conflict in Ethiopia, the Sudan, Mozambique, and Angola contributed to the famine, making delivery of humanitarian aid difficult.[30] According to one report, the U.S. National Security Council had knowledge in the early 1980s of the impending famine but did not act on it, hoping that a famine would either move the Soviet-backed Ethiopian regime to shift allegiance to the United States or destabilize the regime.[31] The last of U.S. food assistance to Ethiopia, a Catholic Relief Services food program, was phasing out. The Reagan administration approached the Ethiopian People's Democratic Front (backed by the Central Intelligence Agency [CIA]) and the Tigrayan People's Liberation Front, but neither group was a workable partner. By October 1984, the public concern over famine in the Horn of Africa pressured the Reagan administration to act. The USAID administrator, M. Peter McPherson, toured Ethiopia in November 1984, but no further action was taken. In the presence of government apathy, Catholic Relief Services, Lutheran World Relief, the Ethiopian Evangelical Church Mekene Yesus, and the Ethiopian Catholic Secretariat formed a consortium to set up feeding centers operated by the PVOs.[32]

In January 1985, with Congress back in session and the Reagan administration downplaying relief to Ethiopia, Congress appropriated $400 million in food aid and $137.5 million in emergency funding and established a $225 million emergency food fund.[33] Feeding the starving became a political quagmire for PVOs, a quagmire of their own doing since many chose to portray the famine as a natural disaster rather than something caused by several factors, including government action and involvement in a civil war. The Ethiopian famine of 1984–85 became a turning point for PVOs in two dimensions.[34] First, delivering humanitarian aid involves political decisions and is never apolitical, a lesson some PVOs learned during the Vietnam War. Second, misrepresenting or not accurately representing a humanitarian crisis to the public can backfire, leading to a lack of confidence in the PVOs and donor apathy.

To improve their relations with the American public and to advocate for food aid more effectively, 16 PVOs formed the Coalition for Food Aid.[35] The mainline Protestant denominations and Lutheran World Relief had already formed an alliance in 1975, setting up a Washington, D.C., office. The Coalition for Food Aid represents some of the largest PVO recipients of P.L. 480, Title II assistance (see table 6.1).

The two largest PVO recipients of food aid, CARE and World Vision (WV), monetize more than half of their nonemergency food aid.[36] The monetization of food is the sale of donated food to obtain currency for other expenses, which may or may not be related to food distribution.[37] Smaller PVOs, such as TechnoServe and Africare, monetize almost all their food aid because they receive little in emergency food assistance.[38] The common cause of the member organizations of the Coalition for Food Aid is the monetization of food aid.

Division among the Evangelicals

World Vision, the only parachurch agency in InterAction in the 1980s, was experiencing evangelical triumphalism.[39] Senator Mark Hatfield (Republican-Oregon), himself an evangelical, served on WV's board of directors. Hatfield sought to internationalize the agency by making it more accountable to people in the countries where WV was working. The opening of the WV Washington office in the late 1970s allowed the agency access to federal funds. It was during this period that WV was maturing as an organization. Part of the process of maturing involved (a) including perspectives of partners outside the United States; (b) learning how to operate large-scale relief and development projects, including the professionalization of staff; (c) working with other PVOs at the organizational level (InterAction) as well as in the field; and (d) preparing to capture significant federal dollars.

World Vision received one of the first Child Survival grants from USAID. The agency was purposefully evolving into a development agency, moving away from child sponsorship as its main focus.[40] Managing multimillion-dollar projects funded by the federal government required a different type of expertise from managing a child sponsorship program. As a result, WV recognized the need for professionalization among its staff.[41] World Vision's largest and most significant federal funding came in the form of $13.5 million in Foreign Disaster Relief Assistance and a P.L. 480 contract for 1.5 million metric tons of food for the famine in Ethiopia. (Note—from table 6.1—that food aid related to Ethiopia put WV into the top five in 1984.) World Vision hired consultants, one of them a former director of the P.L. 480 food program. Moving such a large quantity of food required acquiring 100 trucks and 200 trailers and getting them to Ethiopia to transport food. World Vision had over 1,000 staff people in Ethiopia engaged in relief work. There was such a desperate need in Ethiopia that the Government Accounting Office put a waiver in place stating that it would not audit food programs for a period of time.

By the late 1980s, WV was on a new organizational trajectory. It was moving away from small-scale community development projects toward "area development programs"—clusters of projects focused on development in a microregion. Within World Vision U.S. (WVUS), the development gurus said that a disaster situation such as the Ansokia Valley in Ethiopia could not be transformed into a sustainable development project. The Ansokia Valley consisted of 30 villages in an environmentally decimated area. One feeding center had 70,000 people. World Vision flew in college volunteers to dig latrines. One of the lessons learned from the Ethiopian famine was the disastrous effects of large population feeding centers. The agencies (for example, the United Nations) simply could not address the needs of the refugee population. Within three years, trees were planted, land was reclaimed for agriculture, an aquaculture project was carried out, and 31 villages were reestablished to be famine resistant. The Ansokia Valley is a WV success story in long-term development.

Once the emergency of the Ethiopian famine evolved into a longer-term development issue, the flow of federal and private funds subsided. World Vision saw its total budget go from $46.7 million (in 2005 dollars) in 1985 to $207 million in 1986. In 1987, WV's total revenue dropped to $59.4 million. In 1985, federal dollars provided 93% of WV's total revenue; in 1986, this was 87%, and in 1987, federal sources provided 42.3%.

The leadership within the organization realized that it could not build and function as an organization by going from one disaster situation to another, primarily funded by the federal government.[42] World Vision sought out trained people to work for the organization. It sought world-class technology and professionals in areas such as public health. World Vision set up "skunk works," modeled after Lockheed's working groups. The *skunk works* referred to the location of innovative programs that were developed outside the normal structure of the organization. These programs included water projects in Africa, water sanitation, and child health programs. Agricultural experts were brought in so that WV could learn and understand the issues. This stage of WV's evolution was one of significant professionalization.

As WV became more of a development agency, as it took itself and its work more seriously, the organization became acceptable within the larger relief and development community. Individuals within WV participated in the planning sessions for the merger of PAID with ACVAFS. When InterAction was formed, WV "mainstreamed" by becoming a member, and individuals within WV held positions in InterAction.

InterAction's position in Washington, D.C., as the representative of international PVOs matured. Its staff and leadership sought to influence Congress and increased communication with USAID. The advantages of belonging to an umbrella organization like InterAction were several. Primary among them was that it raised the level of accountability and professionalism within the organization. By participating in a professional association such as InterAction, members benefited from learning from other agencies' experiences, and they exerted pressure on each other to adhere to professional standards. When one agency engages in fraudulent or abusive behavior, it has an impact on the entire PVO community. Interaction was a means of engaging PVOs in discussion and ensuring that they adhered to standards.

In contrast to WV and its mainstreaming into the larger PVO community, AERDO remained apart and independent of the federal government. Its emphasis, like that of InterAction, is on "best practices" for its relief and development member agencies and less on management/financial issues. The organization serves as a means of fostering the exchange of technical and field knowledge, as well as facilitating collaboration. In the sense of cooperation among members, AERDO is "field driven" and not a "headquarters operation."[43] In contrast, InterAction, which is situated in Washington, D.C. (with a paid staff of 35), serves primarily to advocate, convene, coordinate, and educate its members on policy issues and advance their positions in public debates, particularly before Congress.[44]

This advocacy dimension is explicitly absent from AERDO's mandate, which is located in Michigan (staffed by volunteers) and operates in a highly decentralized fashion.

The membership of AERDO includes a few denominations but consists primarily of evangelical parachurches. As a result, most of AERDO's members do not have formal ties to a church hierarchy or church body. Most of these PVOs rely heavily on the Bible's spiritual guidance and evangelism (proselytizing) as the modus operandi of their relief and development work.

In 1980, a counterpart to AERDO, called the Consortium of Evangelical Relief and Development Organizations (COERADO), was formed. USAID suggested that a consortium of evangelical relief and development agencies could better ensure quality control of projects. The USAID-donated block grants to a consortium such as COERADO would improve efficiency, reliability, and delivery of projects. However, USAID never followed through with the suggestion and ended the discussion. The difficulty was not with COERADO but with USAID, which was apprehensive about the legal ramifications of working with evangelical agencies.

Central America and "Low-Intensity Conflict"

The Reagan administration's support of the Contra insurgency in Central America created a major foreign policy debate. President Reagan during his first term preferred to bypass the authorization process in Congress and move the foreign aid appropriation into a continuing resolution.[45] This was to avoid the placement of "killer" stipulations on foreign assistant funds by congressional members. In this manner, the Reagan administration was effective at achieving its foreign policy goals while retaining the integrity of the Foreign Assistance Act.[46]

In March 1981, Reagan approved a $19 million CIA plan to establish a 500-person force to disrupt the Communist Sandinista regime in Nicaragua. By the end of 1983, over 10,000 Contras were engaged in "low-intensity" guerrilla warfare against Nicaragua from their base in Honduras, their host nation. The Boland Amendment of 1982 forbade the use of Contra aid to overthrow the Sandinista government; the official rationale for the Contras was to stop Communism in the backyard of the United States. Congress vacillated on whether to support the Contras or terminate assistance to the paramilitary group.

In 1984, the United States imposed a trade embargo on Nicaragua but exempted humanitarian aid. In 1985, the provision of $27 million in "humanitarian assistance" to the Contras was followed by additional requests for, and heated discussions of, such aid.[47] The approval of non-military assistance to the Contras created a public and acrimonious debate between the Reagan administration and PVOs over what constituted humanitarian aid. In 1986, the State Department was moving toward designating the United Nicaraguan Opposition, the Contra political and military arm, a PVO so that it could qualify for P.L. 480 food and other types of humanitarian assistance. The Reagan administration's request for an additional $30 million in humanitarian aid to the Contras divided the PVO community. Within InterAction, the umbrella organization, PVOs were unable to reach consensus on the issue; as a consequence, the organization was publicly silent on the topic.[48] Eight PVOs sent a letter to Congress expressing their opposition to the funding.[49] The Reagan administration's intense lobbying campaign of legislators who were up for reelection produced congressional approval of $100 million in aid to the Contras. This passage was ironic given that the Gramm-Rudman-Hollings deficit-reduction bill went into effect in fiscal year 1986. With Congress in a fiscally conservative mode, it was a politically difficult climate for the administration to obtain significant funds outside the designated earmarks. Before the funds could be used, the 1987 Iran-Contra congressional hearings exposed the administration's illegal support of the Contras.

P.L. 480 and the Quasi-Governmental PVO

By 1981, the minimal allocation of agricultural commodities to be distributed through PVOs and the U.N. World Food program dropped to 1.2 million metric tons, below the minimum level set for 1973. The increase in P.L. 480 during the Carter administration did not continue under Reagan.

The two largest agencies—Catholic Relief Services and CARE—came under increasing criticism within the PVO community for receiving up to 70% of their annual income from the federal government. These two agencies, with significant P.L. 480 commodities making them the highest recipients of food aid (see table 6.1)—were viewed as agents of the federal government, not private or voluntary or independent. These agencies argued that economies of scale were at play. The lengthy bureaucratic procedure for obtaining P.L. 480 commodities, the specialized staff required for engaging in the distribution of the food commodities, and the required PVO structure to deal with the procedures meant that only a few agencies were qualified.

Another dimension of the food aid debate was its short-term use in relief and disaster situations as opposed to long-term development assistance. Populations in the developing world were dependent on U.S. surplus commodities. Rather than encouraging local agricultural production, PVOs such as Catholic Relief Services and CARE were promoting food dependency, not development. From the perspective of the PVOs with over 50% of their income coming from the federal government, their success was measured by their growth and reliance on their constituencies' perception that the agency engaged in the delivery of food commodities to the poor and in disaster situations, in other words, relief not development.[50]

The two PVOs with the largest share of the P.L. 480 food program, Catholic Relief Services and CARE, presented their food programs as development activities (see table 6.1). In one sense, the work-for-food and school-feeding programs were development projects. Yet, in a systemic structural sense, these programs were stopgap measures that failed to promote the development of local food markets. By the end of the 1980s, the P.L. 480 program was sharply criticized by segments of the American population. The end of the program was seen as essential to creating self-sufficiency in other countries.

The 1990 Farm Bill brought about important changes to the P.L. 480 program. The purpose of the program was clearly stated to be the reduction of global food insecurity. This goal was in sharp contrast to Senator Humphrey's assessment of the soon-to-be-renamed P.L. 480 as the Food for Peace program: "if you are really looking for a way for people to lean on you and to be dependent upon you, in terms of their cooperation with you, it seems to me that food dependence would be terrific."[51]

To improve U.S. delivery of food commodities, the U.S. Department of Agriculture was designated as the responsible authority for surplus food and export market development (Title I). USAID was responsible for Title II and Title III programs. Title III was merged with Title II as all credit programs were phased out and converted to grants. In addition, Congress approved the monetization of food assistance under Title II. The PVOs could sell up to 10% of their food commodities to obtain funds for in-country costs of transporting, storing, and handling food commodities. However, the funds could also be used for nonfood programs. The PVOs continued to advocate successfully for increases in the percentage.[52]

The Parallel Humanitarian Role of the U.S. Military

Historically, military-PVO relations have been one of civilian humanitarian aid being subordinate to military authority. The model was one of the U.S. military entering a region or country as an occupying force with PVOs under the authority of the military command so they did not interfere with military operations. This setup remained the model of PVO-military relations during and after World War II, the Korean War, and the Vietnam War. This model of civil-military relations began to change in the 1980s.

The military was often involved in emergency and disaster relief, providing transportation, engineering and medical skills, communications, and intelligence technology. Transportation was an obvious contribution for the military. Using its aircraft, in 1984 the Office of Humanitarian Assistance of the Department of Defense was authorized to transport PVO supplies on a space-available basis to Central America. In 1985, food airdrops by the air force were critical to supplying refugees in northern Ethiopia. By 1987, under congressional authorization, the Department of Defense was involved in transporting PVO supplies worldwide. This activity, the use of military transportation to deliver relief commodities (food, medicine, blankets), was familiar, harking back to World War II, and was not considered to go beyond the military's mandate.

By the end of the 1980s, the military was engaging in short-term humanitarian assistance related to disasters. In areas where the military operated alongside PVOs, the military thought its mission was to complete a project and move out. In contrast, PVOs were committed to a longer time frame. This difference in perspective caused friction as the military viewed the PVOs as part of the problem. The PVOs viewed the military as failing to address the underlying issues. With the breakup of the Soviet Union in the early 1990s, conflicts increasingly arose, requiring a more efficient military response and coordination with the PVOs. The conflicts that arose would highlight the differences in their respective approaches to humanitarian aid.

Sustainable Development

By the end of the 1980s, PVOs were focusing on the effectiveness of their organizations. Borrowing from the for-profit sector, PVOs were becoming business-like, focusing on cost-efficiency, sound management practices, and organizational strategic planning.[53] "Umbrella" grants were funded by USAID to PVOs that required the PVOs to cultivate local partners by linking their in-country projects with indigenous PVOs.[54]

The idea was that efficient PVOs were in an advantageous position to promote sustainable development. Once PVO sponsorship terminated, projects would continue to operate under local management. For their part, indigenous PVOs were calling for capacity building and not for the provision of services, the traditional method of providing humanitarian aid.

By the end of the 1980s, funding for international development assistance was under scrutiny once again. Developing countries were not improving, and USAID came to the conclusion that "what has haphazardly evolved as development assistance over the past four decades has not worked, has sometimes not even been aimed at the correct objectives, and, above all, has been overtaken by events."[55] By the last phrase, USAID was referring to governments and their people seeking to address their own development issues. Within this new international context of countries exercising their autonomy, global economic institutions and multinational corporations were now the primary catalysts for economic growth. A good example of this approach was the Support of Eastern European Democracy (SEED) Act, which authorized the creation of enterprise funds to assist the development of a private market economy in Central and Eastern Europe. Between 1989 and 1994, the U.S. Congress, through USAID, appropriated $1.3 billion (in current dollars) to establish investment funds known collectively as the Enterprise Funds for Poland and Hungary. From the beginning, USAID structured the Enterprise Funds to be guided by independent boards of directors selected from the upper tiers of the U.S. private sector, who in turn selected the fund's day-to-day operating management.

A shift was occurring within international development, one away from "institution building" to "institutional development."[56] *Institution building* refers to a PVO or organization duplicating its activities overseas. What domestic agencies did well at home, they replicated abroad. By the early 1980s, development strategies were shifting toward institutional development. The U.S. enterprises and agencies worked with local counterparts to assist them in becoming self-sustaining. The focus was fostering indigenous institutions and human capital, so that the U.S. agencies operating internationally would remain intermediaries or become obsolete.

These two trends—private sectors working in global economies and societies forming their own agencies—brought into question the relevance of foreign assistance but in two different ways. Whereas genuine "institutional development" would make U.S.-based PVOs obsolete, private sector and market activities would challenge PVOs to transform themselves and to find their competitive advantage in a changing global environment. The familiar humanitarian paradigm that good intentions automatically lead to good deeds and then to good results was no longer considered legitimate or genuine.

The Reagan administration had a negative view of development assistance as an inefficient sector and sought to marginalize PVOs. After large reductions in personnel during the 1980s, USAID lacked the staff to manage all the activities it was mandated to carry out. By the early 1990s, through contracts as well as grants, USAID required for-profit contractors and PVOs to assume management responsibilities and provide the required accountability. Pressures on USAID to meet minimal levels of support and to show results favored relatively large projects of short duration. Large entities were favored to carry out USAID projects. Opportunities for smaller organizations were increasingly limited through subcontracts. A special House Foreign Affairs Committee task force recommended repealing the Foreign Assistance Act of 1961, passing new legislation with clear objectives, dismantling USAID, and creating a new agency. As had been the case for decades, the executive and the congressional branches of government had differing stances on the future of foreign assistance. The initiative fell to the PVOs to create a third option for their role in international development.

7

The Commercialization of Foreign Aid

Man has almost constant occasion for the help of his
brethren, and it is in vain for him to expect it from their
benevolence only.

—Adam Smith, *The Wealth of Nations*

The disintegration of the Soviet Union brought new opportunities for
relations between private voluntary organizations (PVOs) and the government. Along with the demise of East-West tensions came a changing
geopolitical context and with it new approaches to development. The New
Independent States (NIS) of the former Soviet Union and Eastern Europe
were of primary concern to the United States. The lack of bilateral relations between the United States and these countries meant that PVOs
were going to be instrumental in carrying out U.S. foreign policy in these
regions with weak civil societies.[1] Yet real federal funding of PVOs had
peaked at $1.7 billion in 1986 and was operating at lower levels—between
$1.3 and $1.5 billion—between 1987 and 1991.

In contrast, multilateral institutions were increasing their cooperation with PVOs. The World Bank began focusing its work on poverty
reduction, environmental issues, and natural resource management.
Indigenous, nongovernmental organizations (NGOs) were viewed as a
significant vehicle for carrying out the World Bank's goals. Funding from
international organizations for PVOs was on the rise in the early 1990s
(see table 7.1). Real funding went from $179 million (2005 dollars) in 1989
to $463 million in 1996. The share of total PVO revenue coming from
international organizations went from 3.6% in 1989 to a peak of 7.2% in
1996.

The United Nations established an Office of Humanitarian Affairs,
which coordinated the activities of the U.N. High Commissioner for
Refugees, U.N. Relief and Works Agency for Palestine Refugees (UNRWA),

Table 7.1. PVO funds from international organizations, 1980–2005.

Year	PVO funds from international organizations (millions of 2005 $)	Share of overall PVO funds coming from international organizations
1980	208	0.063
1981	183	0.055
1983	150	0.048
1984	250	0.076
1985	232	0.062
1986	184	0.040
1987	178	0.041
1988	187	0.039
1989	179	0.036
1990	209	0.042
1991	264	0.045
1992	322	0.056
1993	308	0.053
1994	387	0.062
1995	365	0.060
1996	463	0.072
1997	404	0.060
1998	405	0.054
1999	503	0.059
2000	530	0.059
2001	517	0.055
2002	538	0.056
2003	574	0.052
2004	727	0.055
2005	889	0.056

Source: McCleary Private Voluntary Organizations Data Set.

Special Representative for Children and Armed Conflict, Office for the Coordination of Humanitarian Affairs, and International Strategy for Disaster Reduction. Yet U.S. funding to multilateral organizations was conditioned by the Kassebaum-Solomon Amendment, which established a limit to U.S. contributions to the United Nations.[2] The U.S. funding for

PVO activities through the U.N. system was small, mostly used as a stick to secure reforms within the institution.

"Reforming" USAID and the Loss of Competitiveness

From 1993 to 1997, USAID implemented an unprecedented series of reforms and other actions to improve collaboration with the PVO community. Again, USAID was going through a decentralization process that stressed "its strong comparative advantage" in the "experience and competence of its overseas missions."[3] The objectives of the reforms were to "focus and concentrate" USAID operations. With the geopolitical changes taking place since the fall of Communism, USAID began new operations in 30 countries. At the same time that USAID was expanding into NIS and Eastern European countries, the secretary of state announced the closing of 27 USAID field missions, something that had not happened in the history of USAID.

The secretary of state was intent on retaining U.S. direct hires while lowering the number of contractors.[4] In reality, the opposite pattern prevailed. As the agency's budget and workforce were declining, U.S. direct hires from 1992 to 2002 decreased by 34%.[5] Over the lifetime of the agency, U.S. direct hires fell dramatically,[6] from 8,600 in 1962 to 2,000 in 2004. From 1992 to 2002, the number of U.S. direct hires serving in USAID missions decreased by 42%. This shift in the character of the USAID workforce meant that foreign nationals were managing USAID programs in-country or that programs were operating without oversight.

The trend within USAID to hire contractors not only in the form of foreign nationals but also as personal services contractors, and institutional contractors (consulting firms) can be traced back to 1976, when Congress separated USAID operating expenses from its humanitarian and economic development assistance programs (Public Law [P.L.] 94-330). Since 1990, USAID, due to declining direct-hire staff, began relying on contractors. By the beginning of 2003, USAID's worldwide workforce numbered 7,741, of which 1,985 were U.S. citizens. As the number of U.S. direct hires was decreasing, USAID was operating in more countries but from regional offices. There were no U.S. direct-hire personnel in 88 countries, and 45 of these had over $1 million in funding. The combination of declining U.S. direct hires, the decentralization of USAID operations from USAID headquarters and consolidation into regional offices, and the reliance on foreign nationals and contractors meant that many projects lacked adequate management oversight. Furthermore, economic assistance projects as a vehicle of U.S. foreign policy might not be fulfilling the intended strategic objectives and instead might be harming U.S. presence in a country or region through nonmanagement, the use of contractors, and consolidation of activities into large management bundles. A General Accounting Office (GAO) report concluded that USAID was "finding it increasingly difficult to manage the delivery of foreign assistance."[7]

The first part of the "focus-and-concentrate" USAID reform strategy was to rely increasingly on cooperative agreements with PVOs. The second focus-and-concentrate strategy was to wean PVOs from federal funding. For example, in countries with established PVO-USAID relations, USAID would eliminate support and transfer complete responsibility for projects to PVOs. The expectation of USAID was that the PVOs and their local partners would continue operating on private funds.

Complementing the withdrawal of USAID funding for established PVO projects was increasing USAID funding of indigenous PVOs through intermediary or "umbrella" subgrant or contracting arrangements.[8] In contrast to the Matching Grant Program in the 1970s, which did not require a PVO to partner with an indigenous agency, and the umbrella grants of the 1980s, which stipulated that PVO projects in-country had to include the institutional development of indigenous partnering agencies, the umbrella grants of the 1990s focused on capacity building of local PVOs to the point that U.S. PVOs became obsolete. Umbrella grants, like Matching Grants, tended to be awarded to large PVOs. However, USAID noted that umbrella grants were not assisting indigenous PVOs to mature organizationally to the point that they could assume full responsibility for operations.

At the beginning of the Clinton administration in 1993, there were 19 executive branch entities engaged in some aspect of foreign assistance.[9] Foreign aid programs previously operated by USAID were being delegated to other domestic agencies, such as the Departments of Treasury, Health and Human Services, Education, and Labor. The funding by these various agencies was not guided by any overall policy rationale and guidance. Yet their foreign aid disbursements were significant (exceeding $1 billion in nominal dollars in 1993), raising questions about the chaotic implementation of U.S. foreign aid. The issue of a wide and unsupervised disbursement of foreign aid across the executive branch had initially been raised in 1992 at the end of George H. W. Bush's administration as he sought to reorganize foreign assistance.[10] Yet his successors, presidents Clinton and George W. Bush, continued to delegate foreign aid programs to domestic agencies, thereby weakening the policy control of the State Department and USAID over foreign aid. This "incremental approach" or "organizational sprawl" would continue to be discussed by foreign policy experts, becoming in 2007 part of the argument for foreign aid reform.[11]

In 1993, Clinton designated for the first time the administrator of USAID as the special coordinator for international disaster assistance. This structural change centralized in the USAID administrator all U.S. government response to natural and human-caused disasters. Within USAID, administrative oversight for PVOs was consolidated in the Research and Development Bureau.[12] This bureau had been growing in importance, allocating funding for population, health, and environmental programs. In 1993, Congress and the Clinton administration passed legislation and implemented policies that prohibited USAID from funding projects that directly engaged in investment promotion.

In 1993, Congress passed the Government Performance and Results Act of 1993, often called GPRA or the Results Act.[13] This act required federal agencies to develop strategic plans, performance measures, annual performance plans, and performance reporting. Whereas the Reagan administration had viewed PVOs as promoters of private enterprise activity and marginal to a market approach to development, the Clinton administration applied private-sector strategies to the operations of USAID and PVOs. The PVOs, as clients of the federal government, began to experience stricter accounting procedures and requirements focused on results. Questions over measuring results of projects continually arose.[14] Examples of key issues were the quantification of projects and the gathering of consistent data across countries and agencies. The PVOs argued, somewhat pathetically, that USAID was focusing on measurement before achievement.

Commercialization of Aid

Another major setback for PVOs was the increasing reliance by USAID on what it called multiple-award contracts. These contracts, introduced in 1994, were for the performance of the same service by many contracting entities. The main funding instrument is an indefinite quantity contract (IQC). An IQC is a contract for an "indefinite quantity of services to be furnished over a fixed period of time."[15] Prior to 1994, the norm for contracts, with multiple-award contracts requests for proposals (RFPs) were sent to a pool of contractors. Increasingly, the RFP requests were presented as a "bundle" of services of a diverse nature so that they could be satisfactorily provided only by a consortium of contractors.[16] The PVOs were sometimes included as providers in the bundle of services.

The George H. W. Bush administration relied on contractors to implement development projects, as opposed to grants to traditional PVOs. This trend was noted in the 1990s and continued into the new millennium (see tables 1.1 and 1.2 in chapter 1).[17] "With more assignments in the field than staff to perform them, USAID has increasingly turned to contractors...to implement its traditional core programs."[18] It is estimated that, in 2006, one-third of USAID funds were channeled to contracts to for-profit contractors.[19]

The Advisory Committee on Voluntary Foreign Aid (ACVFA) recently published a review of the Foreign Assistance Framework, stating: "The Implementation Working Group is concerned that USAID appears to be moving more toward selecting contracts as the implementation mechanism. The Working Group finds that, in some instances, USAID has failed to assess the nature of the relationship with the implementing organization and the purpose of the award when making its instrument selection decisions...instead, decisions are based, per actual experiences and anecdotal information shared with the Working Group, on preferences by Mission personnel for contracts, a desire to assert federal control over an activity, and/or the misconception that results are not attainable under assistance awards."[20] A review of USAID's Yellow Book (a directory of contracts, grants, and cooperative agreements) found that the same for-profit firms (DAI, Chemonics, Nathan, Checchi, Abt) populated the list of implementers year after year.[21] This criticism from the PVO community is surprising given the pattern of a few PVOs dominating P.L. 480 food aid each year (see table 6.1 from chapter 6). Some of the larger PVOs are able to compete with for-profit firms and secure contracts themselves. However, this competition causes them to behave more like the for-profit firms.[22] In addition, smaller PVOs, which lack the necessary staff and professionalism to engage in the lengthy contracting process, are left out. The HELP Commission noted that any agency that is not seeking to become a general contractor will be excluded from the contract process.

The PVOs perceive the use of IQCs as a top-down approach to implementing development, enabling the government to exercise more control over program activities. This issue continues to stay on the agenda of the PVOs as the InterAction Strategic Goals for 2007–9 include as one of the objectives: "To protect humanitarian and development space from encroachment by external forces, such as the military, contractors, and onerous regulations."[23] However, the process of not using full and open bidding is legal, written into USAID's acquisition regulation.[24] The benefits, then, of using multiple-award contracts are, first, the speediness with which they can be awarded; second, multiple-award contracts permit substantial oversight by USAID; and third, a number of services can be purchased with one contract.

How to Implement Aid

In 1995, with a Republican majority in the U.S. House of Representatives, Republican congressional members, with Senator Jesse Helms leading the offensive, called for a radical overhaul of USAID. Backed by House Speaker Newt Gingrich and Senate Majority Leader Bob Dole, Helms called for a "fundamental and revolutionary reinvention of America's foreign-policy institutions" by making export promotion the primary focus of U.S. foreign policy.[25] Helms proposed that USAID and two other agencies— the U.S. Information Agency and the Arms Control and Disarmament Agency—be integrated into the U.S. Department of State. His proposal was publicly endorsed by Lawrence S. Eagleburger, James A. Baker III, and George P. Shultz, three former secretaries of state.

Representative Sonny Callahan (Republican-Alabama), who was chair of the House Foreign Operations Subcommittee, took the initiative, and the Senate followed. Callahan succeeded in some measures but not in others. The changes focused on specific areas of foreign aid, such as creating a distinct Child Survival and Disease Program Fund.

In 1998, Congress enacted legislation transferring the U.S. Information Agency and the Arms Control and Disarmament Agency to the State Department. Although USAID remained an independent agency, the USAID administrator was required to report and serve under the foreign policy direction of the secretary of state.

In 1995, at the U.N. Social Summit, Vice President Al Gore introduced USAID's New Partnerships Initiative. The organization would apply its results-based approach to indigenous PVOs. This new model was different from previous attempts at fostering the growth of indigenous PVOs in that USAID was actively involved in partnering PVOs with private-sector organizations and local government agencies. The active participation of USAID occurred in the initial setup phase (which the agency described as "participatory conceptualization and design"). Once the projects were operating, USAID took on a support role. The Clinton administration's policy focused on what it termed the "third way"—fostering democratic governance and economically self-sustaining civil societies in the form of PVOs and small business enterprises. The New Partnerships Initiative was an initial part of this third-way approach.[26]

At the end of 1995, USAID introduced flexibility into the cost-sharing aspects of grants for PVOs. Rather than specifying a minimum of 25% of private funding for the total cost of a project, USAID would look case by case, encouraging the "largest reasonable and possible" share of private funding by a PVO on a USAID-funded project. This change in policy was an acknowledgment of the undue burden the privateness rule placed on small PVOs and its discriminatory nature in that USAID, because of the privateness rule, would not award large grants to small PVOs.[27] It appears that this change in policy did not have a net positive effect on PVO participation in foreign aid. By fiscal year 2000, USAID was spending $3 of $4 on for-profit firms, educational institutions, and cooperatives.

Table 7.2 shows numbers of secular PVOs by functional orientation from 1990 to 2005. The increase in total numbers, which began in the

Table 7.2. Numbers of secular PVOs by functional orientation, 1990–2005.

Year	Numbers by type						
	Total	Growth	Relief	Education	Environment	Culture	Health
1990	194	31	66	39	18	1	38
1991	238	36	75	41	32	6	44
1992	284	38	100	50	38	7	47
1993	300	40	109	51	35	8	52
1994	368	45	147	60	39	9	62
1995	352	44	139	53	40	6	63
1996	345	44	142	49	40	6	59
1997	335	45	141	46	38	5	56
1998	332	49	139	45	36	8	52
1999	336	46	141	46	34	9	56
2000	346	44	149	44	36	9	60
2001	359	44	150	49	39	11	62
2002	364	42	157	48	38	11	64
2003	401	45	168	58	40	13	72
2004	380	45	162	47	38	12	71
2005	364	43	154	45	32	12	74

Source: McCleary Private Voluntary Organizations Data Set.
Note that data for 1979–89 are comparable in table 5.1 in chapter 5, and data for the 1960s are comparable in table 4.1 in chapter 4. "Growth" includes economic growth, agricultural development, and engineering and infrastructure; "relief" includes international relief and development; "education" includes education/higher learning and professional societies; "environment" includes conservation, animal protection, solar power, and so forth; "culture" includes communications, culture and society, and foundations; "health" includes medicine and health issues.

mid-1970s, was dramatic in the early 1990s. The number went from 117 in 1986 and 194 in 1990 to 368 in 1994. Concentrating on changes from 1990 to 1994, the rise from 194 to 368 corresponded to a proportionate increase by 90%. This expansion was spread across types. By types, the changes from 1990 to 1994 were as follows: Culture rose from 1 to 9 (an increase by 800%), relief went from 66 to 147 (127%), environment went from 18 to 39 (117%), health expanded from 38 to 62 (63%), growth went from 31 to 45 (45%), and education went from 39 to 54 (54%). In contrast, from 1990 to 1994, religious PVOs went from 81 to 132, an increase by 63%. The largest gains were in the areas of culture, relief, and environment.

By the end of the Clinton administration in 2000, foreign aid was no longer on the administration's agenda. Under the Clinton administration, USAID underwent "a near-death" experience as funding for the agency plummeted.[28] The Overseas Development Council, a Washington, D.C., think tank specializing in development issues, advocated increased funding, as did the PVO umbrella organization, InterAction. The Republican-dominated Congress, intent on budget cuts, viewed foreign aid as discretionary. The PVOs were going through a serious reassessment of their effectiveness and identity as a community of humanitarian agencies. The result of their self-assessment, spearheaded by InterAction, was a standard of PVO behavior in humanitarian crises known as the Sphere Project (http://www.sphereproject.org/).[29]

Initially, it appeared as though foreign policy under the George W. Bush administration would be a low priority. In stump speeches on the campaign trail, candidate Bush was careful to distance himself from the Clinton/Gore foreign policy that had seen the American military stretched in peacekeeping missions in places like Haiti, Somalia, and the Balkans.[30] Bush's priorities appeared largely domestic—education, tax cuts, and the highly touted faith-based initiative, which would not have a foreign assistance component until years later. But, the terrorist attacks on New York City and Washington, D.C., on September 11, 2001, would bring about a change in the way the administration talked about and implemented foreign policy.

The tenure of Andrew Natsios as USAID administrator began in 2001 with a reorganization of the agency around three new "pillar" bureaus and the new Global Development Alliance, designed to foster public-private partnerships.[31] The three pillars were Global Health; Economic Growth and Agriculture; and Conflict Prevention, Democracy/Governance, and Humanitarian Response.[32] In short, the early days of the George W. Bush administration seem to have been occupied with the usual stocktaking and housecleaning that a new leader brings. Meanwhile, the PVO community was concerned mostly with the usual lobbying for increased foreign affairs spending, being better prepared for humanitarian crises, and fighting the HIV/AIDS pandemic.

Since 1973, USAID had become an agency in flux in terms of staffing, accounting procedures, and bureaucratic responsibility. At numerous points from 2002 to 2004, Natsios told legislators not to give his agency more money or responsibility, saying that too much funding could "compromise [USAID's] structures" and noting that USAID programs did not have the "absorptive capacity" for the funding. The Bush administration redirected foreign assistance away from USAID, which was orphaned, placed outside foreign policy decision making and implementation.

The new administrator appeared to want to maintain the trend of decentralization, keeping much of the decision-making authority with the missions in the field. Speaking on the issue of procurement to the ACVFA in 2001, Mark Ward of USAID spoke of a new policy by which all large USAID contracts would be reviewed, preaward, in Washington, D.C. Ward "noted that it was difficult to sell this reform to the Administrator, Natsios, because it went against his desire not to encroach on the authority of the missions."[33]

Years later, Natsios outlined his philosophy in a speech to members of the British Parliament: "The European aid agencies tend to be more highly centralised. Decision-making is undertaken in capital cities, where most of the development staff is also to be found. USAID has most of its staff in the field. You may be surprised to learn that most of the people who work for USAID are not Americans. They are foreigners, many of whom have worked with us for decades....To a great extent, it is people from the developing world, not Washington functionaries, who are running the American aid programme. What I am describing is a highly decentralised system, and a highly desirable one, I might add."[34]

The policy of decentralization extended to the new Global Development Alliance, an agencywide initiative focusing on public-private partnerships. Applicants for prospective alliances are instructed first to submit a concept paper to the mission director for approval.[35] The Global Development Alliance has raised billions of dollars in leveraged resources from the private sector for development assistance programs. This procedure is in keeping with guidelines found elsewhere in USAID policy, namely, the ADS (Automated Directives System) 303—Grants and Cooperative Agreements to Non-Governmental Organizations.[36] These policies all leave significant grant-making authority in the hands of mission directors.

National Security and Foreign Aid

The terrorist attacks of September 11, 2001, and the subsequent armed conflicts in Afghanistan and Iraq changed the landscape in a number of ways. With the conflicts came relief and reconstruction efforts, as well as a trend toward increased involvement by the Department of Defense. They also renewed within the administration, the foreign policy community, and the general public an interest in fragile and failing states. Another heightened concern was the implication for national security of American activity abroad. The National Security Strategy of 2002 articulated that development is now an integral part of national security, elevating it (rhetorically anyway) to the status of defense and diplomacy.[37] It also raised the issue of public diplomacy as it relates to USAID branding, which would become a point of conflict with the PVO community. Another issue was the role of the military in humanitarian efforts. These topics are discussed in further detail in this chapter.

In 2002 and 2003, President Bush announced dramatic increases in U.S. foreign assistance spending. On March 14, 2002, he announced the formation of the Millennium Challenge Account (MCA), designed to foster good governance and reward those countries deemed to be making discernible progress.[38] In his speech, Bush expressed his intention to increase foreign assistance by five billion dollars over the following three years. Then, in the 2003 State of the Union Address, he announced the President's Emergency Plan for AIDS Relief (PEPFAR), a $15 billion effort over five years to fight AIDS in selected nations in Africa and the Caribbean. Although this dramatic increase in foreign assistance funding certainly heralded a new era in U.S. humanitarian engagement abroad, it is noteworthy that these expensive new programs entirely bypassed the existing mechanisms for aid delivery that existed within USAID.[39] Therefore, they have varying implications for PVOs that rely heavily on government funding streams.

The MCA is intended to reward those countries that take demonstrable efforts toward increasing good governance. "The Millennium Challenge Account (MCA) is managed by the Millennium Challenge Corporation (MCC) and provides assistance, through a competitive selection process, to developing nations that are pursuing political and economic reforms in three areas: ruling justly, investing in people, and fostering economic freedom."[40] By nature of being aimed at governments, the money from the MCA is granted directly to the foreign governments that enter into what are called MCC "compacts" or agreements. Therefore, American PVOs do not see much MCC money, except what might be granted to them if they approach those governments directly.

Also, PEPFAR bypasses USAID and is directly administered by the global AIDS coordinator, State Department.[41] Some of PEPFAR programs are administered through other agencies, such as Health and Human Services. However, PVOs receive PEPFAR funds, particularly small- and medium-size organizations working in AIDS-afflicted countries. Thus, the response of the PVOs has been more favorable toward PEPFAR. As PEPFAR has evolved, one of the trends (evident elsewhere in foreign assistance programs under George W. Bush) is toward building capacity among smaller PVOs and particularly foreign indigenous NGOs. In the PEPFAR context, this process is known as the New Partner Initiative, announced in December 2005. This initiative is aimed at entities with little or no prior experience working with the U.S. government.[42]

This trend toward relying on smaller, indigenous PVOs in lieu of larger, traditional American PVOs as implementing partners is also seen in the context of USAID. The Office of Private Voluntary Cooperation (PVC) has been the contact point for PVOs within the agency for the past 35 years, the entity at which PVOs registered to become eligible for funding. This office also administered the grants, including matching grants (see chapter 5).

In the organizational review that took place after Natsios assumed the office of administrator in May 2001, a new framework for PVC emerged. In meetings with PVO representatives at InterAction, USAID officials announced that the new framework would "emphasize capacity strengthening and feature efforts designed to work with new/nascent PVOs, promote capacity building of local organizations, and align the office with the new priority areas of the Agency including conflict."[43] This new policy meant that PVC was phasing out the Matching Grants (which officially ended in 2001, with the last grant awarded in 2003). Child Survival, Farmer-to-Farmer, and Development Education Program grants were shifted out of the PVC office. According to InterAction's report of the meeting, "Judy Gilmore (then head of the PVC office) stated that PVC would shift away from funding larger, established PVOs."[44] Hence, the funding would shift toward newer, smaller, less-experienced PVOs that had no prior relationship with indigenous PVOs and USAID.

This move seems to be one in a series that signaled a shift in the administration, trying to assert a measure of independence from large, well-established PVOs that had come to expect substantial amounts of government funding as the norm. The USAID funding priorities had come full circle to their initial purpose in the early 1970s. The change in the policy framework of the PVC was announced in 2002, and shortly thereafter, in spring 2003, a flare-up took place between Administrator

Natsios and the PVO community over remarks made at the InterAction Annual Forum. The conflict stemmed from a speech he gave, apparently "blasting" U.S. PVOs for not doing enough "PR" (public relations) for the U.S. government abroad. There were later attempts to smooth these words over and say it was a misunderstanding. Nevertheless, the statement was viewed as yet another attempt to encroach on the neutrality of PVOs working abroad. Many of the press reports cited notes from InterAction members in attendance at the closed-door meeting, and there was allegedly an error in the transcript of the speech that was released that led to misreporting of its contents. The bottom line is that relations between Natsios and the PVOs were souring.

The Evolving Role of the Military

A turning point in civil-military humanitarian relations occurred with Operation Provide Comfort in 1991. Following Desert Storm, the Kurdish population fled northward toward the Turkish border. A U.S.-led coalition constructed resettlement areas ("safe havens") for the protection of the Kurds. The objectives of Operation Provide Comfort—to provide humanitarian assistance to the Kurds and to secure their safety—were intertwined. The insights and experience gained by the military from Operation Provide Comfort would come to fruition after a series of failures.

The Clinton administration promoted multilateral solutions to international security crises. Within USAID, the Office of Transition Initiatives was set up to handle postconflict situations. In fiscal year 1994, the Clinton administration successfully sought congressional approval for U.S. military participation in U.N. multinational peacekeeping operations in several countries (Somalia, Haiti, Bosnia, Kosovo, and to a lesser extent Cambodia, Angola, Western Sahara, and East Timor). In 1994, the Department of Defense spent $428 million on humanitarian assistance. Before 1994, the total dollars of Department of Defense humanitarian assistance was not separated from funds for peacekeeping operations.[45] A series of U.S. military involvements followed by humanitarian fiascos in Somalia, Haiti, Bosnia, and Rwanda brought legislators to rethink the effectiveness of U.S. involvement in multilateral efforts and humanitarian aid.

By the mid-1990s, Congress limited the role of the U.S. military in the Balkans. The number of American military personnel serving in U.N. peacekeeping missions began to drop. Public debate over the nature of U.S. foreign policy on military intervention in intrastate conflicts around the world produced a retrenching in Congress. Funding for peacekeeping operations decreased, with operations in fiscal year 2002 reaching a low point.[46]

During the 1990s, the military and the PVO community were engaged in a series of meetings through InterAction. The involvement of USAID was minimal, although a proposal floated to place a USAID officer of Foreign Disaster Assistance in each military command. A fundamental organizational mission difference existed between the military and PVOs. The military, in humanitarian activities, sought to address immediate needs and leave whereas, PVOs were more likely to seek to address underlying causes of crises.[47]

Following the conflict in Afghanistan and at the onset of the conflict in Iraq in 2003, members of the PVO community became increasingly vocal in their opposition to the practice of military personnel carrying out relief operations in conflict zones.[48] In some cases, military personnel were even wearing civilian clothing. Blurring the line between combatant and relief worker posed what the PVOs felt was an imminent threat to the safety of their people. If hostiles could no longer distinguish between military personnel and those in the development community, many of whom work hard to maintain a neutral stance, then the latter would become a target for violent attack.[49] The PVOs work with indigenous organizations and staff, minimizing expatriate staff. The PVOs work "below the radar," working at the community level and avoiding large contractor-based programs. InterAction members felt that the military, when carrying out these tasks, tends to ride roughshod over the experience and expertise of relief workers, who have been doing it far longer.

Peter Bell, then president and chief executive officer (CEO) of CARE, cited examples from Afghanistan, saying that "initially yellow food packages were dropped that were confused with yellow cluster bombs. Later, U.S. Special Operation Forces, dressed in civilian clothes and carrying concealed weapons, engaged in building schools and other humanitarian-oriented projects. These operations caused a great deal of confusion. The PVOs registered their complaints that, by such acts, the military was putting PVO staff at risk."[50]

In 2005, the Department of Defense issued what it refers to as the stability operations directive.[51] This directive for the first time elevated stability operations to the same priority as major combat. The directive describes the many postconflict activities the military is now engaging in, from peace operations (peacekeeping and peace enforcement), humanitarian and civic assistance (including developing a representative government), private sector and economic development, counterterrorism, counternarcotics actions, and counterinsurgency assistance.[52] To fulfill the activities put forth in the stability operations directive, the Department of Defense is increasing personnel related to civil affairs, foreign affairs, military police, engineering, and psychological operations. Part of the necessity driving the increase in personnel is that the military, to address humanitarian and peacekeeping issues, deploys a whole brigade. In other words, the cumbersome nature of the military structure is not conducive to the new objectives of maintaining peace. To be more flexible, the military is developing expertise in development and humanitarian work.

In essence, the State Department is being overtaken by the Department of Defense in intelligence and expertise on postconflict stabilization and reconstruction. Congress approved the assistance of the Department of Defense to the Department State in these areas, including the authorization to transfer materials from Defense to State. Congress further authorized the establishment of interagency operating procedures for federal agencies on stabilization and reconstruction operations. The consequence of this strategic view of U.S. foreign policy for PVOs is to integrate them further into the U.S. policy bureaucracy.

There exists a fundamental difference between the post–World War II reconstruction environment and post-9/11. Postreconstruction efforts are now occurring in parts of the world with which the United States shares little cultural and social heritage (as contrasted with Europe). Security interests of the United States are no longer tied to cold war client states but are directly linked to transnational security threats. As the U.S. military increasingly takes on reconstruction and stabilization activities, it is entering areas of social and political development outside its traditional mandate. The military is extending itself into areas where it lacks expertise. If U.S. foreign policy is to be successful, PVOs, who are by nature flexible and adaptable, need to reclaim the terrain of humanitarian aid and development.

Disbanding the PVO Club

The George W. Bush administration viewed foreign aid funding to PVOs as a "closed club." The registration process at USAID allowed those agencies that registered to qualify for set-aside grants and contracts for PVOs. The Procurement Office at USAID, to ensure that PVOs were fiscally sound, used a prevetting process with PVOs as part of registering with USAID. This process created a preferential process because the Contract Office would work only with registered PVOs.

The USAID registration process, contrary to the Bush administration's perception, did not create a closed club as any agency could apply for registration. As my data set shows, there is PVO movement in and out of USAID, and registration is open. Furthermore, in 1994, USAID abolished the 25% cost-sharing requirement by which PVOs had to contribute financially or in-kind to a project.[53] Second, there are now over 500 registered PVOs with USAID. The Faith-Based and Communities Initiatives (FBCI) office at USAID considered the registration process an impediment to new agencies applying for federal funds. The FBCI also correctly understood that some PVOs were using the registration process as a "seal of good housekeeping" even though USAID relied on self-reporting to register agencies. The PVOs themselves were divided on the issue. Natsios refused to eliminate the registration process, but Congress in 2005 made two significant changes to the process, the main one being the elimination of the 20% "privateness" requirement.[54]

It is the case that USAID, exploiting economies of scale, gave large amounts of foreign aid to the larger PVOs, such as Catholic Relief Services, CARE, and World Vision. In the case of contracts, PVOs would receive extensions to their initial awards without going through a competitive process. For example, Child Survival and Health Care Programs were a set-aside for PVOs, as is part of P.L. 480.

The trend away from working with larger, established PVOs was part of the rationale for the "faith-based initiative," on which George W. Bush campaigned for president. Bush established the first of these offices at the White House and five cabinet departments (Housing and Urban Development, Health and Human Services, Education, Labor, and Justice) by executive order immediately after taking office in 2001. On December 12, 2002, he issued Executive Order 13280, which created additional Centers for Faith-Based and Community Initiatives in two additional agencies, USAID and the Department of Agriculture.[55]

According to Terri Hasdorff, director of the FBCI office at USAID, this measure was, at its core, about doing capacity building for small- and medium-size PVOs.[56] Table 7.3 shows that the share of evangelical revenue in revenue of all PVOs went from 6% in 1980 to 12% in 1989, 14% in 1996, 17% in 2002, and 19% in 2005. Comparable shares in revenue of all religious PVOs were 9% in 1980, 25% in 1989, 32% in 1996, and 40% in 2002 and 2005. Evangelicals receive a significant portion of their revenue from private sources, not the federal government. Shares of evangelical PVOs in federal revenues were much lower. The share in federal revenues for all evangelical PVOs (table 7.3) was 2% in 1980, 5% in 1989, 4% in 1996, 3% in 2002, and 4% in 2005. The share of evangelicals in federal

Table 7.3. Evangelical PVOs' total and federal real revenue, 1980–2005.

Year	Real revenue (1)	Real federal revenue (2)	Share in PVO revenue (3)	Share in PVO federal revenue (4)	Share in religious PVO revenue (5)	Share in religious PVO federal revenue (6)
1980	185	33.2	0.057	0.025	0.087	0.042
1981	237	38.2	0.072	0.027	0.116	0.055
1983	213	36.1	0.069	0.028	0.120	0.065
1984	278	39.7	0.085	0.033	0.144	0.065
1985	342	73.2	0.091	0.051	0.151	0.093
1986	576	89.1	0.124	0.052	0.234	0.113
1987	633	85.2	0.146	0.065	0.291	0.173
1988	571	70.2	0.120	0.046	0.249	0.115
1989	585	69.1	0.118	0.046	0.254	0.127
1990	668	60.3	0.134	0.041	0.273	0.104
1991	704	62.0	0.121	0.040	0.241	0.131
1992	743	122	0.128	0.066	0.300	0.183
1993	747	93.7	0.128	0.049	0.312	0.159
1994	890	110	0.142	0.051	0.349	0.172
1995	724	112	0.119	0.055	0.307	0.230
1996	881	81.0	0.136	0.043	0.319	0.150
1997	1,080	93.4	0.160	0.051	0.384	0.246
1998	1,060	88.6	0.141	0.046	0.318	0.193
1999	1,270	97.4	0.150	0.045	0.338	0.210
2000	1,570	90.8	0.176	0.037	0.400	0.140
2001	1,470	78.8	0.156	0.033	0.386	0.138
2002	1,650	80.0	0.171	0.032	0.404	0.180
2003	1,770	70.9	0.161	0.024	0.357	0.092
2004	2,730	145	0.208	0.043	0.428	0.146
2005	2,970	123	0.187	0.041	0.405	0.163

Source: McCleary Private Voluntary Organizations Data Set.
Note: First column has total real revenue in millions of 2005 dollars for evangelical PVOs, second column has the federal part of this revenue, third column shows the share of evangelical PVO revenue in revenue for all PVOs, fourth column shows the share of evangelical PVO federal revenue in federal revenue for all PVOs, fifth column shows the share of evangelical PVO revenue in revenue for all religious PVOs, sixth column shows the share of evangelical PVO federal revenue in federal revenue for all religious PVOs.

revenues among all religious PVOs was 4% in 1980, 13% in 1989, 15% in 1996, 18% in 2002, and 16% in 2005. Thus, the aim of the Faith-Based Initiative to draw in smaller religious agencies succeeded when it came to evangelical PVOs.

Table 4.3 in chapter 4 shows which evangelical PVOs were in the top 20 lists in selected years. The shift over the years has been from tradi- tional, denominational evangelical PVOs to the evangelical parachurch agencies such as Feed the Children, MAP International, and Samaritan's Purse. The data in tables 7.3 and 4.3 show that the Bush administration succeeded in attracting evangelical agencies to the federal government. Table 1.7 (chapter 1) shows three parachurch evangelical agencies in the top ten in 2005, whereas in 1990 there were none. The attempt on the part of the Bush administration to "level the playing field" has been succeed- ing to some extent.[57]

The Global Development Alliance took some of the impetus away from the larger PVOs that have historically dominated federally funded international relief and development projects. The Global Development Alliance consists of cooperative agreements (an amalgam of a grant and a contract) with private sector enterprises. The Global Development Alliance agreements are collaborations between the U.S. government and private- sector entities to implement, design, and fund development projects.[58] Yet, even with USAID's new focus on public-private cooperation, the agency and Congress have failed to address the fundamental issue of PVOs con- tinuing to be involved in earmarks. In this sense, PVOs behave as an inter- est group, working with congressional staff to ensure continued funding for PVO activities.

Conflict-of-interest questions have been raised about PVOs that accept federal funds and then advocate in Congress for earmarks. Is the advo- cacy work being funded by federal dollars? How do PVOs separate out their functions as relief and development agencies on the one hand versus acting as an interest group on the other? In essence, the criticism leveled against PVOs that engage in public policy advocacy is that they are using federal dollars earmarked for some other purpose for advocacy activity for more federal funding.

Transformational Development

Following the publication of the 2002 National Security Strategy, which emphasized the importance of international development to national secu- rity, USAID published *Foreign Aid in the National Interest*.[59] This document, written mostly by development scholars and academics outside USAID, summarized five decades of development work and the challenges and opportunities for U.S. foreign assistance in the 21st century. In the section about PVOs, it states that, "In 2000 the top 20 USAID-registered PVOs received an average of $43 million in grants and contracts—for a total of about $854 million, or two-thirds of PVO funding by USAID. Within this group, some older PVOs—CARE, Catholic Relief Services, World Vision, and Save the Children—receive significant private contributions (for both domestic and international efforts), ranging from $60 million to almost $380 million. Others also meet the requirement that 20 percent of overseas expenses come from private sources. But more than 30 percent meet it only through exemptions."[60]

The document also says that, in the new century, among the challenges for PVOs would be increasing volunteerism and private contributions to their overseas programs. It also states: "The main challenge for PVOs today is to develop sustainable counterpart institutions that can eventually assume their tasks.... U.S. PVOs must view their role as a bridge toward development, not a permanent fixture."[61]

Building off this document, USAID (2004a) published a White Paper in 2004, *U.S. Foreign Aid: Meeting the Challenges of the Twenty-first Century*. This White Paper articulated, among other things, that foreign aid had other goals besides development, including strengthening fragile states. At the ACVFA public meeting in February 2004, officials from USAID discussed the White Paper with representatives of the PVO community. Barbara Turner, acting assistant administrator at the Bureau for Policy and Program Coordination (USAID), explained that the intent of the White Paper was to have an impact on legislation and the budget process. "Ms. Turner stated that USAID is not abandoning any sectors; it has the right set of tools on the ground. However, it isn't organized as effectively as it could be. There is a need to reorient analytical capabilities, skills, budgets, and reporting."[62]

In January 2006, the *Policy Framework for Bilateral Foreign Aid*[63] was published, bringing together the preceding five years of research into a single document and signaling a change in strategic direction for the agency. This change in direction sought to align USAID with the national security and foreign policy objectives of the administration.[64] "USAID will align budgetary resources according to which of the five goals these resources primarily support and will manage those resources accordingly."[65] In terms of strategy and direction, programs were now to be aligned according to these five goals. This process would include grants and contracts to PVOs and for-profit entities.

Foreign Assistance Reform

At the same time that this new strategic direction for USAID was being codified, a major reform in foreign assistance was announced at the State Department level in January 2006. The move created a new position, the director of foreign assistance (DFA), which was to be held concurrently by the USAID administrator. The new administrator, Randall Tobias, moved his office from USAID headquarters to the State Department and created a new bureau, signified by the single letter "F"—and thus the reform process came to be known as the F-process. Tobias also brought with him to the State Department's USAID's Bureau for Policy Planning and Coordination, "the part of USAID that set goals, policies, and overall budget levels and that saw to their implementation."[66] These changes took place under existing authorities, and Congress was not involved in the process. No legislation or new authority was requested.[67]

"The initial implementation of the 'F process,' which was done hurriedly and could have been better thought through, reinforced the perception that it was a State Department grab for expenditures from foreign assistance coffers at the expense of USAID and State geographical bureaus running individual programs."[68] Meanwhile, the administration maintained that the intent was merely to coordinate international assistance and diplomacy efforts. However, the changes were roundly criticized for the lack of transparency and stakeholder input, as well as for concentrating decision-making authority in the hands of a select few in Washington at the expense of field-level input. Strategic plans were now worked out by country teams and approved by the DFA and the secretary of state.

The reaction of the PVO community to the F-process was largely negative. According to John Ruthrauff of InterAction, they saw it as a takeover of USAID by the State Department, they were not consulted in the process, and they felt it was a cookie-cutter approach to development.[69] Rich Stearns, CEO of World Vision, articulated this sentiment strongly: "Perhaps because of the abbreviated timeframe, so far ACVFA has served the function of reporting to the PVO community what is already underway rather than allowing for real consultation. The process has proceeded without meaningful input from PVOs, communities around the world, or even Congress. Whether or not these reforms survive into the tenure of the next President may depend on how consultative and bipartisan the process is now."[70]

A report issued in November 2007 by the Republican staff of the Senate Foreign Relations Committee detailed numerous problems with the F-process from the perspective of embassies and field staff: "[A]s the process was accelerated to meet budget deadlines, there never developed a sense of common purpose. Pitched battles ensued on just about every-thing. The rushed and muddled start, including the uncertainty due to congressional appropriations delays and the need for a continuing reso-lution, and the abrupt departure in April 2007 of the first Director, has added to the impression that the effort may be doomed, no matter how much sense it may make from a strategic point of view."[71]

The report details complaints from embassy and USAID staff that the F-process created communication problems, unnecessary layers of bureau-cracy, and centralized decision making with little input from the field. Hence, despite paying lip service to the importance of field-level decision making and a decentralized foreign assistance mechanism in its first few years, the Bush administration had now attempted to again centralize USAID mecha-nisms in Washington and, more specifically, at the State Department.

It is important to note that the F-Process, while purporting to streamline "foreign assistance" in general, in reality affects only those programs housed at the State Department and USAID. "The new director of foreign assistance lacks formal, statutory authority even over the Offices of the Coordinator for Reconstruction and Stabilization and the Global AIDS Coordinator within the State Department—let alone over the assistance programs administered by the Departments of Defense or Agriculture, for instance, or the myriad of other U.S. foreign assistance activities housed in other agencies."[72]

One report puts the percentage of the U.S. foreign aid budget managed by the State Department and USAID at around 55%, with the Department of Defense and other independent agencies (which fall outside the author-ity of the DFA) managing the rest.[73] This dispersing pattern is due largely to the creation of new entities by the Bush administration that fund foreign assistance outside traditional mechanisms within USAID.

The proliferation of programs and new foreign aid mechanisms, such as PEPFAR and MCC that fall outside USAID, have caused traditional aid programs to suffer funding shortfalls. A November 2003 policy paper from InterAction noted that, with the launch of new programs, "Over $350 million was cut from other accounts to fund these new initiatives and new approaches to development."[74] A 2006 report to the Committee on Foreign Relations found similar programs declining at the field level based on interviews with staff in Honduras, Mongolia, and Mozambique.[75] However, in our data set, real federal revenue of PVOs rose from $1.85 bil-lion in 1997 to $3.38 billion in 2004, followed by a decline to $3.00 billion in 2005. Overall, there may have been changes in composition since the late 1990s but nothing that looks like cutting of federal support overall.

Sam Worthington, CEO of InterAction, testified before Congress in June 2007 on the dwindling operating expense account at USAID.

"Operating expense constraints, among other things, have resulted in the hyper-centralization of USAID planning and program design, and in the months since Secretary Rice's announcement of Transformational Diplomacy in January 2006, that hyper-centralization has even manifested itself in the suggestion that some missions should close in certain 'non-strategic' countries around the globe."[76]

Worthington said in his testimony before the committee that InterAction members with substantial USAID grant portfolios had noted a significant slowdown in the availability of new USAID grant proposals in 2007 compared to 2006. He also said that members reported a longer time lapse in which USAID was notifying awardees.

Table 7.4 shows that grants rose from about 50% of federal revenue to about 80% from 1990 to 2005 (data for 2006 and 2007 have not been released by USAID); P.L. 480 food fell from 24% to 6%. Freight fell from

Table 7.4. Composition of PVO federal revenue, 1990–2005 (shares of P.L. 480 food, freight, grants, and contracts).

Year	P.L. 480 food	Freight	Grants	Contracts
1990	0.24	0.09	0.54	0.14
1991	0.21	0.10	0.50	0.19
1992	0.21	0.10	0.55	0.14
1993	0.16	0.09	0.61	0.14
1994	0.15	0.07	0.59	0.19
1995	0.15	0.09	0.62	0.17
1996	0.10	0.04	0.68	0.18
1997	0.10	0.05	0.65	0.19
1998	0.10	0.05	0.70	0.16
1999	0.11	0.06	0.70	0.16
2000	0.08	0.08	0.70	0.13
2001	0.08	0.05	0.74	0.13
2002	0.06	0.04	0.78	0.13
2003	0.09	0.06	0.74	0.10
2004	0.10	0.06	0.76	0.07
2005	0.06	0.05	0.80	0.09

Source: McCleary Private Voluntary Organizations Data Set.
Note: Excess property is zero throughout this period. Each cell shows the share of the indicated component in the total federal revenue received by registered PVOs.

9%–10% to 5%. Contracts first rose from 14% to 19%, then fell to 9%. If there was a slowdown in grants, as Worthington suggests, then it occurred after 2005.

Food Aid

While funding sources in the PVC office and the overall Development Assistance budget seem to be dwindling, the PVOs also face a threat to another trusted source of income: P.L. 480, Title II. Established in 1954, at the time intended primarily as a means of dealing with domestic agricultural surplus, P.L. 480 has evolved over the years. The PVOs became major players in the 1990s, as donors increasingly relied on nongovernmental actors for the distribution of food. Title II of P.L. 480, which is managed by USAID, has come to represent 74% of the total of in-kind food aid allocations, most in the form of emergency assistance.[77]

Also in the 1990s, the PVOs were successful in pushing for increases in the amount of food they were allowed to sell for cash in recipient countries, a process known as *monetization*. In this way, food became another stream of revenue, albeit a vastly inefficient one, by which PVOs funded their programs—both those related to food insecurity and others. According to a GAO report, "between 2001 and 2006, NGOs received 94% of non-emergency Title II resources."[78]

While food aid in general and monetization in particular have come under increasing criticism for lack of efficiency and potential harmful effects on local markets, they are protected by the "iron triangle" of domestic food producers, maritime interests, and the PVO community.[79] Many PVOs acknowledge the flaws of the P.L. 480 system but fear that if it was removed as a source of funding it would not be replaced with anything else. Overall, the P.L. 480 budget for nonemergencies under Bush declined in nominal dollars from $1.2 billion in 2001 to the 2006 value of $698 million.[80]

Food assistance was on the radar screen of the Bush administration very early. The President's Management Agenda in 2002 chose P.L. 480 as one of nine agency-specific programs that it targeted for reform.[81] Specifically, the document highlighted monetization as economically inefficient. It appears that Bush tried repeatedly to cut the practice of monetization, most recently proposing that up to 25% of emergency food aid funds be used to purchase food locally in crisis situations. Congress, lobbied by subgroups with vested interests in preserving the status quo, killed the proposal when the president raised it as a part of Farm Bill reauthorizations.[82] And, while U.S. agribusiness and shipping interests have joined PVOs in lobbying to oppose Bush's proposed changes in P.L. 480, there are signs that the bigger PVOs, most notably CARE and Catholic Relief Services, have come around to the president's way of thinking on the issue of monetization.[83] In 2007, CARE decided to no longer distribute P.L. 480 food commodities, shifting its policy toward fostering local markets.[84]

In the most recent flare-up over the 2008 Farm Bill, the administration battled Congress for more flexibility and control over how P.L. 480 money is spent. Along with the ability to purchase up to 25% of food locally, the administration wanted the ability to use funds as needed for emergency situations. Congress wanted to set aside a specified fraction of the P.L. 480 budget for use only in nonemergency, long-term development situations. The House and Senate versions of the bill varied on the amounts to be set aside, but Jerry Moran (Republican-Kansas), who added the House provision, said he did so on behalf of several international aid organizations that "repeatedly have seen money for their long-term development programs taken away for emergency aid."[85] This case is a prime example of PVOs not getting what they want from the Bush administration and then going straight to Congress with their concerns.

The Catholic Relief Services press release on the matter reads in part: "Catholic Relief Services and more than a dozen other humanitarian agencies support the safebox as a way to protect vitally important food-aid programs that increase food security over the long term. Such initiatives enable extremely poor and chronically hungry people to feed themselves and break out of the cycle of poverty and hunger."[86] Note that, along with CARE, Catholic Relief Services was dominant historically in P.L. 480 (see table 6.1 in chapter 6).

The Future of Foreign Aid

The U.S. foreign policy objectives determine to some degree the type of funding instruments used to disburse federal assistance. For example, there has been a continued upward trend in the use of grants (see table 7.4). The reason for these changes varied over the decades. In the 1970s, when grants were introduced, the rationale for relying heavily on grants was to permit domestic PVOs to export their activities and duplicate overseas what they did well in the United States. From the perspective of PVOs, grants were the best funding mechanism because they gave agencies freedom to operate their projects with minimal government interference.

From the perspective of the federal government, grants were the most efficacious funding mechanism because they required minimal staff oversight. But, more important, grants allowed the federal government to extend its presence into geographic areas of the world where there was no official U.S. presence. The PVOs were viewed, via the grants, as agents of the U.S. government. In the 1980s, this situation began to change. As the federal government sought to gain more control over the types of activities of the PVOs and Congress demanded stricter financial accountability, contracts were increasingly used, and cooperative grants were introduced.

Historically, Congress values the work of PVOs. And, PVOs have been successful in garnering support among members of Congress. By contrast, the role of the executive is to implement the president's foreign policy and ensure that PVOs are subsumed under it. The tension between U.S. foreign policy objectives and humanitarian assistance (in the form of relief and development) is continually at play. Many administrations have sought to make it clear that foreign assistance is an instrument of U.S. foreign policy.

Once a type of federal funding is instituted, such as P.L. 480 and ocean freight, it is very difficult to terminate. Furthermore, as PVOs work in different settings, rather than advocating the end of federal funds, they seek to alter the ways in which they can use the funds. The debate within the PVO community over the type of aid they are engaging in turns on viewing the distribution of food and other commodities as creating a mutual dependency between the PVO and the U.S. federal government. To create self-sufficiency, some agencies will not distribute food and other types of commodities. This interplay goes to the heart of the issue of what kind of foreign aid in which the PVOs should be engaged. And, should the federal government, through its P.L. 480 program, be promoting this type of aid as a form of development?

The field of international relief and development has become increasingly diverse, with PVOs representing a variety of religions as well as engaging in a wide range of activities. Federal real revenue to PVOs has consistently increased since 1992. However, as a share of PVO total federal revenue has been declining since 1963–64. Within the universe of PVOs registered with USAID, there is little circulation among the top ten agencies by revenue (table 1.7). This perspective predicates that larger agencies are better at garnering federal funds than smaller agencies. Economies of scale make it easier for larger PVOs to carry out certain projects. This is in part explained by their staff size and satellite offices in Washington, D.C., allowing larger PVOs more contact with members of Congress and USAID bureaucracy.

The federal government tends to favor agencies that already have experience performing projects. As a result, new agencies and particularly small PVOs are discriminated against through the registration process and by the nature of the requirements. I found that the real revenue of smaller PVOs tended to grow faster over time as long as the organization survived. However, smaller PVOs were also more likely drop out, sometimes through mergers but more often by going out of business or not registering with the government for other reasons. The executive and Congress have contributed in significant ways to the formation of a "closed club" or cartel of large PVOs over the decades.

The PVOs that rely on the federal government for financial assistance develop a dependency on a regular and permanent income. Agencies with on average over 50% of their annual income from the federal government—Catholic Relief Services and CARE—tend to follow the U.S. government's foreign policy direction. In contrast, PVOs that remain financially independent can serve as pressure groups, seeking to shape U.S. foreign policy focus. Among religious PVOs, Catholic Relief Services has maintained an average federal funding share of 60% from 1995 to 2005. Evangelical PVOs take a small percentage of federal dollars, 18% from 1968 to 2005. Faith-founded agencies are growing in presence. By 2005, the number of religious PVOs was only 33% of registered agencies. Yet, in terms of total revenue, that of the average religious PVO was larger than that of the typical secular PVO. The federal share for religious PVOs since 1967 has remained smaller (and become much smaller over time) than that for secular PVOs. From 1986 to 1995, federal shares averaged 38% for secular and 24% for religious, and from 1996 to 2005, the shares averaged 35% for secular and 14% for religious. This means that secular PVOs are becoming more dependent on federal revenue than religious agencies.

Those PVOs that depend solely on voluntary contributions must continually address the development needs of their constituencies overseas to continue to garner private funds to operate. I found support for the idea that federal and international organization funds serve as a magnet or certifying device that leads subsequently to higher growth of private real revenue. Those agencies that are able to capitalize on federal funds they have received to garner private funding are more successful. Federal funds and the financial stability they provide to PVOs transform PVOs into interest groups that seek to ensure continued federal funds by lobbying Congress. Rather than accepting the termination of sources of federal funding, PVOs lobby Congress to retain them.

The relationship between PVOs and the U.S. government is in need of reassessment. Historically, U.S. foreign policy objectives have sought to direct PVO activity. Given the lack of program evaluation data over time, assessing the success of PVO activities and how well they meet U.S. foreign policy objectives is not possible to measure. What is clear from the data findings presented here is that only a small number of PVOs benefit over time from receiving federal funds. The data also show that the federal government initiated change in the field of international relief and development by introducing new funding mechanisms. To the degree that PVOs are "private" and voluntary, their purpose is to serve their constituencies. Who the constituencies of PVOs are is a valid question. Is their constituency their donors? The people and communities they serve internationally? To the degree that PVOs accept federal funds, they are implementers of U.S. foreign policy and take direction from the U.S. government. The tension between these two roles will continue as long as PVOs are recipients of federal funds.

Glossary

Basic needs approach. The "basic needs" approach emphasizes provision for minimum needs of the population and essential health, transportation, and educational services. This approach was advocated by development experts in the 1970s.

Biden-Pell Amendment. In 1981, Congress passed the Biden-Pell Amendment to allocate grants to support public education on international development issues, for example, hunger. The amendment was named after the sponsoring senators, Joseph Biden (Democrat-Delaware) and Claiborne Pell (Democrat-Rhode Island). The U.S. Agency for International Development (USAID) allocated funds to its grant program for development education, and private voluntary organizations (PVOs) were required to match government funding with money from their own budgets, thus stimulating a substantial increase in spending on such activities. By 1993, the program had provided assistance to a wide range of U.S. nonprofit organizations, a total of 88 having received Biden-Pell grants.

Child Survival Grant Program. Begun in 1985 by congressional mandate, the program funds community-based programs implemented by PVOs and their local partners. The goal is to implement projects that improve infant and child health and nutrition, contributing to the reduction of infant and child mortality. The PVOs are encouraged to increase and transfer technical and operational aspects of projects to local partners.

Commodity Credit Corporation (CCC). This entity is located within the U.S. Department of Agriculture. The function of the CCC is to manage export credits, surplus stocks, and the acquisition of commodities as designated by P.L. 480 and section 416(b). Section 416(b) of the Agricultural Act of 1949 stipulates that the Department of Agriculture can procure food commodities for through the CCC for donations overseas.

Comprehensive Program Grants (CPGs). The PVOs receiving funding from the federal government through several grants could receive a CPG to consolidate the administrative work and introduce flexibility into program implementation. By the early 1980s, the only type of CPG being awarded by USAID was the Matching Grant (see Matching Grant program entry).

Consortia grant. This grant was awarded to several PVOs that joined together to carry out specific projects. This grant was not a separate category of PVO grant.

Contracts. Provides defined project parameters, and USAID has greater control over performance and remedies for nonperformance. A contract is usually awarded competitively to provide goods and services meeting USAID specifications. Substantial USAID staff involvement and technical direction comes with a contract. As noted in a General Accounting Office Report (2002), under the rubric of contracts, grants, and cooperative agreements are variations thereof to facilitate federal government-PVO funding relations. The USAID missions and bureaus have the flexibility and autonomy (depending on the circumstances) to select and design the proper funding mechanism for the PVO and the proposed project. (See also specific contract entries in this glossary.)

Cooperative agreement. This type of grant is an amalgam of a contract and a grant, with involvement of USAID staff in the formulation and operation of the grant.

Cooperative Development Program. Initiated in 1961 with the Humphrey Amendment to the Foreign Assistance Act of 1961, U.S. cooperative organizations are funded to promote cooperative systems overseas. Cooperatives specialize in various activities, such as credit, agribusiness, technology transfer, housing, microenterprise, small business development, financing and marketing, rural telephone and electrical services, and insurance.

Cost-sharing. A PVO contributes financially or in-kind to the overall costs of a project awarded to the organization by USAID.

Development Education Program or the Biden-Pell Program. This program began in 1980 under section 316 to the International Security and Development Cooperation Act. These grants fund programs in the United States promoting public education on hunger and poverty. The program supports PVO activities that educate the U.S. public about U.S. humanitarian and relief activities overseas. The goal is to demonstrate the relationship between U.S. domestic activities and international issues on hunger and poverty. The annual budget cannot exceed $750,000, and approximately between five and ten grants are awarded annually.

Development Program Grant (DPG). Implemented by USAID in the 1970s, DPGs provided institutional support to an agency for three years. They were awarded on a first-come, first-served basis at the initiative of PVOs. Small and large PVOs received DPGs to build up their organizational capacity to engage in development projects.

Economic Cooperation Administration. The U.S. government agency that administered the European Recovery Program, more popularly known as the Marshall Plan, after World War II.

Economic Support Funds. Economic Support Funds are a form of bilateral assistance to promote economic and political stability in strategically important regions where the United States has special security interests. The funds are provided on a grant basis and are available for a variety of economic purposes, like infrastructure and development projects. Although not intended for military expenditure, these grants allow the recipient government to free up its own money for military programs.

Excess government property. Items of equipment, new or used, owned by the federal government and no longer needed, but not declared surplus.

Farmer-to-Farmer program. Initially authorized by Congress in the 1985 Agricultural Bill, this program provides technical assistance to farmers overseas. Volunteers with specialization are assigned overseas to assist farmers and agricultural education institutions with the goal of increasing the production, processing, and marketing of food.

Gifts-in-kind programs or donations. In-kind donations can be items such as clothing, household items, children's books, nonperishable food, and other nonmonetary items. The Internal Revenue Service regulates deductions for gifts-in-kind donations.

Grants. Types of this funding mechanism were at one time reserved for PVOs registered with USAID. Over the course of the decades, the requirements for grants and the nature of grants have changed, with many of the reserved funding mechanisms for PVOs eliminated. (See also specific grant entries in this glossary.)

Grants management contract. A contract with an organization to award and manage grants to other PVO organizations.

Indefinite Quantity Contract (IQC). Introduced in 1994, an IQC bundles together the performance of an unlimited number of services that can be widely disparate or similar. The IQC is a term contract that is usually fulfilled by several subcontractors.

Institution-building grant. This type of grant for institutional development and management later became folded into contracts and cooperative agreements (both open to competition). The institution-building grant was reserved for PVOs. Among the types of activities funded by this grant were training workshops and courses developed by USAID for its staff and in which PVO staff could participate.

Institutional support grant. This grant was once reserved only for registered PVOs. By the early1980s it was open to competition regardless of registration status. Although technically not a separate grant category, this grant provided funds for institutional development and management.

Lend-Lease Act. Enacted into law in 1941, this legislation gave the president the power to sell, transfer, exchange, and lend equipment to any country to help it defend itself against the Axis powers. From 1941 to 1945, the federal government channeled $36 billion through the Lend-Lease program.

Matching Grant program. Initiated in 1978, the matching grant program was the primary funding mechanism for assisting U.S.-based PVOs in implementing their community-based programs overseas. Matched dollar for dollar by the PVO's own resources, these grants supported programs that were in-line with USAID mission country development priorities and geographical interests. To apply, PVOs had to demonstrate a proven track record (a minimum of three years). The grants had specific foci: Capacity-Building through Economic Growth, Population and Health, Environment, Democracy and Governance, Human Capacity Development, HIV/AIDS, Conflict Prevention/Resolution, Disaster Relief and Post Disaster Management, Information Technology. These grants were eventually phased out by USAID by 2003.

Millennium Challenge Corporation (MCC). The MCC oversees the Millennium Challenge Account (MCA), which provides economic assistance, through a competitive selection process, to developing nations that pursue political and economic reforms in rule of law, grassroots development and human capital, and fostering of civil liberties.

Multiple-award contract. This contract is for a "bundle" of services, wide-ranging in nature. Usually to fulfill the terms of the contract, multiple contractors bid on the contract.

Mutual Security Act. The Mutual Security Act (1951) created a new, independent agency, the Mutual Security Administration, to supervise all foreign aid programs, including military assistance and economic programs that bolstered the defense capability of U.S. allies. It was amended in 1954 to allow PVOs to qualify for excess government property disbursements. Renewed each year until 1961, when the Foreign Assistance Act of 1961 was enacted, the Mutual Security Act produced annual struggles over the size of the foreign aid budget and the balance between military and economic aid.

National War Fund (NWF).   Started in 1943 and dissolved in 1946, the NWF was composed of 22 war-related agencies during World War II. The NWF raised funds from the American public to support the United Service Organizations (USO) and USO-Camp Shows and to provide care, rehabilitation, food, and shelter to civilian allies of the United States, war victims, and refugees. The PVO umbrella organizations were also recipients of the NWF.

Neutrality Act of 1939.   Passed by Congress on November 4, 1939, this legislation regulated the solicitation and collection of contributions for relief in belligerent countries during World War II. The belligerent countries were France, Germany, Poland, and the United Kingdom (including Australia, Canada, India, New Zealand, Union of South Africa). By November 15, 1941, the list included Norway, Belgium, Luxembourg, Netherlands, Italy, Greece, Yugoslavia, Hungary, and Bulgaria.

Ocean freight reimbursement.   This subsidy began during World War II for shipment of donations and foodstuff. A separate program for P.L. 480 commodities was instituted with the passage of that law in 1954.

Ocean freight reimbursement: worldwide program.   This is the oldest ongoing PVO support program. It was created with the Foreign Assistance Act of 1961 and continues to function, subsidizing transportation costs of humanitarian supplies and equipment for registered PVOs. The funding is in the form of a set-aside grant for PVOs.

Operational Program Grant (OPG).   These grants were intended to allow a PVO to operate specific projects in an individual country and sometimes at a regional level. Regional bureaus and field missions had responsibility for funding these grants. The PVOs awarded an OPG had to match 25% of the funding. Mission-funded OPGs generally were related to the mission's field priorities.

Potsdam Agreement of 1945.   A conference was held in Potsdam, Germany, from July 17 to August 2, 1945, between representatives of the United States, the United Kingdom, and the former Soviet Union. These countries established the political and economic principles governing the treatment of Germany in the initial period of Allied control at the end of World War II and sent an ultimatum to Japan demanding unconditional surrender on pain of utter destruction.

President's Emergency Plan for AIDS Relief (PEPFAR). The PEPFAR, established by President George W. Bush, is the largest commitment ever by any nation for an international health initiative dedicated to a single disease—a five-year, $15 billion, multifaceted approach to combating AIDS around the world. The United States now leads the world in its level of support for the fight against HIV/AIDS. On May 27, 2003, President Bush signed P.L. 108–25, the U.S. Leadership Against Global HIV/AIDS, Tuberculosis, and Malaria Act of 2003, the legislative authorization for PEPFAR.

Private voluntary organization. The term *private voluntary organization* or *PVO* refers to a nonprofit (tax-exempt status) organization that provides charitable social services, such as humanitarian assistance. The term was coined in the early 1970s by John Yulinski, director of the Private and Voluntary Agencies Office of USAID. Probably because of this origin, the term is usually applied to nonprofit organizations engaged in international relief and development. For example, USAID describes PVOs as being U.S.-based nongovernmental, private, and voluntary organizations that conduct or will be conducting activities overseas. In its reporting, USAID treats universities as a separate form of nonprofit organization. InterAction, the largest association of U.S.-based international relief and development organizations, also used the term until around 2006, when it began using NGO (nongovernmental organization). InterAction's membership, which overlaps to a large extent with USAID's PVO registry, includes more than 160 PVOs. Although NGO and INGO (international NGO) are now widely used, I prefer the term PVO to NGO as NGO can be construed to include for-profit companies. When referring to non-U.S.-based PVOs, I use the term *indigenous PVO* or *local PVO*.

Program support. Technical, logistical, and administrative assistance is provided to the grants program for PVOs.

Public Law 480 (P.L. 480). This law was originally legislated in 1954 as the Agricultural Trade and Development Assistance Act. It created the main food assistance program of the U.S. government and PVOs. This program was renamed Food for Peace, and a specific bureau within USAID was created to manage and oversee emergency and project food shipments. The United States supports three food aid programs under P.L. 480. They are Title I, which provides concessional loans to developing countries to buy U.S. agricultural products; Title II, which transfers food supplies to countries in need through PVOs; and Title III, which provides assistance to help improve the recipient nation's food production and distribution systems.

Tranformational diplomacy or **transformational development.** The terms *transformational diplomacy* and *transformational development* are used interchangeably. Transformational development is defined processes that "transform countries, through far-reaching, fundamental changes in institutions of governance, human capacity, and economic structure that enable a country to sustain further economic and social progress without depending on foreign aid." USAID 2004a, 14.

Volagency. Small, specialized PVO that was established with USAID funding starting in the 1960s.

Notes

Chapter 1

1. The term *private voluntary organization* refers to a nonprofit (tax-exempt status) organization that provides charitable social services, such as humanitarian assistance. The term was coined in the early 1970s by John Ulinski, director of the Private and Voluntary Cooperative Office (PVC) of USAID. Probably because of this origin, the term *private voluntary organization* is usually applied to nonprofit organizations engaged in international relief and development. For example, USAID describes PVOs as "voluntary agencies engaged in overseas relief and development." See USAID, "Conditions of Registration," n.d. In its reporting, USAID treats universities as a separate form of nonprofit organization. InterAction, the largest association of U.S.-based international relief and development organizations, also used the term up until around 2006, when it began using NGO (nongovernmental organization). InterAction's membership, which overlaps to a large extent with USAID's PVO registry, includes more than 160 PVOs. Although NGO and INGO (international NGO) are now widely used, I prefer the term PVO to NGO as NGO can be construed to include for-profit companies. When referring to non–U.S.-based PVOs, I use the term *indigenous PVO* or *local PVO*.

2. Bush 2002, 21–23.

3. The terms *transformational diplomacy* and *transformational development* are used interchangeably. Transformational development is defined as a process "to achieve far-reaching, fundamental changes in institutional capacity, human capacity, and economic structure so that further economic and social progress can be sustained without dependence on foreign aid." USAID 2004a, 17.

4. The new director of foreign assistance would assume responsibility for foreign aid programs currently under the direction of the secretary of state as well as USAID programs. Those programs beyond the State Department and USAID's oversight, such as the Millennium Challenge Corporation, the Peace Corps, and the Trade and Development Agency, and certain activities of the Department of Treasury would not be brought under the director of foreign assistance. For a discussion of the responsibilities and authority of the director of foreign assistance, see Congressional Research Service 2007a.

5. Krasner 2006.

6. U.S. HELP Commission 2007. Congress established the HELP Commission in January 2004 by P.L. 108-199, sec. 637 (a). The mandate of the commission was to study U.S. development and humanitarian assistance programs and to propose bold reform recommendations for relevant structures, mechanisms, and incentives.

7. See Birdsall, Patrick, and Vaishnav 2006; Brainard 2007; and Wye River Consensus Group 2008.

8. The key committees are the Senate Finance Committee and the House Oversight and Government Reform Committee. The law referred to is the Revenue Ruling 64–182.

9. Schafer 2006.

10. See Berríos 2000, 48, table 3.2. For a list of the top five contractors from 1996 to 2005, see U.S. Commission 2007, appendix 2.

11. See U.S. General Accounting Office 2002, 27, table 2.

12. See U.S. Commission 2007, 133. For a list of the top for-profit USAID contractors, see U.S. General Accounting Office 2002, 27, table 3. There are other categories of nonprofit organizations receiving USAID funds, such as educational institutions, cooperatives, and medical facilities.

13. See USAID 2006a, 20–21.

14. McCleary and Barro 2008.

15. PVO real revenue (2005 dollars) from federal sources fluctuated over the decades. For example, PVO real revenue (2005 dollars) peaked at $1.55 billion in 1964, fell to $960 million in 1972, rose to $1.71 billion in 1986, fell to $1.45 billion in 1990, was fairly flat through 1998, then rose to $3.38 billion in 2004 and $3.00 billion in 2005. The share of PVO revenue coming from federal sources peaked in 1962–64 at around 60%, fell to 28% in 1973, rose to 43% in 1981, fell to 26% in 1991, rose to 35% in 1994, then fell to 26% in 2004 and 19% in 2005. The last number, 19%, is the lowest since 1952. Although PVO real revenue from federal sources has gone up every year since 1992, the federal share of PVO revenue has been declining since 1981. Because of the longitudinal nature of the data set, I was able to trace the reliance on federal funds over time and show how PVOs respond to changes in the extent of this reliance.

16. USAID has 38 PVO sector activity classifications; see USAID, n.d., *Private Voluntary Organizations, U.S. PVO Registry.*

17. These revenue numbers are less than total revenue because they are multiplied by the fraction of total program outlay going to foreign destinations (to approximate the internationally oriented parts of PVO activities).

18. For mainline Protestant denominations, see Lindner 2002. For Christian ecumenical movements, see McFarland 1924.

19. Steensland et al. 2000.

20. We follow Mark Shibley and Nancy Ammerman on this classification. See Shibley 1996; Ammerman 2005.

21. The GSS, begun in 1972, "is the largest project funded by the Sociology Program of the National Science Foundation. Except for the U.S. Census, the GSS is

the most frequently analyzed source of information in the social sciences. The GSS contains a standard 'core' of demographic and attitudinal questions, plus topics of special interest. Many of the core questions have remained unchanged since 1972 to facilitate time trend studies as well as replication of earlier findings." National Opinion Research Center (NORC) at the University of Chicago, General Social Survey, http://www.norc.org/projects/general+social+survey.htm, accessed July 2006.

22. Quebedeaux 1978, 7; Hunter 1983, 32, 35; and Shibley 1996, 10.

23. The more detailed analysis is as follows: For religious PVOs, real revenue rose from $58 million in 1940 (18% of the total) to $626 million in 1945 (22%) and then peaked at $1.04 billion in 1946 (47%). Subsequently, revenue of religious PVOs fell at a slower rate than secular, so the low point of religious revenue of $398 million in 1952 represented 79% of the total. Thereafter, religious and secular revenue both tended to rise, but religious revenue typically grew at a slower rate. Therefore, the religious share of total revenue fell to 39% in 1995.

24. The Institute for International Education (IIE) had an average federal share of 50.5% from 1980 onward. The IIE is not a paradigmatic PVO. It works closely with the State Department, USAID, and the Department of Energy to carry out American foreign policy objectives.

25. Smith n.d.

26. White House 2002b, 21–23.

27. White House 2003, 22.

28. Foreign Assistance Act of 1961 (P.L. 87-195), enacted September 4, 1961.

29. U.S. Department of Defense 2005.

30. White House 2005, 3.

31. USAID 2004a, 14.

32. U.S. General Accounting Office 2007a, 7.

33. The Millennium Challenge Account (MCA) is part of the U.S. foreign assistance program designed to "reduce poverty through sustainable economic growth" in some of the poorest countries in the world (www.mcc.gov). The MCA is administered by the Millennium Challenge Corporation (MCC), a U.S. government corporation. Established in January 2004, the MCC solicits proposals from developing countries that meet specific criteria in the areas of good governance, controlling corruption and investing in people. See "Title VI, Millennium Act of 2003," http://www.mcc.gov, accessed July 2008.

34. The most recent advocates of this view are Easterly 2002; Clark 2007; Collier 2007; Rajan and Subramanian 2007.

Chapter 2

1. U.S. Congress 1948a, 73.

2. According to Johanna Grombach Wagner (2005) of the International Committee of the Red Cross, "the term 'espace humanitaire' was coined by former Médecins Sans Frontières (MSF) president Rony Brauman, who described it in the mid-1990s as 'a space of freedom in which we are free to evaluate needs, free to monitor the distribution and use of relief goods, and free to have a dialogue

with the people.' " The topic of humanitarian space took on new urgency with the kidnap and murder of CARE International Iraq director Margaret Hassan in 2004.

3. U.S. Department of State, n.d., "Reference Guide." PVOs have raised concerns over the recently created Civilian Stabilization Initiative, an intermediate entity between the military and PVOs. The Civilian Stabilization Initiative is an interagency entity (coordinated from within the State Department's Office of Coordinator of Reconstruction and Stabilization) that oversees the Active Response Corps and the Civilian Reservists. The Active Response Corps coordinates in-country the work of the military, PVOs, multilateral organizations, local governments, and civilians. The Civilian Reservists (estimated at 2,000) are to assume responsibilities that the military has taken on, such as policing, rule of law, economic stabilization, governance issues, agriculture, infrastructure, and providing basic services to the population.

4. The joint resolution, referred to as the "Neutrality Act of 1939," was approved on November 4, 1939, by the 76th Congress, second session, Public Resolution No. 54. Section 8 governed the solicitation and collection of contributions for relief in belligerent countries. The belligerent countries were France, Germany, Poland, and the United Kingdom (including Australia, Canada, India, New Zealand, Union of South Africa). By November 15, 1941, the list included Norway, Belgium, Luxembourg, Netherlands, Italy, Greece, Yugoslavia, Hungary, and Bulgaria.

5. The Lend-Lease Act was passed by Congress on March 11, 1941. This legislation gave President Franklin D. Roosevelt the powers to sell, transfer, exchange, and lend equipment to any country to help it defend itself against the Axis powers. From 1941 to 1945, the federal government channeled $36 billion through the Lend-Lease program.

6. This problem would be solved with the formation of the Committee on National Corporations, which met annually to solicit fewer than 100 national corporations.

7. White House 1942, 1.

8. As part of its oversight authority, the President's War Relief Control Board asked two large labor unions, the AFL (American Federation of Labor) and CIO (Congress of Industrial Organizations), to terminate their individual fund-raising campaigns and join with the Community Chests.

9. The reasons cited by the government were to (a) eliminate inefficiency; (b) eradicate duplication of efforts; (c) ban agencies from engaging in political activism; and (d) balance international humanitarian needs with domestic welfare activities, particularly during the war.

10. White House 1944, 2.

11. The National Budget Committee was formed to report directly to the President's War Relief Control Board on all issues pertaining to fund-raising by agencies.

12. Office of War Information 1943; U.S. Department of State 1946, 10. For a history of the National War Fund, see Seymour 1947.

13. The service agencies were USOs, United Seamen's Service, American Field Service, and War Prisoners Aid, Inc. The private relief umbrella agencies were Belgian War Relief Society, British War Relief Society, United Service to China, American Relief for Czechoslovakia, American Denmark Relief, U.S. Committee for the Care of European Children, American Aid to France, Greek War Relief Association, American Relief for Holland, American Relief for Italy, United Lithuanian Relief Fund of America, Friends of Luxembourg, Near East Foundation, American Relief for Norway, Philippine War Relief, American Relief for Poland, Refugee Relief Trustees, Russian War Relief, War Relief Services-National Catholic Welfare Conference, World Emergency and War Victims Fund of the YWCA, World Student Service Fund, and United Yugoslav Relief Fund of America.

14. This arrangement would continue until the dissolution of the President's War Relief Control Board in 1946 and the suspension that same year of the National War Fund.

15. ACVAFS 1942.

16. Egan 1988; Nichols 1988.

17. U.S. Department of State 1946, 18–19.

18. U.S. Department of State, 1944, 17.

19. The UJA was founded in 1929 and reconstituted in 1939. See Raphael 1982.

20. Warburg 1941.

21. Raphael 1982, 17–19, 22–23.

22. Warburg 1941.

23. For a detailed account of this ideological rupture in the UJA, see Halperin 1960.

24. This was an intentional strategy to deflect anti-Semitic attacks; see Bauer 1981, 39–40.

25. Raphael 1982, 22, 29–30.

26. Ibid., 17.

27. Gallup Brain. Gallup began collecting survey data on religious affiliation in 1943.

28. Foreign Missions Conference of North America was founded in 1893. It was the interdenominational body that coordinated Protestant missions all over the world. It reflected the structures of the various boards of missions. In 1950, it became one of the eight bodies that made up the National Council of Churches. It was renamed the Division of Foreign Missions and in 1965 renamed again as the Division of Overseas Ministries.

29. Rouse and Neill 1968, 370–71.

30. International Missionary Council 1946.

31. The Federal Council of Churches established its own relief effort in 1941, the Committee on Foreign Relief Appeals in the Churches. This was an organization established by member denominations and other participating organizations, which included the already-existing Foreign Missions Conference of North America, the YMCA, and the YWCA, to coordinate war relief efforts.

This committee was changed, and its charge expanded in 1942, to become the Church Committee on Overseas Relief and Reconstruction. In 1946, the committee became the Church World Service under the National Council of Churches. The committee registered for two years with the President's War Relief Control Board but never registered with the National War Fund. The funds it raised were negligible.

32. Genizi 1983, 112, 123–24, 128; 1987, 261–76, especially 264.

33. Nichols 1988, 58–59.

34. Seymour 1947, 70–71. For fiscal year 1943–44, War Relief Services received $3,854,162. For fiscal year 1945–46, War Relief Services received $4,791,000. Total National War Fund disbursements to War Relief Services was $10,963,666, making it the fourth-largest recipient of the National War Fund, after United Service to China, United Seamen's Service, and United Social Hygiene Association.

35. The USO was made up of the YMCA, National Catholic Community Service, National Jewish Welfare Board, YWCA, Salvation Army, and National Travelers Aid Association.

36. Moore 1998; Sarna 2004, 266–67.

37. Stewart 1982, 375; Genizi 1983, 96–111; and Sikkink and Regnerus 1996.

38. International Missionary Council 1946, 6.

39. Stewart 1982, 376–83; Genizi 1983, 137–71.

Chapter 3

1. Truman 1947.

2. Truman asked for $400 million for Greece and Turkey. The Truman Doctrine cast the Communist threat in Greece as part of a Soviet grand plan. The Truman Doctrine framed the U.S. position in cold war terms, even though evidence suggested that Soviet intervention and involvement in the Greek civil war was indirect at best. The Balkan states—Albania, Bulgaria, and Yugoslavia—were the primary parties continuing old quarrels over boundaries. The Greek communist insurgency drew significant members among the Slavs, who were primarily interested in an independent Slavophone Macedonia. See Nachmani 1990.

3. Henry Morgenthau, secretary of the treasury under Roosevelt, had developed a plan by which Germany would be an agrarian economy and not return to being an industrialized nation. These ideas are expressed in the Potsdam Agreement, August 2, 1945. James F. Byrnes, U.S. secretary of state, in his "Restatement of Policy on Germany," at Stuttgart, September 6, 1946, reformulated the U.S. position to allow industrial growth in Germany.

4. The Point Four Program was introduced by President Truman in his January 20, 1949, inaugural address. It became H.R. 7346 and later Title IV of H.R. (House of Representatives) 7797, Foreign Assistance Act of 1950.

5. U.S. Congress 1948a, 61. For a description of President Truman's particular interest in forming the Advisory Committee on Voluntary Foreign Aid, see Ringland 1975, [35]–[36]. The agency was initially placed in the Office of the

Assistant Secretary of State for Economic Affairs. In 1953, the committee was transferred to the Foreign Operations Administration. In 1954, it moved to the ICA.

6. McSweeney 1950, 34.

7. Reiss 1985, "ACVAFS: The Organization," 77–79.

8. For a description of the national combined campaign, see U.S. Congress 1948e, 76–85.

9. U.S. Congress 1947. The Relief Resolution of 1947 (P.L. 84) appropriated $5 million for ocean transportation of supplies sent by PVOs to Europe. The Supplementary Appropriations Act of 1948 authorized a further $332 million for PVOs shipping relief supplies to Europe and Asia. The Foreign Assistance Act of 1948 stated that PVOs could receive ocean freight subsidies if they registered with the Advisory Committee on Voluntary Foreign Aid and were recommended by the administrator of that committee for ocean freight.

10. These provisions were found in the Foreign Assistance Act of 1948. ECA reg. no. 3, 13, *Federal Registry* 3783 (1948), "Commercial Freight Shipments of Supplies by Voluntary Non-Profit Relief Agencies"; ECA reg. no. 5, as amended, 13, *Federal Registry* 4706 (1948), "Ocean Freight Shipments of Individual Relief Packages." Foreign Assistance Act of 1948, paragraph 117(c) and amendment to the act paragraph 10(a).

11. When P.L. 480 was enacted, a separate line item was provided in the Foreign Aid Acts of 1954 and 1955 for freight reimbursement on these commodities. In 1965, provision of freight was incorporated into the P.L. 480 legislation.

12. Initially, the Allied Command would only permit a minimum of rations to enter the German zones. With the change in attitude and policy toward Germany, the military placed pressure on the PVOs to step up their aid. See McSweeney 1950, 47, note 98.

13. For an account of the German government setup in American military zone of occupation, see Guardze 1950.

14. These were CRALOG, CARE, and LARA.

15. The U.S. military pressured agencies to engage primarily in refugee and relief work. Many agencies were involved in community development and technical assistance projects, and they resented being relegated to short-term humanitarian work. Cold war politics dominated, and the agencies and their staff were either caught up or intentionally involved in the ideological debate taking place in the United States.

16. U.S. Congress 1950, 55. The Allied Command required German state governments to grant citizenship to refugees of German extraction. Therefore, the refugees were entitled to full civil and political rights.

17. Woodbridge 1950, vol. 1, 108.

18. For a critical assessment of the inadequacies of the UNRRA, see Hoover 1964, vol. 4, 86–87.

19. Woodbridge 1950, vol. 1, 409–507.

20. Agar 1960.

21. See Cazier 1964. Also see Campbell 1990. The original member agencies of CARE were American Christian Committee for Refugees, Inc., American Friends

Service Committee, AJJDC, American Relief for Czechoslovakia, American Relief for France, American Relief for Norway, American Relief for Poland, Committee on Christian Science Wartime Activities for the Mother Church, Congregational Christian Service Committee (later renamed United Church for World Ministries), Cooperative League of the USA, International Rescue and Relief Committee, Labor League for Human Rights (American Federation of Labor, AFL), National CIO (Congress of Industrial Organizations) War Relief Committee, Paderewski Testimonial Fund, Save the Children, Tolstoy Foundation, Unitarian Service Committee, United Lithuanian Relief Fund of America, United Ukrainian American Relief Committee, United Yugoslav Relief Fund of America, War Relief Services, National Catholic Welfare Conference (renamed Catholic Relief Services), and YWCA-World Emergency and War Victims Fund. Lutheran World Relief, based on a commitment to "thoughtful stewardship," did not join CARE. See Bachman 1995, 17.

22. The relationship between UNRRA and voluntary agencies varied from agency to agency. However, overall it could be characterized as contentious due to the lack of U.N. personnel and experience on the one hand and the independent nature of the voluntary agencies on the other. This situation changed in 1946 with the establishment of the Voluntary Agencies Council UNRRA. See Genizi 1993a, 167–92.

23. The American Friends Service Committee (1944), as a peace organization, sought to avoid working under the directions of the military, although the agency did consent to work with UNRRA. The U.S. PVOs working with UNRRA were the American Christian Committee for Refugees, AFL, American Friends Service Committee, AJJDC, American Relief for Italy, American Relief for Czechoslovakia, American *Vaad Hatzala*, Emergency Committee (Jewish orthodox), Brethren Service Committee, Catholic Relief Services (National Catholic Welfare Conference), Church World Service (World Council of Churches/NCCC [National Council of Churches in Christ]), Congregational Christian Service Committee, CIO, Hebrew Immigrant Aid Society (HIAS), International Rescue and Relief Committee, Jewish Agency for Palestine, Lutheran World Relief, Unitarian Service Committee, United Service to China (formerly United China Relief), United States Committee for the Care of European Children, YMCA international, YWCA international, World Student Relief, and World ORT (Obshestvo Remeslenofo zemledelcheskofo Truda).

24. An estimated 1,165 PVO staff and 5,111 UNRRA direct staff were working in Germany by March 1946. See Woodbridge 1950, vol. 1, 70.

25. For the full text of the report by Earl Harrison to President Truman, see Harrison 1945.

26. Woodbridge 1950, vol. 1, 138–43.

27. "Voluntary agency personnel working in the camps wore uniforms with badges carrying both the UNRRA and their agency insignia—as they had done in camps in the Near East." Reiss 1985, "ACVAFS: The Organization," 24.

28. Woodbridge 1950, vol. 1, 140.

29. Charter members of CRALOG were the AFL, American Friends Service Committee, Brethren Service Committee, Committee on Christian Science Wartime Activities of the Mother Church, Church World Service (Church Committee on Overseas Relief and Reconstruction of the Federal Council of Churches of Christ), International Rescue and Relief Committee, Lutheran World Relief, Mennonite Central Committee, Community Service Committee of the CIO, Unitarian Service Committee, and Catholic Relief Services-National Catholic Welfare Conference. CRALOG, when it ended in 1962, had grown to 25 members to include American Baptist Relief; American Fund for Czechoslovak Refugees; AJJDC; Foster Parents' Plan, Inc.; General Council of the Assemblies of God; Heifer Project, Inc.; Russian Children's Welfare Society, Inc.; Salvation Army; Save the Children; Tolstoy Foundation; United Lithuanian Relief Fund of America; United Ukrainian American Relief Committee; World Relief Commission of the National Association of Evangelicals; and YWCA. See Egan and Reiss 1964.

30. U.S. Congress 1948a, 808.

31. The PVOs making up LARA were the American Friends Service Committee, Brethren Service Committee, Church World Service, Labor League for Human Rights-AFL, Lutheran World Relief, Mennonite Central Committee, National CIO Community Services Committee, Salvation Army, War Relief Services-National Catholic Welfare Conference, YMCA-International Committee, and YWCA-National Board.

32. "The Army carried American Relief for Korea supplies without charge from seaports to Korea. Congress eventually provided the money for the ocean transport of voluntary supplies of agencies registered with the Advisory Committee. When the Senate Foreign Relations Committee was marking up Public Law 84 of the 80th Congress, which provided several hundred millions for the provision of food, medical supplies, clothing, fertilizers, pesticides, and seed, I went with Ed O'Connor of the Catholic Relief Services to talk with Senator Alexander Smith. Senator Smith was an intimate associate of Herbert Hoover's and well-informed of all the relief activities of World War I. When he came out I had not met him before, but when I established my identity as an old Hoover man, that was quite sufficient. The upshot of our talk with the Senator was the provision he made for the first appropriation of five million dollars to reimburse the voluntary agencies for their ocean transport costs of supplies determined to be essential supplements to the supplies provided by the general relief assistance program. The 80th Congress established a fruitful precedent and that form of complementary assistance has been carried on ever since in greatly expanded amounts." Ringland 1975, [40]–[42].

33. Cooperation Act of 1948, section 117(c). See note 21 for a list of CARE member agencies.

34. The UJA was formed in 1929 but had a difficult history because of tensions between the pro-Zionist groups and the mainstream Jewish groups.

35. For a history of the UJA, see Raphael 1982.

36. In 1946, there were 608,225 Jews in Palestine. By 1947, the Jewish population rose to 630,000. See IV, Palestine: Arab/Jewish Population (1914–1946) B. Chart; ProCon.org; and Raphael 1982, 39.

37. This would be referred to as the federation system. See Raphael 1982, 26–27.

38. Raphael 1982, 31–37.

39. For a pro-Zionist account of these events, see Halperin 1960. For an institutional, non-Zionist perspective, see Raphael 1980.

40. American Jewish Joint Distribution Committee 1953.

41. "Three years ago we went to the community [i.e. the Jews of the United States] and said this was a special emergency that required one-time giving on an all-out basis. I was assured that that was a fact and told everybody this was one-time and that they would never be asked again. I sincerely believed it. The next year we found we had to get seventy per cent more, and that was not easy. We didn't get it but we raised somewhere between 120 and 125 million dollars. This year we are struggling to raise 250 million." Warburg, quoted in Agar 1960, 224.

42. In 1946, the United States admitted 16,000 Jews; 25,000 in 1947; and 16,000 in 1948.

43. The Advisory Committee on Voluntary Foreign Aid was the designated governmental entity that recommended to ECA the agencies and supplies eligible for ocean transportation.

44. "Fourth, we embark on a bold new program for making the benefits of our scientific advances and industrial progress available for the improvement and growth of under-developed areas." Truman 1949. This became known as the Point Four Program; see note 4. The term *technical assistance* covered a wide range of activities, involving agriculture (particularly with regard to food production), land tenure, health, education, housing, and credit.

45. Pienkos 1991, 95.

46. For a detailed account of the agencies' involvement in resettling displaced persons and refugees, see Reiss 1985, "ACVAFS: Committee on Migration and Refugee Affairs," 25–102.

47. U.S. Congress 1953, 171. Through the American Council on Voluntary Agencies in Foreign Assistance, member agencies coordinated with the U.N. Korea Relief Administration.

48. The PVOs working in Korea were the national Catholic Welfare Conference-War Relief Services; Church World Service; Northern Presbyterian Mission; Southern Presbyterian Mission; Methodist Mission; Seventh-Day Adventist Mission; Maryknoll Sisters; Unitarian Service Committee; Mennonite Central Committee; Friends Service Committee (sponsored by the United States, United Kingdom, and Canada); Australian Presbyterian Mission; Save the Children Federation (United Kingdom); Foster Parents Plan for War Orphans; Christian Children's Fund; Cooperative Remittances for Europe and the Far East (CARE); Korean Red Cross; YMCA; and YWCA.

49. In 1948, several religious organizations pulled out of CARE, contending it should cease operating as the postwar relief efforts in Europe and Asia (Japan, Korea, Okinawa) were being phased out and stocks of surplus military rations were low. Some agencies—Catholic Relief Services, Church World Service, Friends Service Committee, AJJDC, International Rescue Committee, Greek War Relief, American Aid to France—had overseas operations of their own. CARE allowed individuals in the United States to send a package of food to an individual in Europe. In late 1946, CARE began receiving unspecified donations. Several member agencies contended that CARE's mandate did not include deciding where to ship food packages. Rather, undesignated funds should be going to the agencies that were in the business of providing general relief. Some agencies thought that CARE was too politicized, carrying out U.S. foreign policy by only shipping food packages to Western Europe and not Eastern Europe. Hence, in 1948 CARE ceased being an umbrella organization and began operating as a PVO.

50. Foreign Assistance Act of 1948, section 117(c).

51. This is known as U.S. State Department Announcement No. 33, March 1950. For a discussion of the registration process of PVOs, see Harvey 1975. Also see USAID 1974a.

52. Contract data are missing until 1978, except for numbers for 1951 (very small) and 1952.

53. The controversies surrounding the USAID registration of PVOs increased during the Clinton and Bush administrations. During the Clinton administration, the 20 percent privateness rule for PVOs could only be determined if PVOs were required to register and submit financial data to USAID. As a consequence, the PVO registry was kept. The George W. Bush administration sought to eliminate the registration on the grounds that PVO registration created a privileged status for registered agencies to the exclusion of other agencies, particularly evangelical agencies. Although the Bush administration was successful in removing the 20 percent privateness rule from the Foreign Operations Appropriation Bill of 2005, the PVO registry continues.

54. American Council of Voluntary Agencies for Foreign Service 1953, 11–12.

55. Reiss 1985, "ACVAFS: Committee on Development Assistance," 20, 59 footnote.

56. International multilateral organizations operating in the 1950s were the International Refugee Organization, International Labor Organization, U.N. Office of the High Commissioner for Refugees, Intergovernmental Committee for Migration, and the World Health Organization. These organizations not are discussed here. See Beigbeder 1991.

57. Reiss 1985, "ACVAFS: The Organization," 78.

58. My data set is missing data on contracts from 1953 to 1974.

59. Reiss 1985, "ACVAFS: Committee on Development Assistance," 5, 11.

60. There were four titles to the act: Title I covered the sales of Commodity Credit Corporation (CCC) stocks for currencies of other countries; Title II dealt with grants of commodities to other countries; Title III stipulated the distribution

of commodities through PVOs both domestically and internationally; Title IV regulated dollar credit sales of commodities to other countries with long-term repayment agreements.

61. Freight jumped from $35 million in 1954 to $415 million in 1955, but fell back to $116 million in 1956, then rose to $207 million in 1959.

62. In fiscal year 1955, these countries were Afghanistan, Austria, Bolivia, Egypt, Formosa, France, Germany, Greece, Hong Kong, India, Iran, Italy, Jordan, Korea, Pakistan, Peru, Trieste, Vietnam, and Yugoslavia.

63. Reiss 1985, "ACVAFS: Committee on Material Resources," 91–93.

64. For a discussion of the theological and philosophical differences between the mainline Protestant agencies on the one hand and Catholic Relief Services and CARE on the other, see Sullivan 1969.

65. McCleary interview 2008. Protestant agencies were careful to maintain a separation of church and state in their overseas international relief and development work. However, when it came to placing refugees in the United States, Protestant agencies were willing to accept as much government funding as was made available to them. The rationale was that government funds supported the resettling of refugees in the United States through denominational networks (local churches) in the United States and not overseas.

66. The political philosophy of subsidiarity was articulated by Pope Pius XI; see Treacy 1939.

67. United States 1959, 6120–24. Statement by Senator Hubert Humphrey in introducing debate on the bill, S-1711, entitled "International Food for Peace Act of 1959." This was a Democratic version of the P.L. 480 legislation.

68. The percentage of total revenue in the form of P.L. 480 commodities for Catholic Relief Services was 58% in 1953, 58% in 1954, 56% in 1955, 56% in 1956, 55% in 1957, 58% in 1958, 54% in 1959, and 53% in 1960.

69. Bachman 1995, 48.

70. This is known as State Department Announcement No. 33, March 1950. For a discussion of the registration process of PVOs, see Harvey 1975; USAID 1974a.

71. Reiss 1985, "ACVAFS: Committee on Development Assistance." 4.

72. U.S. Department of State 1950.

73. Reiss 1985, "ACVAFS: Committee on Development Assistance," 58–59.

74. Reiss 1988, "ACVAFS: Committee on Development Assistance," 72.

75. Ibid., 94.

Chapter 4

1. Richard W. Cottam (1964) called it "competitive interference."

2. There were three primary recipients of foreign aid during this period: the agencies such as Church World Service, Lutheran World Relief, CRS, and CARE that primarily engaged in humanitarian aid; U.S. cooperatives that set up cooperative organizations overseas; and technical and business associations, consulting firms, and corporations engaged in specialized work primarily related to technology and business management. See Biddle 2006, 4. The Cooperative Development

Program was set up at this time to provide funding to U.S. cooperatives to build organizational capacity and provide technical assistance support and training to local in-country counterparts.

3. The 13 PVOs were American Hospital Association, American Institute for Free Labor Development, American ORT Federation, CARE, Cooperative League of the USA, Council on Social Work Education, Credit Union National Association (CUNA), Institute of International Education, IVS, Industrial Research Institute Research, National Federation of Settlements and Neighborhood Centers, Near East Foundation, and Overseas Education Fund of the League of Women Voters. Except for CARE, all of these agencies offered some type of technical assistance.

4. Reiss 1985, "ACVAFS: Committee on Development Assistance," 72, 92. The exception was the Peace Corps, which refused to contract with religious agencies.

5. For a discussion of the Peace Corps case, see Stedman 1963, especially 611–13.

6. In 1965, the religious agencies negotiating contracts were the AJJDC, CRS, Church World Service, American Friends Service Committee, and Lutheran World Relief.

7. For a detailed account of the interagency struggles to control the Food for Peace program, see Grader 1967, 164–65.

8. The Agricultural Trade Development and Assistance Act was amended in 1961 to allow PVOs to use agricultural commodities as work wages for local personnel and workers. The amendment also permitted PVOs to use food commodities as barter for tools and equipment.

9. The 1960 Mutual Security Act for the first time permitted agencies to use food as payment for work. See Reiss 1985, "ACVAFS: Committee on Material Resources," 110; Bachman 1995, 58.

10. McCracken telephone interview, March 1, 2007; Stenning 1996, 33.

11. Reiss 1985, "ACVAFS: Committee on Material Resources," 111; ACVAFS n.d., 10.

12. Congress authorized $5 billion for the promotion of "more accurate and sympathetic understanding among the peoples of the American Republics through greater interchange of persons, ideas, techniques, and educational, scientific, and cultural achievement." Cited in Fisher 1963, 28. See Reiss 1985, "ACVAFS: Committee on Material Resources," 113–14.

13. USAID 1966.

14. USAID 1974a, 55; White House 1969, 27. The Commodity Credit Corporation distributes stocks of food commodities to registered PVOs. Commodities and transportation costs for P.L. 480, Title II, are provided by the Commodity Credit Corporation under the direction of the secretary of agriculture and administered through the Farm Service Agency.

15. Reiss 1985, "ACVAFS: Committee on Material Resources," 122.

16. Foreign Assistance Act of 1961, 87th Congress, first session 1961 (P.L. 87-195) U.S. Congress 2006, 15–418.

17. Mahajani 1965, 664.

18. Butler 1968, especially 120–21; Viner et al. 1963, 322, 348–50.

19. Title X of the Foreign Assistance Act of 1967, 90th Congress, second session (P.L. 90-137). The USAID funds for population and family planning went from $4.7 million in fiscal year 1967 to $35 million in 1968.

20. Ibid., paragraphs 102, 2079(a).

21. The USAID Advisory Committee on Voluntary Foreign Aid described USAID as being "macro"-focused while the PVOs were "micro"-oriented. See USAID 1974a, 26.

22. For a comprehensive and critical report of the PVO registration process from its inception, see Harvey 1975.

23. Somner 1977, 97.

24. For a history of Vietnam Christian Service, see Bush 2002. For a detailed account, see Stenning 1996, 38–39, 52–53.

25. See Rodell 2002.

26. Ibid., 231, 234.

27. See Kauffman 2005.

28. For a detailed account of CRS and public criticism of its work in Vietnam, see Flipse 2002. Interestingly, the official history of CRS written by Eileen Egan does not discuss the agency's activities in Vietnam; see Egan 1988.

29. For a history of CARE's work in Vietnam, see Pergande 2002.

30. USAID 1975, vol. 1, pt. 1, 20–21.

31. ACVAFS 1968.

32. Garred 2006, 60. Based on experiences in the Sudan and the Philippines, WV began hiring non-Christian staff for field projects and was challenged to "move from a Christian majority mind-set towards a more inclusive approach of working with non-Christians based on a pluralistic approach." This organization's transition from an evangelical agency to a faith-founded one can be dated to the mid-1990s.

33. A *parachurch* is defined as "not-for-profit, organized Christian ministry to spiritual, mental and physical needs, working outside denominational control." Reid et al. 1990, 863–65. For a broader discussion of the term, see Willmer and Schmidt, with Smith, 1998, 12–28.

34. Quebedeaux 1978, 110–11; Stafford 1997, especially 22–23.

35. Zeitz 2000.

36. Raphael 1982, 77.

37. In 1999, United Jewish Communities (UJC) was formed by the merger of three organizations: the UJA, Council of Jewish Federations, and United Israel Appeal.

38. Sarna 2004, 318–23.

39. Silverrnan 1991.

40. Oates 1995.

41. Greeley 1989, 46–47.

42. Nygren and Ukeratis 1993.

43. The social movements of the 1960s have been widely studied. For an overview of the literature, see Skocpol 2003, chapter 4; and Tarrow 2003, chapter 10.

44. By 1989, USAID employed close to 600 former Peace Corps volunteers; see USAID 1989, 64.

45. The original members of PAID were the following organizations with their founding dates in parentheses: Acción International/AITEC (1961), Congregational Christian Service Committee (1947), Emerging Economies Corporation (1970), Fundacion para El Fomento de la Investigación Científica y Tecnológica (1969), Heifer Project International (1944), International Educational Development (1962), IVS (1953), Meals for Millions Foundation (1946), Pan American Development Foundation (1962), Partnership for Productivity Foundation/USA (1969), Save the Children Federation/Community Development Foundation (1957), Technoserve (1969), Volunteers in Technical Assistance (1960), World Crafts Council/USA (1969), and World Education (1957). Formally founded in 1980, PAID was functioning in 1979.

46. USAID 1974a, 117.

47. Section 170 of the Internal Revenue Code relates to surplus property and food. Changes in this code in 1976 allowed for donations up to twice the cost basis. The Katrina Emergency Tax Relief Act of 2005 extended the tax deduction in section 170 to all business entities for donations made between August and December 2005.

Chapter 5

1. Judith Gilmore (1977) detailed the PVO culturally embedded projects as "rural community development, small farmer credit, small-scale enterprise promotion, development of cooperatives and credit unions, low-cost health delivery systems, literacy, vocational and management training, appropriate technology, improved nutrition, and soil and water resources." (3, footnote 2).

2. Schmidt, Blewett, and Henriot 1981, 9.

3. Gilmore 1977, 6.

4. Contracts were used for the procuring of commodities and services to be used by the PVO for designated USAID activities. Agencies with contracts were highly regulated by USAID through the Procurement Office, with USAID retaining oversight for the distribution of the commodities. From the perspective of the PVO, contracts were resource intensive, requiring personnel and time to meet USAID requirements in terms of accountability.

5. For some traditional PVOs, such as Church World Service, the transition from a relief to a development agency was characteristic of agencies that represented various denominations. The member denominations of Church World Service sought to continue to do development work through their missions programs. The denominations were willing to engage jointly in relief and emergency work through Church World Service, but development was their own domain.

6. In 1971, there were 355 agencies operating overseas according to the *U.S. Nonprofit Organizations in Development Assistance Abroad* (American Council of Voluntary Foreign Agencies, 1971). However, their directory for 1971 only accounts for 82 of those agencies operating in 129 countries.

7. For a description of the types of grants and application procedures, see USAID 1974b.

8. In my data set, Africare received its first grant in 1978, the Overseas Education Fund in 1978, and Acción in 1971. Another type of institutional capacity-building grant was ongoing general funding awarded to family-planning agencies such as Pathfinder, Association for Voluntary Sterilization, and Family Planning International Association. This track of funding was separate but consistent with USAID's focus on institutional capacity building. This type of organization is identified by USAID as an "intermediary organization." Included in this category are cooperatives, credit unions, and AFL-CIO (American Federation of Labor-Congress of Industrial Organizations) institutes, as well as family-planning organizations. See USAID 1982b, 5–6.

9. The OPGs brought in PVOs by focusing on projects that "related to employment creation and equitable income distribution and in the priority areas of food and nutrition [a traditional PVO strength], family planning and health, education and human resources development." If a project was ongoing, it would be considered for funding if and only if it brought in PVOs as "implementers for the first time." USAID 1974b, preface i. However, OPGs were large grants, with a minimum of $100,000 per year and for one project. As a result, small PVOs lacking the organizational structure could not qualify. Finally, unlike General Support grants, OPGs, because of their specialized nature (one project), required more USAID oversight in terms of project conception and implementation.

10. The PVO cash contribution levels could be negotiated with the USAID mission; see USAID 1984, 3.

11. On paper, the objective might have been for PVOs with OPGs to conform to USAID's country strategy. In practice, the PVO had to conform to the country context, which was left to the discretion of the mission director. For a brief description of how a country development strategy evolves and is approved, see McGuire and Ruttan 1989, 11.

12. This setup would change in 1977 when USAID mission directors were given the authority to award grants.

13. Gilmore e-mail 2008.

14. The 50% match was required because of the institutional support to the PVO and USAID concern over sustainability. Matching grants later became known as Comprehensive Program Grants, which streamlined several grants a PVO might have been awarded to reduce administrative redundancy and better coordinate program activities.

15. U.S. GAO 1976, 8.

16. Whereas prior to 1974 USAID awarded only General Support grants and Specific Support Grants, the DPGs and OPGs were classified as Specific Support

grants. This new structure meant that USAID had greater oversight for the grant. The two issues PVOs strenuously objected to were (a) clearance of international travel for staff (that is, USAID required all PVOs to provided advance notice of personnel traveling overseas so the relevant USAID mission could be notified) and (b) PVOs objected to USAID approval of subordinate contracts (this requirement was not uniformly enforced).

17. A *cooperative agreement* is a "legal instrument used where the principal purpose is the transfer of money, property, services or anything of value to the recipient in order to accomplish a public purpose of support or stimulation authorized by Federal statute and where substantial involvement by USAID is anticipated." See USAID 2002b, "Glossary," entry "Results-Oriented Assistance."

18. As Judith Gilmore, who was director of the Private Voluntary Cooperative Office from 2000 to 2006, correctly noted, it is impossible to calculate the "privateness" percentage of a PVO because certain types of grants were exempt (telephone interview, July 29, 2008).

19. For an example of this position, see USAID 1976, appendix B.

20. Schmidt, Blewett, and Henriot 1981, 90–100.

21. The General Support grants to the Asia Foundation, Opportunities Industrialization Centers International, and International Executives were earmarked by Congress, and USAID was mandated by Congress to fund them.

22. For a detailed description of congressional review of these three PVOs and USAID's mishandling of their funding, see Schmidt, Blewett, and Henriot 1981, 116–19, especially 117; U.S. GAO 1976, 13–24.

23. Data for PVOs in 1975, 1976, 1977, and 1979 were not published by USAID.

24. The PVC was instrumental in educating and facilitating PVO access to government agencies, bureaus, and U.S. missions overseas.

25. For discussion of the events leading up to the formation of IDCA, see Gilmore 1977, 25–31.

26. For a detailed and nuanced account of political, economic, and humanitarian causes of the famine, see Shepherd 1975.

27. Shepherd 1975, 84.

28. International Development and Food Assistance Act of 1975, P.L. 94-161. In 1974 Congress appropriated $300 million, and in 1975 it appropriated $619 for food and nutrition programs.

29. Public Law 480, Title II, which stipulates agricultural commodities for PVOs, also allocates agricultural goods for disasters. The president of the United States has authority to provide disaster assistance without oversight of Title II.

30. In 1946, the U.N. Economic and Social Council (ECOSOC) granted 41 PVOs consultative status. By 1955, it was clear to the PVOs that they were being sidestepped in favor of universities and other types of institutions.

31. For a discussion of this topic, see chapter 3.

32. U.N. Development Programme 1975.

33. ACVAFS 1980, 9.

34. In 1977, the United States withdrew from the International Labor Organization because it failed to promote human rights. The Carter administration was also frustrated in its attempt to the influence the World Bank and other international financial institutions to tie loans to human rights violations.

35. Schechter 2005, 103.

36. In 1974, Congress recommended the creation of an Office of Human Rights within the Bureau of International Organization Affairs. In 1975, the office was created within the Department of State under a new special assistant on human rights within the office of the deputy secretary of state. In 1977, Congress upgraded the office to that of assistant secretary of state for human rights and humanitarian affairs. In that same year, President Carter created an interagency committee on human rights and foreign assistance.

37. In 1976, Amnesty International opened a Washington, D.C., office. For a history of Amnesty International and this period, see Cmiel 1999. To place Amnesty International within the broader context of the historical development of human rights groups, see Keck and Sikkink 1998. The boomerang effect is when an agent cooperates with an international ally to exert political pressure on its own government.

38. For a detailed account of the subsequent role of the U.S. government and PVOs in mass feeding programs for Vietnamese along the Thai-Cambodia border after 1979, see Mason and Brown 1984.

39. For background information on Vietnam and its political context, both domestic and international, see Charny and Spragnes 1984. The account of how the coalition was formed was obtained in a 2008 interview with Paul F. McCleary, executive director of Church World Service, 1975–84.

40. Lutheran World Relief, which included support from the Lutheran Church-Missouri Synod, the conservative evangelical denomination of the Lutherans, would not politicize itself. The Mennonite Central Committee, a pacifist denomination that sought neutrality and had worked in Vietnam since the 1950s, would not have approved of such a public stance against the U.S. embargo and the implications of doing so.

41. The embargo was eased in 1992 and lifted in 1994.

42. For case studies of the PVOs, see Biberson and Jean 1999; Foreman 1999; Gnaerig and MacCormack 1999; Henry 1999; and Offenheiser, Holcombe, and Hopkins 1999.

43. With regard to the revenue data for PVOs, my data set captures the income agencies report to the U.S. federal government on their 990 forms. For example, WV Australia does not report its income to the U.S. government. In this sense, the data presented here are misleading when it comes to PVOs that have a transnational organizational structure.

44. This argument was laid out by Meyer and Imig 1993 and Tarrow 2003.

45. In fiscal year 2005, Americares Foundation had real revenue of $849 million, and WV had $795 million.

46. For a detailed account of the debate over evangelism versus social action, see Hoge 1976.

47. In 1960, the Federal Communications Commission's ruling on the sale of public interest broadcasting effectively broke the monopoly of the mainline denominations (through the National Council of Churches) on radio and television religious broadcasting. This ruling suddenly introduced competition at the national level, to the disadvantage of mainline churches, which were relying on free airtime, whereas the evangelicals had been willing to pay for airtime on local stations. Mainline churches were not accustomed to raising funds for radio time or packaging their shows to sell to the public. See Hadden and Swann 1981, 77–80; Hadden and Shupe 1988, 51; and Finke and Iannaccone 1993.

48. Yamamori e-mail 2003.

49. See chapter 6 for a discussion of the development of the gifts-in-kind standard.

50. Vallet and Zech 1995, 93–95.

51. Dykstra and Hudnut-Beumler 1992; Olson and Caddell 1993; and Hoge et al. 1996.

52. For a good description of the nature of this relationship, see ACVAFS 1980, 12–13; ACVAFS 1981, 12–13.

53. ACVAFS 1982b, 8.

54. ACVAFS 1944.

55. ACVAFS 1975, November 24. Report of the National Information Bureau, Inc., to ACVAFS stated that "the primary business of World Vision, Inc. is to conduct Christian religious and missionary services, to assist in improving and ameliorating the moral and social conditions of humanity; to promote services to God's people which will enable them to accomplish more quickly the Great Commission of advancing the kingdom of God." A 1981 note in the financial files of ACVAFS stated that the WV membership was pending. ACVAFS files, Special Collections, Rutgers University, Rutgers, New Jersey.

56. U.S. GAO 1976, 32–33; Gilmore 1977, 10, 15.

57. *Chronicle of Philanthropy* 2004.

58. Gal and Gottschalk 2001.

59. Tobin 2001.

60. See Jewish Funders Network.

61. Rimor and Tobin 1990, 159.

62. Rimor and Tobin 1990, 159–60; Tobin 2001, 5–6.

Chapter 6

1. In 1978, Congress took away the exemption from PVO overseas personnel as part of tax legislation. The ACVAFS organized meetings of PVO representatives with senators and representatives to discuss overturning the legislation, which applied only to overseas workers of U.S. oil companies. The law passed in December 1980 was retroactive to January 1979. In essence, the PVOs had lost a privilege that they were successful in having Congress reinstate.

2. The Biden-Pell Amendment, P.L. 96-533, section 316, resulted from the Presidential Commission on World Hunger (1978–80). See Hogan 1989.

3. To meet the goals of the Biden-Pell Amendment, USAID created Development Education grants to PVOs and cooperatives; it set aside up to $750,000 for no more than 12 grants to be awarded by April 1982. In 1981, there existed a plethora of USAID grants: Development Program Grants (DPGs), OPGs, Matching Grants, Consortium Grants, general institutional support, management service grants, cooperative agreements, and grants available from the U.S. government other than those offered through the Bureau of Food for Peace and Voluntary Assistance, USAID.

4. For the first few years, USAID awarded ten grants per year to PVOs. Some of the first grantees were Credit Union National Association of the Mutual Insurance Group, Heifer Project, Pan American Development Foundation, American Forum for Global Education, CARE, Global Tomorrow Coalition, OEF International, International Service Association for Health, YMCA, American Association of School Administrators, and American Jewish World Service. For a discussion of the first seven years of the Biden-Pell grants, see the entire first volume of 1989's *Development Education Annual.*

5. This provision also included the Sahel Development Program, introduced during the presidency of Jimmy Carter in 1978. The purpose of the Sahel program was to provide technical assistance through technology transfer, education and human resources, rural development, agriculture, and nutrition.

6. USAID 1982d.

7. USAID 1982b. One need only read and compare the statement presented by the ACVAFS at the same meeting to see that PAID's statement was strident and openly critical of the changes proposed by USAID, something the ACVAFS was not. See ACVAFS 1982a.

8. USAID 1982b, 1–6, especially 6.

9. For a detailed account of how the "privateness" rule was enacted into law, see USAID 1982b. For a description of the formula used to measure PVO privacy, see Biddle 1986, appendix 1.

10. See chapter 5 for a description of the various kinds of grants. For a brief description of the funding grants available to PVOs in the early 1980s, see USAID 1982d, 11–13.

11. The formula for the Lewis privateness requirement included in-kind contributions, donations, and P.L. 480 commodities, whereas previously they were exempt from total federal revenue. For a discussion of the Lewis Amendment formula, see Biddle 1986, appendix 1, 6–7.

12. Newton e-mail (registrar, OPD/PVC Office, USAID) 2008.

13. USAID 1987, 44.

14. For the discussion of evangelical PVOs accepting a significant percentage of gifts-in-kind donations, see chapter 4, table 4.4, of AERDO 1999.

15. InterAction 2002a. Point 7.6.3 states that InterAction members are to follow AERDO Gifts in Kind (GIK) standards.

16. In 1977, Congressman Charles Wilson (Democrat-California) introduced a bill that required PVOs to disclose their finances prior to a solicitation. Senator

Mark Hatfield (Republican-Oregon), an evangelical, met with several evangelical ministers and urged them to disclose voluntarily their financial statements. *Christianity Today* 1979; Mooneyham n.d.

17. *Christianity Today* 1988a; 1988b; 1989.

18. As a consequence, institutional grants were phased out.

19. Federal Grant and Cooperative Agreement Act 1977.

20. International Development Cooperation Act of 1978 created IDCA.

21. For a discussion of the politics of setting up the IDCA, see McGuire and Ruttan 1989, 15–16.

22. USAID 1982c.

23. USAID 1985, 11.

24. USAID 1982a, 16.

25. Robinson 1997, 59–60

26. For a discussion of these points, see USAID 1987, 18–20.

27. USAID 1983, 50–51.

28. For an account of the journalists' travel to Ethiopia in 1984, see Emergency Nutrition Network 1997. For a firsthand account by a PVO staff person, see Vaux 2001, 43–68.

29. Peter Davies, president of InterAction at the time, agreed to allow InterAction to receive public contributions at the urging of Mickey Leland, chair of the House Select Committee on Hunger. Davies telephone interview 2003.

30. The Ethiopian population was especially at risk, an estimated 70 million. The provinces of Eritrea and Tigray were fighting to secede from Ethiopia. The PVOs were denied access by the Ethiopian government to the two provinces to provide food aid. The Eritrean People's Liberation Front ambushed relief vehicles carrying food, and the Ethiopian government was rightfully concerned that the food aid was feeding rebels, not civilians.

31. Clay 1989, 233, 236.

32. Pezzullo 1989, 223.

33. Congressional Research Service 2006a, 20. The total supplemental aid came to $1 billion for famine relief in Africa for fiscal year 1985. The total humanitarian aid for fiscal year 1985 came to $2.75 billion.

34. For a candid and detailed assessment of PVO response to the Ethiopian famine, see Clay 1989.

35. The member organizations are Adventist Development and Relief Agency International, Agricultural Cooperative Development International/Volunteers in Overseas Cooperative Assistance (ACDI/VOCA), Africare, American Red Cross, CARE, Catholic Relief Services, Counterpart International, Food for the Hungry International, International Orthodox Christian Charities, International Relief and Development, Land O'Lakes, Mercy Corps, Opportunities Industrialization Centers (OIC) International, Project Concern International, Save the Children, and WV.

36. Barrett and Maxwell 2005, 101.

37. This topic is discussed in more detail in chapter 7.

38. Barrett and Maxwell 2005, 101.

39. In 1984, World Vision Relief and Development Organization (WVR&D) was created. It was set up in direct response to the large income ($13.5 million in Foreign Disaster Relief Assistance and P.L. 480 1.5 million metric tons of food) coming in for the famine in Ethiopia. The purpose of WVR&D was to pursue federal funds. It was a paper organization, a nonsectarian organization that took a nonsectarian long-range approach to development projects. The organization was criticized by the more established PVOs as simply being a fund-raising machine for an evangelical child sponsorship program. Within WVUS, WVR&D was buried within the organizational structure. Dean Hirsch, executive director of WVR&D, reported to a vice president, who in turn reported to an executive vice president, who in turn reported to the president of WV; WVR&D was in charge of reporting to USAID. This relationship required negotiating and positioning WVUS vis-à-vis the federal government. The Charitable Choice Act (1997) made it no longer necessary to have a subsidiary entity, and WVR&D ceased to exist. From an interview in 2003 with a former executive of WV who asked to remain anonymous.

40. The Child Survival Grant Program was introduced in 1985. The purpose of the program was to reduce infant mortality. In 2001, the program was moved out of the Office of Private and Voluntary Cooperation into the Global Health Bureau of USAID.

41. World Vision is one of many agencies that viewed their funding relationship with USAID to have positive effect on the professionalization of their staff. The U.S. branch of Plan International (formerly Foster Parents Plan) accepted a Matching Grant even though financially it did not need the funds; Plan International USA accepted the Matching Grant to pressure its international network into introducing technological change into the organization. Gilmore telephone interview 2008.

42. Seiple telephone interview, October 30, 2003.

43. Hancock telephone interview, June 3, 2002.

44. InterAction 2003.

45. Congress passes and the president signs into law a Continuing Resolution Authority (CRA), which provides budget authority to federal agencies to continue operations for a specified length of time or until regular appropriations are enacted. The CRA is a temporary appropriation enacted to provide authority for specific ongoing activities in the event that regular appropriations have not been enacted by the beginning of the fiscal year or the expiration of the previous CRA. A CRA has a fixed life and provides the authority necessary to allow operations to continue in the absence of appropriations. See Congressional Research Service 1997, 2.

46. The appropriations subcommittees of the House and Senate since the mid-1980s have come to wield significant power. For a discussion of how this came to be, see Flickner 2007, 225–45. Carol Lancaster and David Obey (1988) interpreted the Reagan administration's use of continuing resolutions as a political reality.

By the 1980s, the U.S. public lost its interest in funding foreign aid, and bipartisan support for foreign aid in Congress no longer existed as it had in previous decades.

47. A detailed account of congressional approval of the $27 million "humanitarian assistance" and where it went is given in Kornbluh 1987, 196–201.

48. Catholic Relief Services withdrew from InterAction, stating that the organization no longer represented its interests. American Friends Service Committee issued a statement arguing that the U.S. government had violated the neutrality of humanitarian aid. The American Friends Service Committee offered assistance to Nicaraguan civilians. Oxfam took a similar position to that of the American Friends Service Committee, arguing for neutrality and giving aid to both sides of the conflict.

49. The agencies that signed the letter were American Friends Service Committee, Church World Service, Oxfam America, Heifer Project International, Medical Mission Sisters, Unitarian Universalist Service Committee, Mennonite Central Committee, and Lutheran World Relief.

50. Agencies that began by sponsoring children, such as Save the Children, Foster Parents Plan, WV, and, to a lesser extent, Christian Children's Fund, also engaged in a "reality gap" between the ongoing programs of the agency and its public image so constituents were not lost. But, unlike Catholic Relief Services and CARE, which sought to present P.L. 480 food programs as development, the children's agencies moved away from solely sponsoring children into development programs with child sponsorship as a component of the program.

51. Quoted in Ruttan 1993, 87.

52. For a discussion of the monetization of the Title II program, see Barrett and Maxwell 2005, 101–3.

53. USAID 1988.

54. Umbrella activities involve a USAID award to a lead organization, which then makes subgrants to a number of other PVOs. Capacity building of subgrantees would become an increasingly important part of umbrella activities, particularly for indigenous subgrantees, who stood to benefit from the expertise and contacts of the lead agency.

55. USAID 1989, 120.

56. Korten (1983) coined the terminology.

Chapter 7

1. USAID 1992a.

2. "No payment may be made for an assessed contribution to the United Nations or its specialized agencies in excess of 20 percent of the total annual budget of the United Nations or its specialized agencies (respectively) for the United States Fiscal Year 1987 and following years" unless the U.N. grants voting rights "proportionate to the contribution of each such member state to the budget of the United Nations and its specialized agencies on matters of budgetary consequence." Section 143, P.L. 99-93 (99 Stat 424).

3. USAID 1992b, 2.

4. USAID 1995a, 21; 1995b, 7, 22.

5. U.S. GAO 1992; U.S. GAO 2003, 6.

6. Congressional Research Service 2005, 28, footnote 20.

7. U.S. GAO 2003, 6.

8. In October 1993, USAID introduced its new principles on participatory development.

9. In 1993, the Office of Management and Budget (Presidential Review Directive No. 20) looked at the number of domestic agencies involved in foreign assistance. By 2006, the list had grown to include 28 government entities, among them: USAID, MCC, Peace Corps, Inter-American Foundation, African Development Foundation, Overseas Private Investment Corporation, Trade and Development Agency, Department of the Treasury, Department of Agriculture, Department of Commerce, Department of Defense, Department of Energy, Department of Health and Human Services–Centers for Disease Control, Department of Justice, Department of Labor, Department of the Interior, Department of Transportation, the Ex-Im Bank, Federal Trade Commission, National Endowment for Democracy, National Science Foundation, National Institutes of Health, U.S. Institute for Peace, and U.S. Postal Service, Homeland Security, and the recently formed Coalition Provisional Authority (CPA) for Iraq reconstruction. For a brief description of the funding going through these executive entities, see Congressional Research Service 2005, 23–25. For another list, see Congressional Research Service 2007d, 27. In fiscal year 2005, an estimated $5.8 billion in foreign aid disbursements were made by the Department of Agriculture, Department of Health and Human Services, Department of Energy, Department of Labor, Department of Commerce, Homeland Security, Department of Justice, Department of Interior, and Department of Transportation. See Congressional Research Service 2006a, 5.

10. Congressional Research Service 2007c.

11. Brainard 2007, 37; Nowels 2007, 273.

12. This bureau had several offices: Office of Agriculture, Office of Environment and Office of Natural Resources, and Office of Research.

13. Senator William V. Roth, Jr. (Republican-Delaware), proposed and actively supported the legislation.

14. The PVOs expressed their concerns at meetings of the Advisory Committee of Voluntary Foreign Aid. See USAID 1998a; USAID 1998b.

15. U.S. GAO 1996, 3, footnote 5; USAID 2006e, 23.

16. The HELP Commission final report, *Beyond Assistance,* described IQCs as "limiting awards to entities willing to be all-purpose, worldwide USAID grantees or contractors. Combining tourism with hydro-electric power generation and climate change into a single contract, for instance, does not attract prime bidders with genuine expertise and global reputation in any one of these discipline." U.S. Commission on Helping 2007, 133; see also 123–24.

17. See Berríos 2000, 13. A GAO investigation conducted in 1996 at the request of Benjamin Gilman, chair of the House Committee on International Relations,

did not find favoritism and concentration of contracts in the largest contractors. See U.S. GAO 1996.

18. U.S. Congress 2007, 22.

19. Goiza telephone interview 2007. A comprehensive list of all for-profit contractors and their federal awards is not made public. The closest, albeit inaccurate, to a comprehensive list made public can be found in the HELP Commission's report (U.S. Commission on Helping 2007), 146–48.

20. USAID 2008a, 2.

21. Dichter 2006, 32.

22. See Cooley and Ron 2002.

23. InterAction 2007a.

24. USAID acquisition regulation, section 706.302–70, USAID 1997b, 1–3.

25. *Sierra Magazine* 1995.

26. USAID 1995a; USAID 1997a.

27. U.S. GAO 1995, 35.

28. Carol Lancaster, deputy administrator of USAID, describes the situation at that time (2007, 83–91).

29. For a history and analysis of the process of developing the standards, see Buchanan-Smith 2003. For an assessment of the Sphere Project, see van Dycke and Waldman 2004.

30. *Washington Post* 2003.

31. The Global Development Alliance is a funding mechanism within USAID that has sidestepped PVOs, minimizing their role in international development. See http://www.usaid.gov/our_work/global_partnerships/gda/, accessed May 2008.

32. These three bureaus—Bureau for Democracy, Conflict, and Humanitarian Response; Bureau for Economic Growth, Agriculture, and Trade; and the Bureau of Global Health—came out of two bureaus previously known as the Global Bureau and the Bureau of Humanitarian Response.

33. USAID 2001, 18.

34. Natsios 2006, 136. For a presentation of the data for July 2002 to August 2003, see U.S. GAO 2003. The GAO data findings show that during that time period, USAID staff and operations were centralized in the Washington, D.C., headquarters.

35. USAID 2008b, 7.

36. See USAID 2008c.

37. The MCC is an independent entity of both the State Department and USAID. The PEPFAR funds are directly managed by the State Department.

38. White House 2002b, 21–23.

39. Congressional Research Service 2005b, 3.

40. Congressional Research Service 2007a, "Summary," n.p.

41. The global AIDS coordinator reports directly to the secretary of state.

42. USAID 2006c.

43. InterAction 2002b. Meeting held at InterAction on the future strategies of USAID/PVC, n.p.

44. Ibid.

45. USAID 1995, 13, figure 14.

46. See Congressional Research Service 2006b, table 1.

47. The PVOs tend to see relief and development on a continuum from saving life (relief) to restoring normal, daily existence (development). When going into a country for relief purposes, PVOs will assess their institutional capacity toward a longer-term commitment: (a) Does the agency have the technical skills required to carry out a program in the situation? Is it within the PVO's mission? (b) What level of security/stability is present? How much risk will the PVO assume? (c) Is there funding to carry out a longer-term project? Or is there potential for funding?

48. See U.S. Institute of Peace 2005.

49. Preserving PVO neutrality is an issue that comes up time and again. World Vision's food distribution activities in Somalia could only be carried out with the protection of U.S. military convoys. The identification of humanitarian relief work with the military started World Vision along a slippery slope. The close identification with the U.S. military destroyed credibility and trust necessary for humanitarian work. "It puts the humanitarian community at risk. They, too, become a legitimate target rather than remaining neutral." Getman telephone interview, November 4, 2003.

50. USAID 2003, 22.

51. U.S. Department of Defense 2005.

52. See Congressional Research Service 2006b, 6–7.

53. The requirement was change to a case-by-case determination, thereby introducing flexibility into the cost-sharing of projects.

54. The other change was refining the classification of agencies that receive federal funds. See USAID 2006f, 5.

55. *Federal Register* 69, no. 109, June 7, 2004.

56. Hasdorff e-mail 2008. "World Vision made every mistake you could possibly make in international development 3 times before 1965," World Vision U.S. president Rich Stearns told *Christianity Today* (2006) in a recent interview. "I urge megachurches to get that expertise on their teams—hire it, partner with it—so when you begin your development programs, you're going to avoid many of these mistakes." This quotation shows how far World Vision has moved from being an upstart in the PVO community to becoming an established PVO.

57. The appointment of Chad Hayward, formerly of the Center for Faith-Based and Community Initiatives at USAID, as executive director of Association of Evangelical Relief and Development Organizations further demonstrates the closeness between the Bush administration and the evangelical community.

58. "The Global Development Alliance has proven itself enormously successful with more than 680 alliances formed with over 1,700 distinct partners, leveraging more than $9 billion in combined public-private sector resources." USAID 2007, 5.

59. USAID 2002.

60. Ibid., 141.

61. Ibid., 141.
62. USAID 2004b, 11.
63. See USAID 2006b.
64. The *Policy Framework* articulated five core goals for foreign aid: promote transformational development; strengthen fragile states; support strategic states; provide humanitarian relief; and address global issues and other special, self-standing concerns. See USAID 2006b, 4–5.
65. USAID 2006b, 5.
66. Hyman 2008, 5.
67. Congressional Research Service 2007c, 21.
68. U.S. Congress 2007, 2.
69. Ruthrauff e-mail (InterAction) 2008.
70. USAID 2006d, 23.
71. U.S. Congress 2007, 12.
72. Brainard 2007, 33–66, especially 38.
73. Congressional Research Service 2006a.
74. InterAction 2003, 10.
75. U.S. Congress 2007, 2.
76. InterAction 2007, 3.
77. This is the case from 2004 onward.
78. U.S. GAO 2007, 14.
79. Barrett and Maxwell 2005, 87.
80. U.S. GAO 2007, 10.
81. White House 2002a.
82. *International Herald Tribune* 2007, 1–2.
83. See *International Herald Tribune* 2007; CARE 2006.
84. CARE 2006.
85. *USA Today* 2008.
86. Catholic Relief Services 2008, 1.

Bibliography

Agar, Herbert. 1960. *The Saving Remnant: An Account of Jewish Survival.* New York: Viking.

American Council of Voluntary Agencies for Foreign Service, Inc. 1942, December 20. "Private International Service Organizations in Post-War Relief." ACVAFS Archives, Special Collections and University Archives, Archibald S. Alexander Library, Rutgers University, Rutgers, NJ.

———. 1944, August 31. "Memorandum to All Member Agencies." ACVAFS Archives, Special Collections and University Archives, Archibald S. Alexander Library, Rutgers University, Rutgers, NJ.

———. 1952, July 23. "Historical Background and Current Programs Joint Distribution Committee, 1946–1952." ACVAFS Archives, Special Collections and University Archives, Archibald S. Alexander Library, Rutgers University, Rutgers, NJ.

———. 1953. *American Council of Voluntary Agencies for Foreign Service: The Role of Voluntary Agencies in Technical Assistance.* New York: American Council of Voluntary Agencies for Foreign Assistance, Committee on Technical Assistance and Projects.

———. 1968, November. *South Vietnam: Technical Assistance Programs of U.S. Non-profit Organizations, including Voluntary Agencies, Missions, and Foundations Directory.* New York: American Council of Voluntary Agencies for Foreign Service, Technical Assistance Clearing House.

———. 1971, May. *U.S. Non-profit Organizations in Development Assistance Abroad: including Voluntary Agencies, Missions and Foundations.* Edited by Barbara Crosby and Stuart J. Smyth. Two vols. TAICH Directory. New York: Technical Assistance Information Clearing House.

———. 1974, December. *U.S. Non-profit Organizations in Development Assistance Abroad: A Supplement to the TAICH 1971 Directory.* TAICH Profile Report, no. 3. New York: American Council of Voluntary Agencies for Foreign Service, Technical Assistance Information Clearing House.

———. 1975, November 24. Report of the National Information Bureau, Inc., to ACVAFS. ACVAFS Archives, Special Collections and University Archives, Archibald S. Alexander Library, Rutgers University, Rutgers, NJ.

American Council of Voluntary Agencies for Foreign Service, Inc. 1980. *1980 Annual Report.* ACVAFS Archives, Special Collections and University Archives, Archibald S. Alexander Library, Rutgers University, Rutgers, NJ.

———. 1981. *1981 Annual Report.* ACVAFS Archives, Special Collections and University Archives, Archibald S. Alexander Library, Rutgers University, Rutgers, NJ.

———. 1982a, March 11. "Discussion Paper." ACVAFS Archives, Special Collections and University Archives, Archibald S. Alexander Library, Rutgers University, Rutgers, NJ.

———. 1982b. *1982 Annual Report.* New York: American Council of Voluntary Agencies for Foreign Service. ACVAFS Archives, Special Collections and University Archives, Archibald S. Alexander Library, Rutgers University, Rutgers, NJ.

———. n.d. "Development Assistance Committee." Photocopy of the typed meeting notes. ACVAFS Archives, Special Collections and University Archives, Archibald S. Alexander Library, Rutgers University, Rutgers, NJ.

American Friends Service Committee. 1944, November 20. "Draft of a Foreign Service Policy." American Friends Service Committee: FS, 1944, Policy. Cited in Genizi 1983, 212.

American Jewish Joint Distribution Committee. 1953, October 26. "Historical Background and Current Programs. Joint Distribution Committee, 1946–1951." Unpublished document, American Council for Voluntary Agencies in Foreign Assistance. Rutgers University Library Special Collection, American Council for Voluntary Agencies in Foreign Assistance Files, Rutgers, NJ.

Ammerman, Nancy. 2005. *Pillars of Faith: American Congregations and Their Partners.* Berkeley: University of California Press.

Association of Evangelical Relief and Development Organizations (AERDO). 1999, January. "AERDO Interagency GIK Standards." http://www.aerdo.net/gik_standards/gik_index.php. Accessed May 2008.

Bachman, John W. 1995. *Together in Hope. 50 Years of Lutheran World Relief.* New York: Lutheran World Relief.

Barrett, Christopher B., and Daniel G. Maxwell. 2005. *Food Aid for Fifty Years: Recasting Its Role.* London: Routledge.

Bauer, Yehuda. 1981. *American Jewry and the Holocaust. The American Jewish Joint Distribution Committee, 1939–1945.* Institute of Contemporary Jewry, Hebrew University. Detroit, MI: Wayne State University Press.

Beigbeder, Yves. 1991. *The Role and Status of International Humanitarian Volunteers and Organizations.* Dordrecht, Netherlands: Kluwer Academic.

Berríos, Rubén. 2000. *Contracting for Development: The Role of For-Profit Contractors in U.S. Foreign Development Assistance.* Westport, CT: Praeger.

Biberson, Philippe, and François Jean. 1999. "The Challenges of Globalization of International Relief and Development." *Nonprofit and Voluntary Sector Quarterly* 28, no. 4 (Supplement): 104–8.

Biddle, C. Stark. 1986. *Dependency of Private Voluntary Organizations on Federal Sources of Support*. Washington, DC: USAID, Bureau for Food for Peace and Voluntary Assistance, Office of Private and Voluntary Cooperation.

———. 2006. "The Work of the Office of the Private and Voluntary Cooperation, Thirty-Five Years of Change and Accomplishment." Unpublished manuscript provided by the author.

Birdsall, Nancy, Stewart Patrick, and Milan Vaishnav. 2006, February. *Reforming U.S. Development Policy: Four Critical Fixes*. Center for Global Development Essay. Washington, DC: Center for Global Development.

Brainard, Lael. 2007. "Organizing U.S. Foreign Assistance to Meet the Twenty-first Century Challenges." In Lael Brainard (ed.), *Security by Other Means: Foreign Assistance, Global Poverty, and American Leadership*. Washington, DC: Center for Strategic and International Studies and Brookings Institution Press, 33–66.

Buchanan-Smith, Margie. 2003, July. *How the Sphere Project Came into Being: A Case Study of Policy-Making in the Humanitarian Aid Sector and the Relative Influence of Research*. Working Paper 215. London: Overseas Development Institute.

Bush, Perry. 2002. "The Political Education of Vietnam Christian Services, 1954–1975." *Peace and Change* 27, no. 2 (April): 198–224.

Butler, Brian E. 1968. "Title IX of the Foreign Assistance Act: Foreign Aid and Political Development." *Law and Society Review* 3, no. 1: 115–52.

Byrnes, James F. 1946, September 6. "Restatement of Policy on Germany." Stuttgart, Germany. http://usa.usembassy.de/etexts/ga4–460906.html. Accessed May 2008.

Campbell, Wallace J. 1990. *The History of CARE. A Personal Account*. New York: Praeger.

CARE. 2006, June 6. *White Paper on Food Aid Policy, CARE USA*. http://www.care.org/newsroom/publications/whitepapers/food_aid_whitepaper.pdf. Accessed May 2008.

Catholic Relief Services. 2008, March 11. "Catholic Relief Services Urges Congress to Preserve the Food Aid Safebox." http://crs.org/newsroom/releases/release.cfm?ID=1416. Accessed May 2008.

Cazier, Stanford O. 1964. "CARE: A Study in Cooperative Voluntary Relief." Ph.D. dissertation. University of Wisconsin.

Chandler, Edgar H. S. 1959. *The High Tower of Refuge: The Inspiring Story of Refugee Relief throughout the World*. London: Long Acre and Odhams.

Charny, Joel, and John Spragnes, Jr. 1984. *Obstacles to Recovery in Kampuchea*. Boston: Oxfam America.

Christianity Today. 1979. "Accountability in Fund Raising," Editorials, 23, no. 13 (April 16): 10, 48–49.

———. 1986. "A Year of Major Tests for Evangelical Relief Agencies." Randall L. Frame, 30, no. 1 (January 17): 32–33.

———. 1988a. "Full Disclosure. Broadcast Ministries Can No Longer Have Financial Secrets." Thomas C. Oden, 32, no. 5 (March 18): 40–41.

Christianity Today. 1988b. "Cleaning House: ECFA Expels Members." 32, no. 14 (October 7): 44–45.

———. 1989. "ECFA Celebrates Ten Years." 33, no. 15 (October 20): 44.

———. 2006. "Q & A with Rich Stearns, President of World Vision US." 50, no. 10 (October): 27.

Chronicle of Philanthropy. 2004, November 25. "Jewish Giving's New Era: Established Groups Face Growing Competition for Funds." Debra Nussbaum Cohen, vol. 14. http://philanthropy.com/free/articles/v17/i04/04000701.htm. Accessed May 2005.

Clark, Gregory. 2007. *Farewell to Alms: A Brief Economic History of the World.* Princeton, NJ: Princeton University Press.

Clay, Jason W. 1989. "Ethiopian Famine and the Relief Agencies." In Bruce Nichols and Gil Loescher (eds.), *The Moral Nation: Humanitarianism and U.S. Foreign Policy Today.* Notre Dame, IN: University of Notre Dame Press, 232–77.

Cmiel, Kenneth. 1999. "The Emergence of Human Rights Politics in the United States." *The Journal of American History* 86, no. 3 (December): 1231–50.

Collier, Paul. 2007. *The Bottom Billion: Why the Poorest Countries Are Failing and What Can Be Done about It.* Cambridge, UK: Oxford University Press.

Comptroller General of the United States. 1974. *Information Concerning Voluntary Foreign Aid Programs: Agency for International Development, Department of State.* Report to the Subcommittee on Children and Youth, Committee on Labor and Public Welfare United States Senate. Washington, DC: U.S. General Accounting Office, 74–0170.

Congressional Research Service. 1997, September 26. *Continuing Appropriations Acts: Brief Overview of Recent Practices.* Sandy Streeter, analyst in American National Government, Government Division. CRS Report for Congress. Washington, DC: Library of Congress.

———. 2005a, January 19. *Foreign Aid: An Introductory Overview of U.S. Programs and Policy.* CRS Report for Congress. Washington, DC: Library of Congress.

———. 2005b, July 1. *Millennium Challenge Account: Implementation of a New U.S. Foreign Aid Initiative.* CRS Report for Congress. Washington, DC: Library of Congress.

———. 2006a, June 16. *Restructuring U.S. Foreign Aid: The Role of the Director of Foreign Assistance.* CRS Report for Congress. Washington, DC: Library of Congress.

———. 2006b, July 13. *Peacekeeping and Related Stability Operations: Issues of U.S. Military Involvement.* Nina Serafino. CRS Report for Congress. Washington, DC: Library of Congress.

———. 2007a, January 3. *Millennium Challenge Account: Report to Congress.* Washington, DC: Library of Congress. Curt Tarnoff, specialist in foreign affairs, Foreign Affairs, Defense, and Trade Division. CRS Report for Congress. Washington, DC: Library of Congress.

———. 2007b, January 23. *Restructuring U.S. Foreign Aid: The Role of the Director of Foreign Assistance in Transformational Development.* Connie Veillette, specialist in foreign affairs, Foreign Affairs, Defense, and Trade Division. CRS Report for Congress. Washington, DC: Library of Congress.

———. 2007c, August 23. *Diplomacy for the 21st Century: Transformational Diplomacy.* Report for Congress. Washington, DC: Library of Congress.

———. 2007d, November 7. *Foreign Aid Reform: Issues for Congress and Policy Options.* Report to Congress. Washington, DC: Library of Congress.

Cooley, Alexander, and James Ron. 2002. "The NGO Scramble: Organizational Insecurity and the Political Economy of Transnational Action." *International Security* 27, no. 1 (Summer): 5–39.

Cottam, Richard W. 1967. *Competitive Interference and Twentieth Century Diplomacy.* Pittsburgh, PA: University of Pittsburgh Press.

———. 2006. "Foreign Aid Policy: Old Wine in New Bottles?" *Foreign Service Journal* 83, no. 6 (June): 28–34.

Dykstra, Craig, and James Hudnut-Beumler. 1992. "The National Organizational Structures of Protestant Denominations: An Invitation to a Conversation." In Milton J. Coatler, John W. Mulder, and Louis B. Weeks (eds.), *The Organizational Revolution: Presbyterians and American Denominationalism.* Louisville, KY: Westminster John Knox, 307–31.

Easterly, William. 2002. *The Elusive Quest for Growth: Economists' Adventures and Misadventures in the Tropics.* Cambridge, MA: MIT Press, 2002.

Egan, Eileen. 1988. *Catholic Relief Services: The Beginning Years.* New York: Catholic Relief Services.

Egan, Eileen, and Elizabeth Clark Reiss. 1964. *Transfigured Night: The CRALOG Experience.* Philadelphia: Livingston.

Emergency Nutrition Network. 1997. "What Became of . . . " Written and researched by Killian Forde. *Field Exchange* 2 (August). http://www.ennonline.net/fex/02/wo23.html. Accessed May 2008.

Fisher, Paul. 1963. *A Short History of the U.S. Aid Program: The Development of Key Aid Concepts.* Document # PN-ABT-602. Washington, DC: USAID.

Flickner, Charles. 2007. "Removing Impediments to an Effective Partnership with Congress." In Lael Brainard (ed.), *Security by Other Means: Foreign Assistance, Global Poverty, and American Leadership.* Washington, DC: Center for Strategic and International Studies and Brookings Institution Press, 225–54.

Flipse, Scott. 2002. "The Latest Casualty of War: Catholic Relief Services, Humanitarianism, and the War in Vietnam, 1967–1968." *Peace and Change* 27, no. 2 (April): 245–70.

Foreman, Karen. 1999. "Evolving Global Structures and the Challenges Facing International Relief and Development Organizations." *Nonprofit and Voluntary Sector Quarterly* 28, no. 4 (Supplement): 178–97.

Forsythe, David P. 1989. "Humanitarian Assistance in U.S. Foreign Policy, 1947–1987." In Bruce Nichols and Gil Loescher (eds.), *The Moral Nation: Humanitarianism and U.S. Foreign Policy Today.* Notre Dame, IN: Notre Dame University Press, 63–90.

Gal, Allon, and Alfred Gottschalk (eds.). 2001. *Beyond Survival and Philanthropy: American Jewry and Israel.* Cincinnati, OH: Hebrew Union College Press.

Gallup Brain. http://brain.gallup.com. Accessed July 18, 2007.

Garred, Michelle (ed.), with Mohammed Abu-Nimer. 2006. *A Shared Future: Local Capabilities for Peace in Community Development*. Monrovia, CA: World Vision International.

Genizi, Haim. 1983. *American Apathy: The Plight of Christian Refugees from Nazism*. Ramat-Gan, Israel: Bar Ilan University Press.

———. 1987. "Christian Charity: The Unitarian Service Committee's Relief Activities on Behalf of Refugees from Nazism, 1940–1945." *Holocaust and Genocide Studies* 2, no. 2: 261–76.

———. 1993a. "American Lutherans and Lutheran Refugees, 1933–1952." In Frank H. Littell, Alan L. Berger, and Hurbert G. Locke (eds.), *What Have We Learned? Telling the Story and Teaching the Lessons of the Holocaust*. Symposium Series, Vol. 30. Lewiston, UK: Edwin Mellen, 167–92.

———. 1993b. *America's Fair Share: The Admission and Resettlement of Displaced Persons, 1945–1952*. Detroit, MI: Wayne State University Press.

Gilmore, Judith. 1977. *A.I.D.'s "New Directions" with Private and Voluntary Organizations*. Development Studies Program VI. Washington, DC: USAID.

Gnaerig, Burkhard, and Charles F. MacCormack. 1999. "The Challenges of Globalization: Save the Children." *Nonprofit and Voluntary Sector Quarterly* 28, no. 4 (Supplement): 140–46.

Grader, Charles Raymond. 1967, January. *Public Law 480: A Study in United States Government Policy Formation*. Ph.D. thesis. Tufts University.

Greeley, Andrew M. 1989. *Religious Change in America*. Third printing, 1996. Cambridge, MA: Harvard University Press.

Guardze, Heinz. 1950. "The Laenderrat: Landmark of German Reconstruction." *The Western Political Quarterly* 3, no. 2: 190–213.

Hadden, Jeffrey K., and Anson Shupe. 1988. *Televangelism: Power and Politics on God's Frontier*. New York: Henry Holt.

Hadden, Jeffrey K., and Charles E. Swann. 1981. *Prime Time Preachers: The Rising Power of Televangelism*. Reading, MA: Addison-Wesley.

Halperin, Samuel. 1960. "Ideology or Philanthropy? The Politics of Zionist Fund-Raising." *The Western Political Quarterly* 13, no. 4 (December): 950–73.

Harrison, Earl. 1945. Report to President Truman. http://www.ushmm.org/museum/exhibit/online/dp/resourc1.htm. Accessed June 2007.

Harvey, Bartlett. 1975, January 31. *Registration and Approval of Voluntary Foreign Aid Agencies by the Voluntary Committee on Voluntary Foreign Aid of the Agency for International Development*. A Report to the Committee and the Agency. Washington, DC: USAID.

Henry, Kevin M. 1999. "CARE International: Evolving to Meet the Challenges of the 21st Century." *Nonprofit and Voluntary Sector Quarterly* 28, no. 4 (Supplement): 109–20.

Hogan, Elizabeth. 1989. "The Biden-Pell Program: Catalyst for Sustainable Development Education, an Interview with Elizabeth Hogan, Coordinator,

USAID Biden-Pell Program." *Development Education Annual* 1: 6–7. New York: National Clearinghouse on Development Education.

Hoge, Dean R. 1976. *Division in the Protestant House: The Basic Reasons behind the Intra-Church Conflicts.* Philadelphia: Westminster.

Hoge, Dean R., Charles E. Zech, Patrick H. McNamara, and Michael J. Donohue. 1996. *Money Matters: Personal Giving in American Churches.* Louisville, KY: Westminster John Knox.

Hoover, Herbert. 1964. *An American Epic: The Guns Cease Killing and the Saving of Life from Famine Begins, 1939–1963.* Vol. 4. Chicago: Henry Regnery.

Hunter, James Davison. 1983. *American Evangelism: Conservative Religion and the Quandary of Modernity.* Rutgers, NJ: Rutgers University Press.

Hyman, Gerald F. 2008, February. *Assessing Secretary Rice's Reform of U.S. Foreign Assistance.* Carnegie Papers. Democracy and Rule of Law Program, no. 90. Washington, DC: Carnegie Endowment for International Peace.

InterAction. 2002a. "InterAction's Private Voluntary Organization (PVO) Standards," point 7.6.3. http://www.interaction.org/disaster/pvostandards. html. Accessed May 2008.

———. 2002b, February 21. "Notes from Meeting at InterAction on USAID/PVC's Future Plans." John Ruthrauff. http://www.interaction.org/library/detail. php?id=918.

———. 2003, November. *Foreign Assistance in Focus: Emerging Trends.* An InterAction Policy Paper. Washington, DC: InterAction. http://www.interaction.org/ campaign/emerging_trends.html#Emer.

———. 2007a, April 1. "InterAction Strategic Goals: 2007–2009." http://www. interaction.org/library/detail.php?id=5739. Accessed May 2008.

———. 2007b, July 2. Letter from InterAction Samuel A. Worthington to the Honorable Richard Lugar. http://www.interaction.org/library/detail.php? id=5866. Accessed May 2008.

International Herald Tribune. 2007, April 21. "Bush gains support for new approach on Global Food Aid." Celia Dugger. http://www.iht.com/articles/2007/04/ 21/america/web-0421food-35235.php. Accessed May 2008.

International Missionary Council. 1946. *The International Missionary Council and Continental Missions in the War of 1939–1945.* London: Morrison and Gibb.

Jewish Funders Network. "About JFN." http://www.jfunders.org/about_us/ about_us.html. Accessed February 2005.

Kauffman, Christopher J. 2005. "Politics, Programs, and Protests: Catholic Relief Services in Vietnam, 1954–1975." *The Catholic Historical Review* 91, no. 2: 223–50.

Keck, Margaret, and Kathryn Sikkink. 1998. *Activists Beyond Borders: Advocacy Networks in International Politics.* Ithaca, NY: Cornell University Press.

Kornbluh, Peter. 1987. *Nicaragua: The Price of Intervention. Reagan's War against the Sandinistas.* Washington, DC: Institute for Policy Studies.

Korten, David. 1983. *Learning from U.S.A.I.D. Field Experience: Institutional Development and the Dynamics of Project Process.* National Association of Schools and Public Affairs and Administration. Washington, DC: Bureau for Science and Technology, USAID.

Krasner, Stephen. 2006, January 20. Director of Policy Planning, State Department "Transformational Diplomacy." Presentation at the Center for Global Development, Washington, DC.

Lancaster, Carol. 2007. *Foreign Aid: Diplomacy, Development, Domestic Politics.* Chicago: University of Chicago Press.

Lindner, Eileen W. (ed.). 2002. *Yearbook of American and Canadian Churches 2002.* Prepared and edited for the National Council of the Churches of Christ in the U.S.A. Nashville, KY: Abingdon.

Mahajani, Usha. 1965. "Kennedy and the Strategy of AID: The Clay Report and After." *The Western Political Quarterly* 18, no. 3 (September): 656–68.

Mason, Linda, and Roger Brown.1981. *Rice, Rivalry, and Politics: Managing the Cambodian Relief.* Notre Dame, IN: University of Notre Dame Press.

McCleary, Rachel M., and Robert J. Barro. 2008. "U.S.-Based Private Voluntary Organizations: Religious and Secular PVOs Engaged in International Relief and Development, 1939–2004." *Nonprofit Voluntary Sector Quarterly* 37, no. 2: 512–36.

McFarland, Charles S. 1924. *International Christian Movements.* New York: Fleming H. Revell.

McGuire, Mark F., and Vernon W. Ruttan. 1989. *Lost Directions: U.S. Foreign Assistance Policy since New Directions.* Bulletin 89–5. Minneapolis: University of Minnesota, Economic Development Center.

McSweeney, Edward. 1950. *American Voluntary Aid for Germany, 1945–1950.* Freiburg, Germany: Caritas-Verlag.

Meyer, David S., and Douglas R. Imig. 1993. "Political Opportunity and the Rise and Decline of Interest Group Sectors." *Social Science Journal* 30, no. 3: 253–70.

Millennium Challenge Account. http://www.mcc.gov. Accessed July 2008.

Mooneyham, W. Stanley. n.d. "The History of the Evangelical Council for Financial Accountability." Unpublished document provided to the author by Ted Engstrom.

Moore, Deborah Dash. 1998. "Jewish GIs and the Creation of the Judeo-Christian Tradition." *Religion and American Culture* 8, no. 1: 31–53.

Nachmani, Amikam. 1990. "Civil War and Foreign Intervention in Greece: 1946–49." *Journal of Contemporary History* 25, no. 4 (October): 489–522.

National Opinion Research Center (NORC). 2006. "General Social Survey." http://www.norc.org/projects/general+social+survey.htm. Accessed July 2006.

Natsios, Andrew S. 2006. "Five Debates on International Development: The U.S. Perspective." *Development Policy Review* 24, no. 2 (March): 131–39.

Nichols, J. Bruce. 1988. *The Uneasy Alliance: Religion, Refugee Work, and U.S. Foreign Policy.* New York: Oxford University Press.

Nowels, Larry. 2007. "Foreign Aid Reform Commissions, Task Forces, and Initiatives: From Kennedy to Present." In Lael Brainard (ed.), *Security by Other*

Means: Foreign Assistance, Global Poverty, and American Leadership. Washington, DC: Center for Strategic and International Studies and Brookings Institution Press, 255–76.

Nygren, David, and Miriam Ukeratis. 1993. *The Future of Religious Orders in the United States.* Westport, CT: Praeger.

Oates, Mary J. 1995. *Catholic Philanthropic Tradition in America.* Indianapolis: Indiana University Press.

Obey, David R., and Carol Lancaster. 1988. "Funding Foreign Aid." *Foreign Policy* 71 (Summer): 141–55.

Offenheiser, Raymond, Susan Holcombe, and Nancy Hopkins. 1999. "Grappling with Globalization: Partnership, and Learning: A Look Inside Oxfam America." *Nonprofit and Voluntary Sector Quarterly* 28, no. 4 (Supplement): 121–39.

Office of War Information. 1943, January 13. "National War Fund." OWI-1099. Memorandum. Compilation of Documents: President's Committee on War Relief Agencies and President's War Relief Control Board. Harvard University, Widener Library.

Olson, Daniel V. A., and David Caddell. 1993, March. "Causes of Financial Giving to United Church of Christ Congregations." Paper presented to the Catholic University Seminar on Religious Giving. Washington, DC: Catholic University of America.

Parker, Joseph I. (ed). 1938. *Interpretative Statistical Survey of the World Mission of the Christian Church. Summary and Detailed Statistics of Churches and Missionary Societies, Interpretative Articles, and Indices.* New York: International Missionary Council.

Pergande, Delia T. 2002. "Private Voluntary Aid and National Building in South Vietnam: The Humanitarian Politics of CARE, 1954–1961." *Peace and Change* 27, no. 2 (April): 165–97.

Pezzullo, Lawrence A. 1989. "Catholic Relief Services in Ethiopia: A Case Study." In Bruce Nichols and Gil Loescher (eds.), *The Moral Nation: Humanitarianism and U.S. Foreign Policy Today.* Notre Dame, IN: University of Notre Dame Press, 213–31.

Philips, Rosemarie. 1989. "Seven Years of Biden-Pell: What We Learned about Education Development: Lessons Learned." *Development Education Annual,* vol. 1. New York: National Clearinghouse on Development Education.

Pienkos, Donald E. 1991. *For Your Freedom and through Ours: Polish American Efforts on Poland's Behalf, 1863–1991.* New York: East European Monographs; Columbia University Press.

ProCon.org. http://www.israelipalestinianprocon.org/populationpalestine.html. Accessed July 2008.

Quebedeaux, Richard. 1978. *The Worldly Evangelicals.* New York: Harper and Row.

Rajan, Raghuram G., and Arvind Subramanian. 2007. "Does Aid Work?" *American Economic Review* 97, no. 2 (May): 322–27.

Raphael, Marc Lee. 1982. *A History of the United Jewish Appeal, 1939–1982.* Brown Judaic Studies 34. Providence, RI: Scholars Press.

Reid, Daniel G., Robert Dean Linder, Bruce L. Shelley, and Harry S. Stout (eds.). 1990. *Dictionary of Christianity in America*. Downers Grove, IL: Intervarsity.

Reiss, Elizabeth Clark. 1985. *ACVAFS : Four Monographs*. New York: American Council of Voluntary Agencies for Foreign Service.

Rimor, Mordechai, and Gary A. Tobin. 1990. "Jewish Giving Patterns to Jewish and Non-Jewish Philanthropy." In Robert Wuthnow, Virginia A. Hodgkinson, and associates, *Faith and Philanthropy in America: Exploring the Role of Religion in America's Voluntary Sector*. San Francisco: Jossey-Bass (Independent Sector), 134–64.

Ringland, Arthur C. 1954, March 15. "The Organization of Voluntary Foreign Aid, 1939–1953." *The Department of State Bulletin*. Washington, DC: U.S. Department of State, 383–92.

———. 1975, July 14. Oral history interview. Consultant, National Defense Advisory Commission and President's War Relief Control Board, 1940–46; executive director, Advisory Committee on Voluntary Foreign Aid, U.S. Department of State, 1946–53. Washington, D.C. by Richard D. McKinzie. Harry S. Truman Library, http://www.trumanlibrary.org/oralhist/ringland.htm. Accessed April 2006.

Robinson, Mark. 1997. "Privatising the Voluntary Sector: NGOs and Public Service Contractors?" In David Hume and Michael Edwards (eds.), *NGOs, States and Donors. Too Close for Comfort?* Houndsmills, UK: Macmillan in association with Save the Children, 59–78.

Rodell, Paul A. 2002. "International Voluntary Services in Vietnam: War and the Birth of Activism, 1958–1967." *Peace and Change* 27, no. 2 (April): 225–44.

Rouse, Ruth, and Stephen Charles Neill (eds.). 1968. *A History of the Ecumenical Movement, 1517–1948*. 2nd ed. with revised bibliography. Philadelphia: Westminster.

Ruttan, V. W. (ed.). 1993. *Why Food Aid?* Baltimore, MD: Johns Hopkins University Press.

Sarna, Jonathan D. 2004. *American Judaism: A History*. New Haven, CT: Yale University Press.

Schafer, Jacqueline E. 2006, July 27. Assistant administrator, Bureau of Economic Growth Agriculture and Trade. "USAID's Progress in Implementing the Microenterprise Results and Accountability Act of 2004." Testimony before the Subcommittee on Africa, Global Human Rights and International Operations, Committee on International Relations, U.S. House of Representatives. http://www.usaid.gov/press/speeches/2006/ty060727.html. Accessed May 2008.

Schechter, Michael G. 2005. *United Nations Global Conferences*. London: Routledge.

Schmidt, Elizabeth, Jane Blewett, and Peter Henriot. 1981. *Religious Private Voluntary Organizations and the Question of Government Funding*. Final Report. Maryknoll, NY: Orbis.

Seymour, Harold J. 1947. *Design for Giving: The Story of the National War Fund, Inc. 1943–1947*, with a foreword by Winthrop W. Aldrich. New York: Harper and Brothers.

Shepherd, Jack. 1975. *The Politics of Starvation*. New York: Carnegie Endowment for International Peace.

Shibley, Mark. 1996. *Resurgent Evangelicalism in the United States: Mapping Cultural Change since 1970*. Columbia: University of South Carolina Press.

Sierra Magazine. 1995, July–August. "Jesse Helms' Family Plan—Plan to Shut Down U.S. Agency for International Development." B. J. Bergman. http://findarticles.com/p/articles/mi_m1525/is_/ai_17160370. Accessed May 2008.

Sikkink, David, and Mark Regnerus. 1996. "For God and Fatherland: Protestant Symbolic Worlds and the Rise of German National Socialism." In Christian Smith (ed.), *Disruptive Religion: The Force of Faith in Social Movement Activism*. New York: Routledge, 147–66.

Silverman, Ira. 1991. "The New Jewish Philanthropies." In Barry A. Kosmin and Paul Ritterband (eds.), *Contemporary Jewish Philanthropy in America*. Savage, MD: Rowman and Littlefield, 205–18.

Skocpol, Theda. *Diminished Democracy: From Membership to Management in American Civic Life*. Norman: University of Oklahoma, 2003.

Smith, Tom. n.d. "Humanitarian Assistance (HA) Program." U.S. Department of Defense, Defense Security Cooperation Agency. Office of Humanitarian Assistance, Disaster Relief, and Mine Action (HDM), document no. 601-3657. http://www.dsca.osd.mil/programs/HA/HA.htm. Accessed July 2008.

Somner, John. 1977. *Beyond Charity: U.S. Voluntary Aid for a Changing Third World*. Washington, DC: Overseas Development Council.

Stafford, Tim. 1997. "Anatomy of a Giver." *Christianity Today* 6 (May 19): 20–24.

Stedman, Murray S., Jr. 1963. "Church, State, People: The Eternal Triangle." *The Western Political Quarterly* 16, no. 3 (September): 610–23.

Steensland, Brian, Jerry Z. Park, Mark D. Regnerus, Lynn D. Robinson, W. Bradford Wilcox, and Robert D. Woodberry. 2000. "The Measure of American Religion: Toward Improving the State of the Art." *Social Forces* 79, no. 1: 291–318.

Stenning, Ronald E. 1996. *Church World Service: Fifty Years of Help and Hope*. Foreword by Senator Paul Simon. New York: Friendship Press.

Stewart, Barbara McDonald. 1982. *United States Government Policy on Refugees from Nazism, 1933–1940*. New York: Garland.

Sullivan, Robert R. 1969. "The Politics of Altruism: The American Church-State Conflict in the Food-for-Peace Program." *A Journal of Church and State* 11, no. 1: 47–61.

Tarrow, Sidney. 2003. *Power in Movement: Social Movements and Contentious Politics*. 2nd ed. Cambridge: Cambridge University Press.

Tobin, Gary A. 2001. *The Transition of Communal Values and Behavior in Jewish Philanthropy*. San Francisco: Institute for Jewish and Community Research.

Treacy, Gerald C. 1939. *Five Great Encyclicals: Labor, Education, Marriage, Reconstructing the Social Order, Atheistic Communism*. New York: Paulist Press.

Truman, Harry S. 1947, March 12. "Recommendation for Assistance to Greece and Turkey: Address of the President of the United States Delivered before a Joint Session of the Senate and the House of Representatives." 80th Congress,

1st session, House of Representatives doc. no. 171, vii–xi. Washington, D.C.: Government Printing Office.

―――. 1949, January 20. Inaugural address. http://www.trumanlibrary.org/calendar/viewpapers.php?pid=1030. Accessed July 2008.

U.N. Development Programme. 1975, January 21. "Strengthening Collaboration with Non-government Organizations." New York: United Nations Development Programme.

United States. 1959, April 16. *Congressional Record, Proceedings and Debates of the 86th Congress, 1st Session*. Vol. 105, pt. 5, p. 6124. Washington, DC: Government Printing Office.

U.S. Agency for International Development. 1966. Advisory Committee on Voluntary Foreign Aid. *Food for Peace and the Voluntary Agencies*. Report of the Task Force. Washington, DC: USAID, February 6.

―――. 1974a, April. The Advisory Committee on Voluntary Foreign Aid. *The Rise of Voluntary Agencies in International Assistance: A Look Forward*. Washington, DC: Advisory Committee on Voluntary Foreign Aid.

―――. 1974b, October 22. "Report of the Workshop on Grant Procedures." Washington, DC: USAID and Advisory Committee on Voluntary Foreign Aid.

―――. 1975, December. *United States Economic Assistance to South Viet Nam, 1954–1975*. Vols. 1, 2a, 2b, and 3. Prepared by the Asia Bureau, Office of Residual Indochina Affairs, Viet Nam Desk. Washington, DC: USAID.

―――. 1976, November 15–17. "Report of the Crystal City Conference of Thirty-One Private Voluntary Agencies as Recipients of AID Development Program Grants." Washington, DC: USAID and Advisory Committee on Voluntary Foreign Aid.

―――. 1982a. Advisory Committee on Voluntary Foreign Aid. *Cooperation between American Corporations and Private Voluntary Organizations in the Developing World*. Public report of meeting March 25–26. Washington, DC: USAID.

―――. 1982b, March 16, Advisory Committee on Voluntary Foreign Aid. *Public Report of Meeting March 25–26, 1982.Cooperation between American Corporations and Private Voluntary Organizations in the Developing World*. Prepared by Inter-American Development Institute. Annex 3: "PVO Testimony Written Statements." Report by Private Agencies in International Development, "Comments on Proposed AID Policy Statement on Programs of Private and Voluntary Organizations." Washington, DC: USAID, 1–6.

―――. 1982c, May. *Private Enterprise Development*. AID Policy Paper. Bureau for Program and Policy Coordination. Washington, DC: USAID.

―――. 1982d, September. *AID Partnership in International Development with Private and Voluntary Organizations*. AID Policy Paper. Bureau for Program and Policy Coordination. Washington, DC: USAID.

―――. 1983. Advisory Committee on Voluntary Foreign Aid. *Theme: World Hunger*. Quarterly meeting report, September 15–16. Washington, DC: Newman and Hermanson.

———. 1984. Office of Private and Voluntary Cooperation, Bureau of Food for Peace and Voluntary Assistance. *The AID-PVO Partnership: Sharing Goals and Resources in the Work of Development.* Washington, DC: USAID.

———. 1985, March. *Private Enterprise Development (revised).* AID Policy Paper. Washington, DC: USAID.

———. 1987a, May 25. M. Peter McPherson, letter to the Honorable Malcolm Wallop. Cited in Mark Huber, "'Private Voluntary Organizations' Betray Their Trust." *Backgrounders* 619 (March 7, 1988), 1–15, especially p. 4. Washington, DC: The Heritage Foundation.

———. 1987b, September 3. *A Study of AID/PVO Collaboration* (draft). Washington, DC: USAID.

———. 1988. Advisory Committee on Voluntary Foreign Aid. *The Effectiveness of Private Voluntary Organizations.* Washington, DC: USAID.

———. 1989, February 17. *Development and the National Interest: U.S. Economic Assistance in the 21st Century.* A report by the administration of the Agency for International Development. Washington, DC: USAID.

———. 1992a, February 25–26. Advisory Committee on Voluntary Foreign Aid. *The New Independent States and the Implications for Private Voluntary Organizations.* Quarterly meeting report. Washington, DC: USAID.

———. 1992b, May 19–20. Advisory Committee on Voluntary Foreign Aid. *The A.I.D./PVO Relationship. The Operational Aspects of the Partnership.* Quarterly Meeting.

———. 1995a, July 21. *Toward the New USAID: An NPR Report.* Washington, DC: USAID.

———. 1995b, October. *Reinventing Foreign Assistance for the 21st Century: USAID Proposal for the Second Phase of Reengineering Government.* Washington, DC: USAID

———. 1997a, January. Advisory Committee on Voluntary Foreign Aid. *USAID/ PVO Partnership Assessment.* Washington, DC: USAID.

———. 1997b, July 10. *Contract Information Bulletin 97-16 (CIB-97-16).* Washington, DC: USAID.

———. 1998a, June 10. Advisory Committee on Voluntary Foreign Aid. *Measuring Results: Perspectives of USAID, Partners, Stakeholders.* ACVFA Quarterly Report. Washington, DC: USAID.

———. 1998b, September 17. Advisory Committee on Voluntary Foreign Aid. ACVFA Quarterly Report. Washington, DC: USAID.

———. 1999, June 3. Advisory Committee on Voluntary Foreign Aid. *Whither Foreign Aid?* ACVFA Quarterly Report. Washington, DC: USAID.

———. 2001, October 17 Advisory Committee on Voluntary Foreign Aid. *USAID's Strategies for Conflict Prevention, Procurement Reform, the Global Development Alliance, and HIV/AIDS.* Meeting report. Washington, DC: USAID.

———. 2002a. *Foreign Aid in the National Interest. Promoting Freedom, Security, and Opportunity.* Washington, DC: USAID. http://www.usaid.gov/fani/Full_ Report—Foreign_Aid_in_the_National_Interest.pdf. Accessed March 2006.

U.S. Agency for International Development. 2002b, October 10. *Sourcebook.* http://www.usaid.gov/pubs/sourcebook/usgov/glos.html. Accessed June 2008.

———. 2003, May 14. Advisory Committee on Voluntary Foreign Aid. *U.S. Foreign Assistance Strategy—A New Role for NGOs and USAID?* Meeting report. Washington, DC: USAID.

———. 2004a, January. Bureau for Policy and Program Coordination. *U.S. Foreign Aid: Meeting the Challenges of the Twenty-first Century.* White paper. http://www.usaid.gov/policy/pdabz3221.pdf. Accessed March 2006.

———. 2004b, February 25. Advisory Committee on Voluntary Foreign Aid. *The Changing Face of Foreign Assistance: New Opportunities and Challenges.* Meeting report. Washington, DC: USAID.

———. 2006a, January. *The Global Development Alliance: Public-Private Alliances for Transformational Development.* Office of Global Development Alliances. Washington, DC: USAID.

———. 2006b, January. *Policy Framework for Bilateral Foreign Aid. Implementing Transformational Diplomacy through Development.* Washington, DC: USAID. http://www.usaid.gov/policy/policy_framework_jan06.html. Accessed May 2008.

———. 2006c, June 7. Advisory Committee on Voluntary Foreign Aid. Public meeting. Washington, DC: USAID.

———. 2006d, October 25. Advisory Committee on Voluntary Foreign Aid. Public meeting report. Washington, DC: USAID.

———. 2006e. *USAID Primer: What We Do and How We Do It.* Washington, DC: USAID.

———. 2006f. *VOLAG Report of Voluntary Agencies.* Washington, DC: USAID.

———. 2007. Office of Development Partners. *Public Private Alliances. FY 2009 Annual Program Statement.* Washington, DC: USAID.

———. 2008a, February. Advisory Committee on Voluntary Foreign Aid. *Reviewing the Foreign Assistance Framework.* Washington, DC: USAID..

———. 2008b. USAID Office of Development Partners. *Public-Private Alliances. FY 2008 Annual Program Statement.* Washington, DC: USAID.

———. 2008c, April 21. *The ADS. A Guide to UASAID's Automated Directives System.* Electronic booklet. http://www.usaid.gov/policy/ads/adsbooklet.pdf. Accessed December 2008.

———. n.d. "Conditions of Registration for U.S. Organizations." http://www.usaid.gov/our_work/cross-cutting/private_voluntary_cooperation/conditions_us_organizations.pdf. Accessed July 2008.

———. n.d. "The Green Book." http://qesdb.usaid.gov/gbk/. Accessed July 2008.

———. n.d. "Results-Oriented Assistance: A Source Book." http://www.usaid.gov/pubs/sourcebook/usgov/glos.html. Accessed July 2008.

U.S. Commission on Helping to Enhance the Livelihood of People around the Globe (HELP). 2007. *Beyond Assistance: The HELP Commission Report on Foreign Assistance Reform.* http://www.helpcommission.gov/portals/0/Beyond%20Assistance_HELP_Commission_Report.pdf. Accessed July 2008.

U.S. Congress. 1947. House Select Committee on Foreign Aid. *Final Report on Foreign Aid*. 80th Congress, 1st session, pt. 4, 5122 ff. Washington, DC: U.S. Government Printing Office.

———. 1948a. Committee on Foreign Affairs. *Voluntary Foreign Aid: The Nature and Scope of Postwar Private American Assistance Abroad, with Special Reference to Europe. A Study by a Special Subcommittee of the Committee on Foreign Affairs*. 80th Congress, 2nd session. Washington, DC: U.S. Government Printing Office.

———. 1948b. Foreign Assistance Act of 1948. ECA Reg. No. 3, 13. *Federal Register* 3783 (1948), "Commercial Freight Shipments of Supplies by Voluntary Non-Profit Relief Agencies."

———. 1948c. Foreign Assistance Act of 1948. Public Law 472, 80th Congress, 2nd session (April 3, 1948), 144–67, *U.S. Code* [S. 2202].

———. 1948d. Foreign Assistance Act of 1948. Reg. No. 5, as amended 13, *Federal Register* 4706 (1948), "Ocean Freight Shipments of Individual Relief Packages."

———. 1948e. House Select Committee on Foreign Aid. *Final Report on Foreign Aid*. H.R. Rep. No. 1845, 80th Congress, 2nd session. Washington, DC: U.S. Government Printing Office.

———. 1950. House Special Subcommittee on the Committee on the Judiciary. *Expellees and Refugees of German Ethnic Origin*. Report of the Special Subcommittee of the Committee on the Judiciary, House of Representatives, Pursuant to H. Res. No. 238, 81st Congress, 2nd session, report no. 1441. Washington, DC: U.S. Government Printing Office.

———. 1953. House of Representatives. *Hearings before a Subcommittee of the Committee on Government Operations*. 83rd Congress, 2nd session, October 13, 14, and 16. Washington, DC: U.S. Government Printing Office.

———. 1954. *U.S. Congressional Record, Proceedings and Debates of the 86th Congress, 1st Session*. Washington, DC: Government Printing Office.

———. 1961. Foreign Assistance Act of 1961. Public Law 87-195, 87th Congress, 1st session (September 4, 1961), 470–519, *U.S. Code* [S1983].

———. 1975. International Development and Food Assistance Act of 1975. Public Law 94-161 94th Congress, 1st session (December 20, 1975), *U.S. Code* 89 Stat. 849.

———. 1976. Foreign Assistance and Related Programs Appropriation Act of 1976. Public Law 94-330, 94th Congress, 2nd session (June 30, 1976), *U.S Code* 90 Stat. 771.

———. 1985. Foreign Relations Authorization Act, Fiscal Years 1986 and 1987. Public Law 99-93, 99th Congress, 1st session (August 16, 1985), *U.S. Code* [99 Stat 405].

———. 2004. Consolidated Appropriations Act of 2004. Public Law 108-199 (January 23, 2004), 108th Congress, 2nd session, *U.S. Code* [118 Stat. 3].

———. 2006, January. Committee on International Relations and Committee on Foreign Relations. *Legislation on Foreign Relations through 2005*. Vol. 1-A. Washington, DC: Government Printing Office.

U.S. Congress. 2006, April. Committee on International Relations and Committee on Foreign Relations. *Legislation on Foreign Relations through 2005.* Vol. 1-B. Washington, DC: Government Printing Office.

———. 2007, November 16. Committee on Foreign Relations, U.S. Senate. *Embassies Grapple to Guide Foreign Aid.* 110th Congress, 1st session. Washington, DC: U.S. Government Printing Office.

U.S. Department of Defense. 2005, November 28. "Military Support for Stability, Security, Transition, and Reconstruction (SSTR) Operations." Directive 3000.05. http://www.dtic.mil/whs/directives/corres/pdf/300005p.pdf. Accessed May 2008.

———. n.d. Overseas Humanitarian, Disaster and Civic Aid Appropriation (OHDACA). "Humanitarian Assistance (HA) Program" prepared by Tom Smith, HDM, 601-3657. http://www.dsca.osd.mil/programs/HA/HA.htm. Accessed May 2008.

U.S. Department of State. 1944, April 22. President's War Relief Control Board. "Requirements and Licensing Procedure Governing Private Relief Society Exports." Memorandum to All Registered Agencies for Foreign Aid. U.S. National Archives, Washington, DC. Records of Temporary Committees, Commissions, and Boards, President's War Relief Control Board, (Record Group 220) 1893–1996 (bulk 1924–93) 220.5.6.

———. 1946. President's War Relief Control Board. *Voluntary War Relief during World War II. A Report to the President by the President's War Relief Control Board.* Washington, DC: U.S. Government Printing Office.

———. 1950. "Other Council Development Assistance Activities." Department of State Announcement 33. ACVAFS Archives, Special Collections and University Archives, Archibald S. Alexander Library, Rutgers University, Rutgers, NJ.

———. n.d. *Compilation of Documents: President's Committee on War Relief Agencies and President's War Relief Control Board.* Cambridge, MA: Harvard University Press.

———. n.d. *Private Voluntary Organizations, U.S. PVO Registry.* http://pvo.usaid.gov/usaid/. Accessed July 2008.

———. n.d. "Reference Guide to the President's FY 2009 Budget Request for the Civilian Stabilization Initiative." http://www.crs.state.gov/index.cfm?fuseaction=public.display&id=a91e832f-d628–4d1b-8fa9-a7c39876acb0. Accessed July 2008.

U.S. General Accounting Office. 1976. Comptroller General. *Channeling Foreign Aid through Private and Voluntary Organizations.* Washington, DC: U.S. GAO.

———. 1992, April 2. *Foreign Assistance: A Profile of the Agency for International Development.* Washington, DC: U.S. GAO.

———. 1995, December. *Foreign Assistance: Private Voluntary Organizations' Contributions and Limitations.* Washington, DC: U.S. GAO.

———. 1996, November 27. Letter from Benjamin F. Nelson, director, International Relations and Trade Issues, GAO, to the Honorable Benjamin A. Gilman, chairman, House Committee on International Relations. Washington, DC: U.S. GAO.

———. 2002, April. *Foreign Assistance: USAID Relies Heavily on Nongovernmental Organizations, but Better Data Needed to Evaluate Approaches*. Washington, DC: U.S. GAO.

———. 2003, September 23. *Foreign Assistance: USAID Needs to Improve Its Workforce Planning and Operating Expense Accounting*. Washington, DC: U.S. GAO.

———. 2004, June 7. *Federal Register* 69, no. 109.

———. 2007a, March. *Foreign Assistance: Actions Needed to Better Assess the Impact of Agencies' Marking and Publicizing Efforts*. Washington, DC: U.S. GAO.

———. 2007b, May 24. *Various Challenges Impede the Efficiency and Effectiveness of U.S. Food Aid*. Statement of Thomas Melito, director of International Affairs and Trade. Washington, DC: Government Accountability Office.

U.S. Institute of Peace. 2005, September. *Provincial Reconstruction Teams and Military Relations with International Nongovernmental Organizations in Afghanistan*. Special Report 147. Washington, DC: U.S. Institute of Peace.

USA Today. 2008. "Capitol Hill Food Fight Threatens Aid for Millions." January 16. http://www.usatoday.com/news/washington/2008-01-16-foodaid_n.htm. Accessed May 2008.

Vallet, Ronald E., and Charles E. Zech. 1995. *The Mainline Church's Funding Crisis: Issues and Possibilities*. Grand Rapids, MI: William B. Eerdmans.

van Dycke, Marci, and Ronald Waldman. 2004, January. *The Sphere Project Evaluation Report*. New York: Center for Global Health and Economic Development, Program on Forced Migration and Health, Columbia University.

Vaux, Tony. 2001. *The Selfish Altruist. Relief Work in Famine and War*. London: Earthscan Publications, Ltd.

Viner, Jacob, George Meany, Fowler Hamilton, Otto Passman, and Paul Hoffman. 1963. "The Report of the Clay Committee on Foreign Aid: A Symposium." *Political Science Quarterly* 78, no. 3 (September): 321–61.

Wagner, Johanna Grombach. 2005. "An IHL/ICRC Perspective on 'Humanitarian Space.'" *Humanitarian Exchange Magazine* 32 (December): 24–26. Humanitarian Practice Network. http://www.odihpn.org/report.asp?ID=2765. Accessed June 2008.

Warburg, Edward M. M. 1941, May 27. Letter to the Honorable Joseph E. Davies, chairman, President's War Relief Control Board archives, U.S. National Archives, attached handwritten note by Joseph E. Davies.

Washington Post. 2003, February 26. "Bush Backs into Nation Building." Terry M. Neal. http://www.informationclearinghouse.info/article1710.htm. Accessed May 2008.

White House. 1942, July 24. "Establishing the President's War Relief Control Board and Defining Its Functions and Duties." Executive Order 9205. U.S. National Archives, Washington, DC. Records of Temporary Committees, Commissions, and Boards, President's War Relief Control Board, (Record Group 220) 1893–1996 (bulk 1924–93) 220.5.6.

———. 1944, June 6. President's War Relief Control Board. Press release. Bruno-Re 3175. OWI-3271. *Compilation of Documents. President's Committee on War Relief*

Agencies and President's War Relief Control Board. Cambridge, MA: Harvard University, 1947.

White House. 1946. President's War Relief Control Board. *Voluntary War Relief during World War II: A Report to the President.* Washington, DC: U.S. Printing Office.

———. 1969, April 22. *Food for Peace: Annual Report on Public Law 480.* Washington, DC: White House.

———. 1993. Office of Management and Budget. Presidential Review Directive No. 20.

———. 2002a. Executive Office of the President, Office of Management and Budget, 65–68. http://www.whitehouse.gov/omb/budget/fy2002/mgmt.pdf. Accessed May 2008.

———. 2002b, September. *The National Security Strategy of the United States of America.* Washington, DC: White House.

———. 2003, February. *National Strategy for Combating Terrorism.* Washington, DC: White House.

———. 2005, December 7. *National Security Presidential Directive/NSPD-44.* Washington, DC: White House.

Willmer, Wesley K., and J. David Schmidt, with Martyn Smith. 1998. *The Prospering Parachurch: Enlarging the Boundaries of God's Kingdom.* San Francisco: Jossey-Bass.

Woodbridge, George. 1950. *UNRRA: The History of the United Nations Relief and Rehabilitation Administration.* Three vols. New York: Columbia University Press.

Wye River Consensus Group. 2008, June. *New Day, New Way: U.S. Foreign Assistance for the 21st Century.* A proposal for modernizing foreign assistance network. http://www.cgdev.org/content/publications/detail/16210/. Accessed June 2008.

Zeitz, Joshua Michael. 2000. "'If I Am Not Myself….' The American Jewish Establishment in the Aftermath of the Six Day War." *American Jewish History* 88, no. 2 (June): 253–86.

Personal Correspondence and Interviews

Ainsworth, Robert. September 25, 2003: telephone interview.
Ballard, Jerry. May 13, 2003; October 20, 2004: e-mail correspondence.
Borton, Nan. May 19, 2008: e-mail correspondence.
Davies, Peter. May 7, 2003: telephone interview.
De Haan, John. November 28, 2003: telephone interview; June 3, 2003; June 4, 2003: e-mail correspondence.
Duss, Serge. August 3, 2003; August 14, 2003; September 3, 2003; March 29, 2007; April 2, 2007: e-mail correspondence.
Elliot, Evan. April 10, 2008: e-mail correspondence.
Engstrom, Ted. November 3, 2003: telephone interview.
Farris, Colonel Karl. June 2, 2008: e-mail correspondence.

Fox, Tom. November 17, 2003: interview, Washington, DC.

Getman, Thomas. October 29, 2003; November 4, 2003: telephone interview; October 28, 2003; November 13, 2003; March 17, 2004; July 29, 2004: e-mail correspondence.

Gilmore, Judith. November 20, 2003: telephone interview; March 26, 2007: telephone interview; July 29, 2008: e-mail correspondence and telephone interview.

Goiza, Vanessa. March, 2, 2007: telephone interview.

Hammock, John. November 25, 2003: interview, Cambridge, MA.

Hancock, Robert "Bud." June 3, 2002; September 9, 2003: telephone interview; June 15, 2003; July 5, 2003; July 13, 2003; September 10, 2003; September 14, 2004: e-mail correspondence.

Hasdorff, Terri. February 13, 2008.: e-mail correspondence.

Kiehne, Frank. June 9, 2003; September 6, 2003: e-mail correspondence; June 13, 2003: telephone interview.

McCleary, Paul. March 9, 2003: e-mail correspondence; July 31, 2008: interview, Bozeman, MT.

McCracken, James. February 27, 2007; March 1, 2007; March 5, 2007; July 17, 2007: telephone interviews.

Natsios, Andrew. February 2, 2007: interview, Washington, DC.

Newton, Mary Q. August 7, 2008: e-mail correspondence.

Ruthrauff, John. April 2, 2008: e-mail correspondence.

Seiple, Robert. October 30, 2003: telephone interview.

Smith, Elise Fiber. November 17, 2003: interview, Washington, DC.

Taft, Julia. June 9, 2003: e-mail correspondence.

Yamamori, Ted. November 29, 2003: e-mail correspondence.

Index